|o|

Living History Museums

Undoing History
through Performance

D1534938

Scott Magelssen

THE SCARECROW PRESS, INC.
Lanham, Maryland • Toronto • Plymouth, UK
2007

SCARECROW PRESS, INC.

Published in the United States of America
by Scarecrow Press, Inc.
A wholly owned subsidary of
The Rowman & Littlefield Publishing Group, Inc.
4501 Forbes Boulevard, Suite 200, Lanham, Maryland 20706
www.scarecrowpress.com

Estover Road
Plymouth PL6 7PY
United Kingdom

British Library Cataloguing in Publication Information Available

Library of Congress Cataloging-in-Publication Data

Magelssen, Scott, 1974–
    Living history museums : undoing history through performance / Scott Magelssen.
    p. cm.
    Includes bibliographical references and index.
    ISBN-13: 978-0-8108-5865-7 (pbk. : alk. paper)
    ISBN-10: 0-8108-5865-7 (pbk. : alk. paper)
    1. Historical museums—United States. 2. Historic sites—Interpretive programs—
United States. 3. Performing arts—United States—Philosophy. 4. Performing arts—
United States—Technique. 5. Historical reenactments—United States. 6. Historical
museums—Public relations—United States. 7. Public history—United States. I. Title.
E172.M23 2007
973.075—dc22   2006029941

For Theresa and Trygg

A play is a blueprint of an event: a way of creating and rewriting history through the medium of literature. Since history is a recorded or remembered event, theatre, for me, is the perfect place to "make" history. . . . Theatre is an incubator for the creation of historical events—and, as in the case of artificial insemination, the baby is no less human.

—Suzan-Lori Parks, "Possession"

If one doesn't talk about a thing, it has never happened.

—Oscar Wilde, *The Picture of Dorian Gray*

~

Contents

~

Acknowledgments

Unlike many authors of works on living museums, I am neither a participant-observer in the field, nor a living history hobbyist. While this "outsider" status permits me the necessary scholarly (and political) distance for a critical analysis of museum performance practices, it denies me any illusions of carte blanche access to the inner world of curators and costumed interpreters. Much of the material the reader will find in this book, then, is here by virtue of practitioners' generosity in spending time answering a theatre scholar's questions, providing him with helpful contact information, and sharing with him their impressions, beliefs, and goals.

In order to do my research for this book, I left the comfortable womb of the academic institution and transgressed into spaces that were not my own. Most of the time, equipped with notebooks, a tape recorder, and a camera, I was not unlike many of the tourists who frequent living history museums with a genuine love of historical information and a desire to record their experiences. I could blend in, becoming a tourist myself, and my subjects were happy to treat me as such. Other times were less comfortable, such as one afternoon when there had been a lack of communication, a missed phone call, and I found myself in a museum staff lounge, unannounced and unexpected, with interpreters in various states of costume staring at me—a voyeur who had broken through the membrane between the touristic colonial environment and their offstage world. Fortunately, these were gracious people, and after piecing together what had happened, they were more than willing to accommodate me and make me comfortable, even volunteering to answer my questions despite my protests. In fact, through conversations that day, I gained some of my most valuable insights about living history and museum interpretation. To these individuals, I express my sincerest gratitude.

Likewise, the curators and administrative staff at these sites were more than helpful in my project. Welcoming me into their just-slightly backstage offices or indulging me in telephone interviews, these individuals were responsible for the majority of the information on the current incarnation of living history museums in the United States treated here. Specifically, I appreciated the help of Jim Bradley, Rosemarie McAphee, and Berry Hoak at Colonial Williamsburg; Walt Woodward and Michelle Pecoraro at Plimoth Plantation; and Jack Larkin at Old Sturbridge Village. I am grateful, too, for the generosity of Christy Coleman Matthews, president of the Charles H. Wright Museum of African-American History in Detroit, who took time to talk with me about her experiences with the 1994 Estate Auction reenactment at Colonial Williamsburg. Finally, there were those cheerful, knowledgeable women and men whose roles are outside the scope of this book, yet without whom living history museums would not function. I refer to the volunteers and support staff behind welcome desks and information booths, at the other end of phones, and on-site in museum uniform. I would not have gotten far without their willingness to help me out, direct me to people they knew I ought to talk to, and give me those connections I could not necessarily have made for myself.

My sincere thanks also go to Tony Wise, Andrea Marple Wittwer, John "Little Bird" Anderson, Lee at the Plymouth Public Library, Harvey Bakari, Karen Wicker, Mark Howell, Toni Brennan, Bentley Boyd, Robert Jackson, Emily James, Caroline Travers, Jane Hetrick, Michael Hall, Marge Bruchac, Thomas Shaw, the Wampanoag Interpretation Program staff, Bruce McConachie, Bill Worthen, Spencer Golub, Jorge Huerta, Joanne Tompkins, Karen Till, Leigh Clemons, Harry Elam, Daniel Brewer, Lou Bellamy, Josephine Lee, Cesare Casarino, Cathy Choy, Luis Montero, Gordon Murdock, Karla Erickson, Stuart Andrews, Matthew Wagner, Lisa Arnold, Natalya Baldyga, Alan Sikes, Lisa Peschl, Patricia Ybarra, Gary Hesser, Jeff Coussens, Gil and Patty Koenigsaecker, Susan Walters, Grace Ebron, Serena Leigh Krombach, Jason Hallman, Peter Kivisto, Jeff Abernathy, and Don and Kathy Nanstad.

Very special thanks to Tamara Underiner, Ellen Stekert, Aleksandra Wolska, and Sonja Kuftinec, who read my earliest drafts of this project; to Michal Kobialka, who guided and mentored me throughout my work on living museums for my doctoral thesis; and to Rose Bank, who generously provided invaluable editorial advice in composing a book manuscript. Thank you to my wife, Theresa Magelssen, for reading multiple drafts of my manuscript every step of the way. And many, many thanks to Renée Camus and Kellie Hagan at Scarecrow Press, for working with this project and bringing it to print.

Portions of this book appeared in earlier form in the *California State University Stanislaus Journal of Research* ("The Vulgar Representation of Time: Time Space and Living History Museums"), *Theatre Survey* ("Living History Museums and the Construction of the Real through Performance," reprinted with permission from Cambridge University Press), *Theatre History Studies* ("Performance Practices of [Living] Open-Air Museums [And a New Look at 'Skansen' in American Living Museum Discourse]"), *Theatre Annual* ("Stepping Back in Time: The Construction of Different Temporal Spaces at Living History Museums in the United States"), and *Theatre Journal*, Johns Hopkins University Press ("Making History in the 'Second-Person': Post-Touristic Considerations for Living Historical Interpretation"). My thanks to these journals for allowing me to reprint this material here.

~

Introduction

Wall: This loam, this rough-cast, and this stone doth show
    That I am that same wall; the truth is so;
    And this the cranny is, right and sinister,
    Through which the fearful lovers are to whisper.
Theseus: Would you desire lime and hair to speak better?

—William Shakespeare, A *Midsummer Night's Dream*

Snout, one of the rude mechanicals presenting *Pyramus and Thisby* before the court in Shakespeare's Athens, seeks to establish for the spectators his credibility and authenticity as the wall that separated the famous title characters of their drama. To do so, it isn't enough for the tinker to merely resemble a wall; he augments his visual appearance by pointing to the details that comprise it—the loam, the rough-cast, the stone, and the cranny—indicating that these very features corresponded to those of the "vile Wall which did these lovers sunder." Thus, Snout does not represent the wall; he *is* that same wall: "the truth is so."

Of course, Theseus and his court do not accept Snout or his fellows as the same wall, moon, lovers, or any other element of the original story. At best, the performers are sloppy referents of that which they signify, recognizable only by the handful of details that all individuals present have agreed upon as conventions of the familiar narrative. Because this band of naive "hempen homespuns" is significantly below the social level of the Duke, because of the poor quality of the entertainment, and because the court has not granted the rude mechanicals any legitimacy as serious performers, structures are in place that preclude any of what Samuel Taylor Coleridge would call "a willing suspension of disbelief."[1] Rather, this representation invites unmasking, derision, and sport from the audience. To take Snout for a real wall, historical or otherwise, would be ludicrous.

Today, living history museums engage strategies in their performance of the past similar to those of Snout—claiming to be real history by virtue of their attention to detail. However, museum environments are much more complex than the stage for *Pyramus and Thisby* and do not offer their visitors the same conditions for simple unmasking. Not only do these places offer total, three-dimensional environments in which the visitor can encounter costumed personas from past eras in history, but the experience is heightened—made more *real*—by the curatorial machinery of the museum. Brochures, signage, and costumed interpreters link each visual image to an archived *fact*: this thatched-roof hovel is based on archaeological digs, this street corresponds to the layout of an eighteenth-century map, the tone in this interpreter's voice is based on careful interpretation of a Pilgrim's 1627 diary entry. Thus, living history museums do not merely *represent* the past; they make historical "truth" for the visitor.

* * *

Living history is a form of theatre. Participants use performance to create a world, tell a story, entertain, and teach lessons, regardless of whether they are playing "characters" or speaking in the third person. Living museums are also historiographic operations, that is, they produce history, as does any textbook, history film, or classroom lecture. This book examines the ways living history museums have practiced costumed reenactment in order to represent historical periods for visitors. Specifically, it articulates the performance practices, philosophies, and curatorial methods these museums have used to "stage" the past throughout the twentieth century and into the twenty-first, and how these museums see themselves as the very products of these practices.

Approaching my material from a background in theatre history and theory, I address and critique currently circulating scholarship on living history and position my own discourse in relation to this scholarship with theories from postmodernism and new historiography. Simply put, history is no longer to be seen as the reconstruction of past events through scientific analysis. As Michel Foucault reminds us, the language of origins is silent. Therefore, since the original event is irrecoverable, the function of the historian is to create the event anew in the present, each time it is enunciated. The idea that history can be "brought to life" through combining research and performance needs to be rethought. If living history museums are not making windows into *real* past moments, what *is* being produced?

As I will show in this book, living history museums currently default to what Agamben calls a "vulgar representation of time as a precise and homogeneous continuum" grounded in nineteenth-century notions of time and space. "Undoing history," a term circulating in the living history field, implies that museum staff can retrace history, backward, along a developmental timeline in order to arrive at the past event. If time is viewed as a homogeneous continuum in this model, then the assumption is that one simply needs to reverse the formula and work backward in order to "undo" the progress that has accompanied the elapse of time. Hayden White poses a question about the culture out of which such conceptions of time emerge. In "The Value of Narrativity in the Representation of Reality," he asks, "What kind of notion of reality authorizes the construction of a narrative account of reality in which continuity rather than discontinuity governs the articulation of discourse?"[2]

Because museum curators and scholars operate with this view of time as a homogeneous continuum, the current scholarship on living history is, it would seem, limited to addressing whether or not museums are achieving accuracy in their programming and the barriers that lie in the way. For example, in essays like Kate Stover's "Is It *Real* History Yet?" or *Early American Life*'s "Living History: Getting Closer to Getting It Right," the questions focus on the continuing pursuit of historical documents or archaeological evidence that would close the gaps in the understanding of the past. Other critics suggest living history museums ought to work harder to include stories of those formerly relegated to the margins of history: blacks, women, the poor, native peoples, and others (much of history has covered up or downplayed the unfair or degrading practices in America, while celebrating the deeds and ideals of the "founding fathers").

While I do hold that leaving aspects of historical racism and violence unaddressed in a representation of a time period is unethical, I will not be focusing on this as a lack of "accuracy," nor will I dwell on pinpointing inaccuracies in living history museums. The subject of this book moves in a different direction. Accuracy and objectivity are neither achievable goals nor transcendent qualities (Peter Novick has established that objectivity—since the end of the Cold War, during which it enjoyed a return to favor by the American historical profession—"has become more problematic than ever before").[3] Accuracy and authenticity are socially constructed relationships.

The degree to which a museum's historical environment is authentic has less to do with an ontological category of "authenticity," or how long and hard it has worked to get there, and much more to do with how the museum has managed its reputation as a rigorous, authoritative institution, and the degree to which visitors perceive and put stock in this reputation. In other words, instead of asking whether or not the staging of the past can be accurate, my question is: How have Colonial Williamsburg, Sturbridge Village, Plimoth Plantation, and other living history museums used performance to *make* accuracy and authenticity? To answer this, I look at conceptions of time and space, modes of performance, and the fields of relationships in the twentieth century that determined the conditions that allowed living history to emerge.

What is at stake? Living history museums have been critiqued for many things in the past thirty years. The major criticisms, according to Jay Anderson, fall into two categories: first, that living history "beautifies" historical periods and events, favoring aesthetically pleasing, utopian images of the past over more "accurate," dirtier ones; and second, that even if institutions try to accurately portray historical events, the enormous gap in historical data between the present and the past makes it impossible to claim any sort of accuracy. Both claims are valid, but only if based on the logic that the quality of representation is directly related to the degree of accuracy obtained. The touchstone of this logic is the assumption that the ideal reality of the original historical event, although physically unachievable, can be closely approached if the institutions can collect a quantitative amount of data or a qualitative understanding of the past through research. The idea that the closer one can get to the real or authentic original, the better the representation, implies that accuracy is the criterion for ethically good academic and touristic practices. With this criterion as the basis for institutional inquiry, the ethical problems of living history museums are, in a sense, solvable, or at least one can work toward a greater sense of ethical (re)presentation by means of more research. However, since accuracy and authenticity are constructions relative to the political and philosophical perceptions of the institution, these institutions produce what Gilles Deleuze and Félix Guattari call "fabulations," articulating intersections of present sensibilities informed by the current state of affairs.[4]

Have books like this one been written before? Not exactly. The major study on living history in general is *Time Machines: The World of Living History*, written by Jay Anderson in 1984. Anderson divides living history into three distinct categories: living history for educational purposes, living history as a research tool, and living history as recreation (for "history buffs").

Educational living history uses reenactment to animate restored forts, villages, and so forth for museum purposes. These museums are usually funded, often accredited, and use costumed enactment programming in lieu of, or in addition to, traditional collections. Living history as a research tool is conducted mainly by archaeologists and social scientists, who use reconstructive, experimental, or imitative techniques in outdoor laboratories in order to generate "new data" about a historic time. Examples of living history as a research tool include Thor Heyerdahl's *Kon Tiki* and experimental ancient farms like Buster Farms in England, which reconstruct primitive or historical agricultural practices. Living-history buffs are those nonprofessionals who reenact history for personal reasons, for play, or to get away from everyday life or what Alvin Toffler termed "future shock." These buffs are to be found all over the country, engaging in "mock" Civil War battles, "rendezvous" gatherings, and craft fairs, often rivaling the rigor of their professional counterparts in their attention to detail.

Anderson devotes a portion of his book to each of these types of living history. His writing is anecdotal and is based largely on his own experience working on the curatorial and performance staffs of several of the larger museums. Anderson also posits a general narrative of living history museums, beginning in 1881 with Sweden's Skansen, which he considers the first open-air museum, and progressively developing toward maturity in the 1980s with museum reenactment in the United States.

My approach differs in that, rather than addressing my subjects by placing each of them into a different mode of living history, I specifically articulate the relationships between beliefs and practices within institutional museum sites that use costumed interpretation as a historiographic practice. I also resituate living history museums into a genealogy of performance that departs from Anderson's traditionally accepted model of the linear evolution of museum display.

Other book-length studies treat specific living history institutions as their subjects. Stephen Eddy Snow's book on Plimoth Plantation, *Performing the Pilgrims*, includes a history of the changes that have occurred in museum practices with a move toward revisionist history. Central to Snow's argument is the question of whether or not the programming at Plimoth Plantation can be considered "theatre." Snow maintains that Plimoth indeed features a "theatre of the Pilgrims," presenting his case using both comparative analysis and his own experience in theatre and performance.[5] However, Snow limits his performance narrative to traditional, mainstream realism, then opens it up to a larger discussion of what Victor Turner speaks of as ritual or aesthetic performance and Richard Schechner's analogy between ancestor worship and theatre. The problem is that Snow chooses to include only those events in the Pilgrims' and Plimoth's history that fit into patterns of cyclical conflict-and-resolution stories. While dramatically interesting, the vast majority of other histories are erased.

Most notably, the inclusion of a discussion of the Wampanoag village, Hobbamock's Homesite, remains absent in Snow's account, since the Native interpreters do not "reenact" according to mainstream theatrical techniques. Snow chooses not to include a history and analysis of the Wampanoag Interpretation Program at the plantation because, in his words, "the Native American interpreters for the most part no longer employ the first person role-playing technique" with the exception of a fur trade between Hobbamock and three Pilgrim characters—the main point of contact between the Pilgrims and Native interpreters at the time of Snow's writing.

While Snow's book remains the essential work on performance, ethnography, and anthropology at Plimoth Plantation, I believe that there are several questions he leaves unanswered. The primary one concerns adequately addressing Plimoth Plantation's Wampanoag Interpretation Program and why it does not include programming that fits a traditional, psychological-realism approach to performance. The performance practices that these interpreters *do* engage in are very intriguing and deserve more attention. The Native interpreters choose not to speak in seventeenth-century dialects, but instead speak from a contemporary position, allowing the voicing of the history of genocide and treaty violations that would need to be left silenced if they were to limit themselves to the time-specific voice of their neighbors in the 1627 Pilgrim Village.

The second large question concerns whether we can analyze the performance at Plimoth with theories other than the now-conservative models of the nineteenth- and early twentieth-century realists and naturalists. Though Snow does treat Brechtian techniques briefly,[6] his understanding of such concepts as Brecht's *Verfremdungseffekt* might be more helpfully applied. Finally, Snow invokes a discussion of postmodernism by saying that Plimoth is comprised of a postmodern thrust toward a "blurring of genres."[7] With Schechner, he states that "historical restoration is actually a version of the postmodern. It assumes that spectators, and restorers, can shift temporal channels."[8] While his discussion focuses on how Plimoth Plantation is part of a postmodern milieu in which art, tourism, and culture are all at play, he does not use postmodern practices in his work. Rather, he sticks to a very conservative course, including a history of first-person interpretation that reads like cultural Darwinism in the evolutionary development of a kind of superior form of interpretation, latently awaiting emergence with the shift to costumed role-playing in the late 1960s.

Richard Handler and Eric Gable's large, comprehensive work, *The New History in an Old Museum: Creating the Past at Colonial Williamsburg*, treats this living history museum's shift to social history, especially in regard to the representation of Williamsburg's black slaves. Handler and Gable refer to the controversy over the newer portrayal of colonial history as a "culture war."[9] They identify two current strains of historic scholarship at Colonial Williamsburg. The "realist/objectivist" historians consider themselves getting progressively closer to the real history every day. They base historic truth on the weight of evidence and do not consider that there could be many histories, each truer than the next based on the subjectivity of the historian.[10] Realist/objectivists promote reenactment as "mimetic" or "progressive realism," with accuracy as an achievable aim. In this sense, history can be resuscitated again, for educational purposes, and the past can "come alive."[11] The "constructionist" historians, on the other hand, advocate a model of presentation that comments on the lives and history of their historical subjects, while at the same time foregrounding the fact that the history as we know it is subject to change. They recognize the inherent gaps of a history based upon certain documents that were allowed to survive only because they belonged to those who held positions of power in a dominant hegemony.

Handler and Gable conclude that the museum is not a "living history," no matter what it claims. "Colonial Williamsburg, like any other museum and historic site, is a present-day reality. . . . It is not, nor can it be, the past brought to life. It is not, nor can it be 'authentic.'"[12] The crowning irony of the situation, they write, is that Colonial Williamsburg historians are the first to admit this. But the view does not make it to the "frontline" interpretive staff, who often feel they must stick to the conservative, party-line version of history promoted by their institution. Museums like Williamsburg, moreover, confuse the visiting public by "claiming authority based on the institutional possession of a historic reality," with harmful results.[13] Not only does the mimetic realism of Colonial Williamsburg "destroy history" by making various erasures based on specific political and cultural values, but as a consequence it also "deadens the historical sensibility of the public. It teaches people not to question the historians' stories, not to imagine other, alternative histories, but to accept an embodied tableau as the really real."[14]

Cary Carson, vice president of research at Colonial Williamsburg, in a *Journal of American History* essay responded to Handler and Gable's initial critiques, calling their view of Williamsburg's disparity between the curators' view of history and that of frontline interpretation "sophomore-level 'cultural hegemony' theory."[15] Carson counters the critiques point by point, arguing that, with the move to social history programming, interpreters have more freedom in what they share with the visitor—indeed, that they have the equivalent of their own classroom. "The process can be opened to admit even more sunshine, to be sure, but the notion that upper-echelon administrators are the message-makers at Colonial Williamsburg and interpreters merely their mouth pieces is an anthropologist's fairy tale."[16] Carson offers his own condensed history of interpretive programming at Colonial Williamsburg in an issue of the *Public Historian*. He describes the pitfalls of administering the museum, from making extensive changes in a huge organizational structure to overcoming obsolete pedagogical strategies (i.e., moving from the "ordinary off-the-shelf, standard-fourth-of-July, patriotic rhetoric" of the Cold War to making room for ordinary people with the emergence of social history in the later decades of the twentieth century).[17]

The most recent book-length account of the history of Williamsburg is Anders Greenspan's *Creating Colonial Williamsburg*, though this work does not focus as much attention on the performance aspects of the museum as it does on institutional and policy changes throughout its seventy-five years (the author prefers the term *restoration* to *living museum*). Greenspan categorizes the roles of Williamsburg into eras, starting in the 1920s, when it functioned as a perceived bulwark against foreign ideas that threatened "American Values." In the 1930s, Williamsburg promoted individual initiative in the darkest days of the Depression. By the 1950s, it was a participant in the Cold War and a promoter of the representational model of government in the rest of the world. With the arrival of social history in the 1970s, Greenspan writes, Colonial Williamsburg "achieved maturity." The most valuable aspect of Greenspan's study is that it takes on the question of why African-American narratives were such a late addition to Williamsburg's institutional history, as well as to the history of colonial Virginia it produced. Greenspan cites the pervasive racism of the segregationist South in much of the twentieth century and how it was reflected in Williamsburg's labor and visitor policies. Even with the Civil Rights Movement, the museum and its curators were unforgivably reluctant to present black history on "an equal basis with that of the white founding fathers."[18] Greenspan posits that these decisions were indicative of a conservative strategy that has plagued Williamsburg for decades: steering a middle course between seeking to be better at history but not offending its conservative supporters—a strategy that, more often than not, damned them on both counts.[19]

In addition to general works such as Anderson's *Time Machines* and specific works on individual sites, other volumes are devoted to techniques for historical reconstruction, thematic programming, costumed reenactment, and performance at living history sites. Stacy F. Roth's *Past into Present: Effective Techniques for First-Person Historical Interpretation* (1998) and William

T. Alderson and Shirley Payne Low's *Interpretation of Historic Sites* (1985) take a more prescriptive approach to living history programming, as does Freeman Tilden's *Interpreting Our Heritage* (1977).

Several master's and doctoral theses treat living museums. Susan K. Irwin's master's thesis, "Popular History: Living-History Sites, Historical Interpretation, and the Public" (Bowling Green State University, 1993), critiques museums' claims to historical accuracy. Three important doctoral studies treat the manner in which popular living museums deal with Native and African-American histories in their programming: Laura Peers' "'Playing Ourselves': Native Histories, Native Interpreters, and Living History Sites" (McMaster University, 1996), Anna Logan Lawson's "'The Other Half': Making African-American History at Colonial Williamsburg" (University of Virginia, 1995), and Rex Ellis's "Presenting the Past: Education, Interpretation, and the Teaching of Black History at Colonial Williamsburg" (College of William and Mary, 1989).

Most of the other published material on living history and tourism consists of either tourist literature, items in popular magazines and newspapers, or critiques in academic journals. Michael Wallace's 1981 essay, "Visiting the Past: History Museums in the United States," originally appearing in the *Radical History Review*, calls the capitalist motives of popular living history sites into question, in addition to offering his own genealogy of museums (stemming from Skansen, much like Anderson's account). Several articles address specific instances of conflicts that have occurred at these sites in recent years. The decision to reenact a slave auction at Colonial Williamsburg in 1994, for example, received much attention in the press. However, it would appear that no large studies treat the broader subject of living history museums in terms of historiographic practices, the creation of identity, curatorial agendas, or the modes of institutional representation of time and space. Little has been written about challenging the fundamental ideals and procedures that serve as the modus operandi of these institutions. These are the questions I will examine.

Methodologies, Strategies, and Procedures

This book is grounded in theories of performance and historiography and involves primary research and recent interviews at current living history museums in the United States. Chapter 1 traces the manner in which living history museums' "history" has been written. Teasing out the limits of an evolutionary development of costumed interpretation, as held by Anderson, and examining the notions of time and space in physics and popular understandings that inform and are reflected by representational practices in living history museums, I indicate the dilemmas in living interpretation, from misleading visitors about both time and history to perpetuating outmoded views of progress in museum programming.

Chapter 2 offers a new genealogy of living museum performance, reexamining the shifts in the nineteenth and twentieth centuries in terms of economics, how time and space have been defined, how national identity was produced and instilled, and how major living history museums have answered to each of these relationships. My movement through this terrain is spatial rather than linear—one which stops to select certain enunciations that define an epistemological field.

In chapter 3, I consider the specific performance practices used in the programming at these living history museums and examine these practices in relation to the institutions' notions of time and space and recent shifts in curatorial goals and policies. With a new historiography come new possibilities of historical display and reenactment that break from the limited dichotomy of linear past and present.

The primary institutions in my research are Plimoth Plantation in Massachusetts, Colonial Williamsburg in Virginia, and Old Sturbridge Village in Massachusetts. These sites represent three different "historical periods" in what is now the eastern United States: early colonization of the "New World," pre-Revolutionary Colonial America, and 1830s New England, respectively. Each of these museums practices costumed interpretation in simulated past environments. Each has been granted a significant amount of authority by virtue of its educational programs and popular appeal. Furthermore, all three have been critiqued on their commitment to accuracy and have negotiated within their programming in order to address these issues. I conducted additional research at Living History Farms (Iowa), Greenfield Village (Michigan), Historic Fort Snelling (Minnesota), Old World Wisconsin, Strawbery Banke (New Hampshire), Pioneer Village (Massachusetts), Jamestown Settlement and Yorktown Victory Center (Virginia), Mystic Seaport (Connecticut), Conner Prairie (Indiana), Old Fort William (Ontario, Canada), and Skansen (Stockholm, Sweden), as well as numerous small-scale pioneer villages and community historical society sites.

Use of Terms

Living History
Living history is a somewhat ironic and misleading term in that it implies, on the one hand, that other forms of history are "dead" and, on the other, that

one can bring history back to life by way of performance. It is a blanket term used in popular discourse to cover individuals or groups that engage in practices that evoke a different historical time from the present. These practices include costuming, pageantry, battle reenactment, buckskinning, rendezvous, pioneer villages, living history museums, imitative research institutions, cemetery walks, living dioramas, and the production of crafts by artisans using time-specific methods.

Barbara Kirshenblatt-Gimblett states that museums boasting "living heritage" engage in false advertisement. "Heritage signifies death, whether actual or imminent," she writes. "'Heritage,' the term and concept, endows the dead and the dying with a second life, an *afterlife*, through the instrumentalities of exhibition and performance. It is in this sense that heritage productions are 'resurrection theatre.'"[20] Kirshenblatt-Gimblett's phrase "resurrection theatre" echoes Joseph Roach's "cities of the dead," which Roach defines as commemorations through acts of surrogation of a lost history.[21] Plimoth Plantation, a "living museum" since 1969, speaks to this irony, claiming to be a living representation of history. But the reason this history is so attractive is precisely because it has been dead for so long. No living episode of American history could evoke as much nostalgia, since nostalgia is not produced until the very moment of loss. The idea of an irrevocable age or of a "dying race," such as Native Americans in traditional garb signify, hearkens a nostalgia, which, according to Dean MacCannell, taps into a reverence for a threatened element of life. "The negative attitude so prevalent in society toward anything which is old, *dépassé* or alien dissolves into sentimentality and respect whenever the object in question is the last of its kind."[22]

Living History Museum
While not all institutions I include in my study advertise themselves as "living history museums," I use the term to describe those institutions (whether for-profit or not-for-profit) that practice costumed interpretation within reconstructed or restored sites and that depict a particular time in history for educational purposes. These attractions are sites to which tourists travel in order to engage in what is advertised as a different temporal space, to interact with a simulation of a past time as part of an educational or recreational enterprise. Colonial Williamsburg, Old Sturbridge Village, and Plimoth Plantation are examples of living history museums. These sites are not actual pasts—that is, they are not the historic actualities that they reference. Rather, they are what Jean Baudrillard would term *simulacra*: images that are better and more real than any lived events or spaces by virtue of the institutional authority that legitimizes them.[23]

In addition to being sites of leisure, living history museums arrange the records and acquired rationalizations of the past in order to present certain stagings of history. Traditional historic reenactments utilize a form of representation based on linear narratives that must choose to portray certain elements and relationships while repressing others. These sites are simulations, but an examination of these sites that is grounded solely in the criteria normally reserved for realistic and naturalistic modes of representation can only be limited to focusing on the relationship between the simulations and the actualities they reference.

First-Person and Third-Person Costumed Interpretation

Interpretation is the industry term for museum programming in the form of educational interaction between museum staff and museum visitors.[24] There is a considerable amount of hairsplitting to be done, however, over the distinction between "first-person" and "third-person." At the most basic level, the difference between the two is that first-person interpreters speak in the first-person, present indicative tense when informing visitors about the lives and times they are portraying in the museum's environment. That is, they perform their roles as if they were the subject on display: a costumed black slave interpreter at Colonial Williamsburg would say, "Lord Dunmore has offered freedom to those of us who would take up arms against the colonists advocating freedom from England." Third-person interpreters, often in historic costume, also interpret the lives of the people the museum displays, but in a third-person, preterit verb tense: "The townspeople who lived here in the nineteenth century used the same breed of cattle for work, dairy products, meat, and tallow for candles," costumed farm workers tell visitors to Old Sturbridge Village. While it would be easy to define the first type of interpreter as an actor and the second as a docent, both are modes of performance, and oftentimes neither one will consider himself or herself an actor.

Now comes the hairsplitting: there are several modes of interpretation within the first and third persons. At many sites, the first-person interpreters will never "break character." They do not outwardly recognize any time after the established day of their interpretation and will refuse to acknowledge that the visitors asking them questions are from the "future." These interpreters will treat the visitors as if they were fellow colonists, social equals or betters (rarely treating them as inferior in class or race) from far away. Plimoth Plantation is known for the quality of its first-person interpreters and their rock-solid characters that cannot be cracked by even the peskiest of "Pilgrim-Baiters" (described in Snow's book as those gadflies who make a game out of trying to poke holes in the interpreters' façades).

Such restrictive practices open first-person interpretation to the criticism that it limits the learning to a small period of history and prevents making connections with the present. First-person interpreters use various means to negotiate around this dilemma. Patrick Henry (interpreted by Richard Schumann), whom I met in June 2000 at Colonial Williamsburg, fielded questions from the spectators asking about events after 1775, saying:

> At this time I will be very pleased to answer to any queries or curiosities you may have of me, be they regarding my person or our general state of affairs. I have even been known upon many occasions in past, to be able to speculate into the future with some great accuracy. But I certainly would not wish to style myself a soothsayer.[25]

Schumann told me afterward that he can get away with this because, in some accounts, Henry is described as being prone to forecast future events and political climates with sometimes surprising accuracy.

Elsewhere, at sites like Historic Fort Snelling, the interpreters will address the visitor in first person until being asked a question the interpreter cannot answer without breaking character and speaking in a present-day voice. At that point, rather than continuing in the first person, they will transition (smoothly or choppily, depending on the experience and talent of the interpreter) into the third person, introduce themselves as the present-day individual, and answer the question using the past tense. This mode, says Stephen Osman, the Fort Snelling site manager, allows visitors to be comfortable in asking questions, rather than making them feel as if the interpreters are standoffish on matters not directly related to nineteenth-century Minnesota.[26] Other museum interpreters will employ the "my time-your time" technique, which allows for more comparison and contrast. "My musket is the most advanced firearm of my day," says a Continental soldier at Yorktown Victory Center, "but I am told that in your time, there are automatic rifles which do not require reloading before every discharge."

Yet another mode of the first person, employed in some programming at Colonial Williamsburg, is to have a visitor from the past, speaking in first-person present, in a modern venue (Stacy Roth refers to this as "ghost interpretation").[27] I attended an "Audience with Thomas Jefferson" in the DeWitt Wallace Fine Arts Gallery at Colonial Williamsburg in June 2000. Mr. Jefferson (Bill Barker) informed us, after commenting on the strange architecture of the modern auditorium, that he was a visitor to our time and would answer questions stemming from our time, but reminded us that he could answer only from his knowledge and experience from his own time.

A practice not as common in the living history field is "second-person in-terpretation." This refers to the "hands-on" activities and programming of-fered by living history museums in which visitors may try out various prac-tices such as weaving, cooking, or musket loading and can imagine that they are interpreting the past through physical means. Living History Farms even begins its visitor orientation by handing out work gloves stamped with the museum logo. Not only does this encourage visitors to help patch a cabin wall with mud or to try their hand at the plow but it also gives them a take-home souvenir, reminding them of their visit to the past.

Recently, some museums have begun to give visitors even more of a char-acter role in second-person programming. Old Sturbridge Village's Summer-Shops program gives children the chance to play nineteenth-century New Englanders for a week. In April 2004, I participated in "Follow the North Star" at Conner Prairie, a living history museum depicting nineteenth-century Indiana. In this program, daytime visitors return to the museum at night and step into the roles of fugitive black slaves seeking freedom in the north. Several times a night in the spring and summer months, forty Conner Prairie staff members, performing slave owners, bounty hunters, helpful Quakers, and so on, lead small groups of participants from point to point, un-der cover of darkness through a simulated threatening environment, seeking to teach the history of slavery in Indiana in the nineteenth century.[28] Colo-nial Williamsburg's "Enslaving Virginia" program casts "admission-paying tourists" as slaves and, according to one account, "has evoked such strong emotions that some audience members have attacked actors playing the role of slave owners."[29]

The Museum Visitor

Because of their multiple roles, I employ the terms *visitors*, *spectators*, and *tourists* interchangeably to describe those individuals who attend living his-tory museums. David Carr advocates the term *user* or *learner*, rather than merely "visitor," since this individual is an "actor and thinking receiver" who is "embedded in an environment."[30] Parks Canada, which operates Canadian historical sites, refers to its museums' visitors as "interpreters," since it holds that *they* are the ones doing the interpreting (the costumed staff are referred to as "performers").[31] The currently preferred industry term in the United States tends to be "visitor."

The reader will not find a substantial ethnography of the museum visitor in this book. While I recognize that a discussion of representational practices is not a one-sided affair, I have limited this project to the curatorial and performative procedures of living history institutions and to the manner in which these practices have been disseminated, celebrated, and critiqued in scholarship and other literature. Determining the extent to which visitors believe the history represented at these museums is *real* would be a difficult task, since each touristic experience is subjective and relative to the individual. Asking on-site visitors, "Do you believe this is real?" or a similar question to that effect would bar a complex analysis, since, in my estimation, the answer would always be no. No one would go as far as to equate living environments with the *actual* past (although there are always the stories of the visitors to Plimoth who, not realizing this is a performance, conflate the Pilgrim interpreters with contemporary sects, believing them to be akin to the similarly dressed Amish).

Many studies have already taken the tourist as the main subject of inquiry, most notably Dean MacCannell's *The Tourist: A New Theory of the Leisure Class*.[32] The idea of the tourist, however, is changing. Maxine Feifer and John Urry have pointed to the emergence of what they each call the new tourist, or "post-tourist," who is no longer a generalized seeker of the "authentic." Feifer writes that the post-tourist is one who has an eye for, and can buy, a piece of touristic kitsch without making a fetish out of it and who recognizes "the glossy tourist brochure is an interesting piece of pop culture, maybe, but not 'reality.'"[33] Urry adds, in *The Tourist Gaze*, that

> "post tourists" almost delight in the inauthenticity of the normal tourist experience. "Post tourists" find pleasure in the multiplicity of tourist games. They know that there is *no* authentic tourist experience, that there are merely a series of games or texts that can be played.[34]

Above all, he says, "The post-tourist is . . . self-conscious, 'cool' and role-distanced."[35]

Living museums do not yet appear to cater to the post-tourist and still emphasize accuracy and authenticity in programming, signage, and travel literature. In the post-touristic, post-9/11 landscape of the twenty-first century, with dramatically fluctuating gasoline prices and a seemingly ever-expanding number of options from which families may choose what John H. Falk and Lynn D. Dierking term "free-choice learning" activities, time will tell whether living museum audiences will constitute a major segment of tourist destinations.[36] (According to Leo Landis, curator of agriculture and rural life at Greenfield Village, there is toughening competition for tourists' leisure time and dollars, forcing many historic sites to cut back on programming.[37] A recent *Washington Post* article reports, too, that many museums increasingly find it necessary to offer historically inaccurate programs, for example,

Christmas celebrations with anachronistic Christmas trees and Santa Clauses, in an effort to combat slipping attendance.[38] Meanwhile, Colonial Williamsburg has added a new "Podcasting" program in which listeners may download MP3 files from Williamsburg's "Past and Present" series onto their iPods, as a way of moving museum-user experience into the twenty-first century.)[39] Museums are, and will continue to be, purveyors of knowledge and culture. They won't go away soon, but they're no longer going to be the same meccas of authenticity they were in the nineteenth and twentieth centuries.

* * *

Like Snout the tinker's Wall, living history museums *become* the real past, not by transporting their spectators back in time but by emphasizing their historical authenticity aloud. My project is to maneuver through the space of these enunciations, noting where they are similar, organizing them according to the discourses that link them, and searching for their reverberations in the field and in the archives. Unfortunately, these statements do not exist in the same way as when they were first enunciated. Instead, as Foucault describes them, they exist in *remanence*—preserved residually by virtue of a number of supports and material techniques (i.e., in a book). They survive by their material existence and by the techniques that put them into operation, and it is against these statements that memory can be deployed.[40] Like any historiographic labor, mine is not the last word on my subject. Rather, I hope it will function as a *threshold* in discourse surrounding living history museums: a culmination of knowledge that pushes thought (my own and others') in a new direction.

Notes

1. Samuel Taylor Coleridge, "Progress of the Drama," in *Dramatic Theory and Criticism: Greeks to Grotowski*, ed. Bernard E. Dukore (Fort Worth, TX: Harcourt, 1976), 586–88.

2. Hayden White, "The Value of Narrativity in the Representation of Reality," *Critical Inquiry* 7.1 (Autumn 1980), 5–27.

3. Peter Novick, *That Noble Dream: The "Objectivity Question" and the American Historical Profession* (Cambridge, UK: Cambridge University Press, 1998), 17.

4. Gilles Deleuze and Félix Guattari, *What Is Philosophy?*, trans. Hugh Tomlinson and Graham Burchell (New York: Columbia University Press, 1994), 167–68.

5. Stephen Eddy Snow, *Performing the Pilgrims: A Study of Ethnohistorical Role-Playing at Plimoth Plantation* (Jackson: University Press of Mississippi, 1993), 5.

6. Snow, *Performing the Pilgrims*, 147–48, 181.

7. Snow, *Performing the Pilgrims*, 191.

8. Snow, *Performing the Pilgrims*, 191.

9. Richard Handler and Eric Gable, *The New History in an Old Museum: Creating the Past at Colonial Williamsburg* (Durham, NC: Duke University Press, 1997), 7.

10. Handler and Gable, *New History in an Old Museum*, 59, 60.

11. Handler and Gable, *New History in an Old Museum*, 70.

12. Handler and Gable, *New History in an Old Museum*, 223.

13. Handler and Gable, *New History in an Old Museum*, 223. If one wonders whether Handler and Gable's accusation of Colonial Williamsburg having a monopoly on history is correct, one need only look at the address of its website: www.history.org. Apparently, when one logs on to this site, he or she is not just downloading a tourist attraction or museum onto their browser; they are downloading "history." The museum's toll-free number similarly points to the "institutional possession of a historic reality": 1-800-HISTORY.

14. Handler and Gable, *New History in an Old Museum*, 224.

15. Cary Carson, "Lost in the Fun House: A Commentary on Anthropologists' First Contact with History Museums," *Journal of American History* 81.1 (June 1994): 137–45.

16. Carson, "Lost in the Fun House."

17. Cary Carson, "Colonial Williamsburg and the Practice of Interpretive Planning in American History Museums," *Public Historian* 20.3 (Summer 1998): 30.

18. Anders Greenspan, *Creating Colonial Williamsburg* (Washington, DC: Smithsonian Institution Press, 2002), 122.

19. Greenspan, *Creating Colonial Williamsburg*, 151.

20. Barbara Kirshenblatt-Gimblett, "Afterlives," *Performance Research* 2.2 (Summer 1997): 4.

21. Joseph Roach, *Cities of the Dead: Circum-Atlantic Performance* (New York: Columbia University Press, 1996).

22. Dean MacCannell, *The Tourist: A New Theory of the Leisure Class* (Berkeley: University of California Press, 1999), 88.

23. Jean Baudrillard, "The Precession of Simulacra," in *Simulacra and Simulation*, trans. Sheila Faria Glaser (Ann Arbor: University of Michigan Press, 1994), 6.

24. Various American institutions have experimented with other terminology. Borrowing from cultural anthropology, for instance, Plimoth Plantation briefly called its interpreters "informants," from whom the visitors (the interpreters) would learn about the culture and time of the Pilgrims. See James Deetz, "The Link from Object to Person to Concept," in *Museums, Adults, and the Humanities*, ed. Zipporah W. Collins (Washington, DC: American Association of Museums, 1981), 32.

25. "A Public Audience with Patrick Henry," 6 June 2000, Palace Garden, Colonial Williamsburg.

26. Stephen Osman, personal interview, 13 May 2000.

27. Stacy F. Roth, *Past into Present: Effective Techniques for First-Person Historical Interpretation* (Chapel Hill: University of North Carolina Press, 1998), 17.

28. See my article "'This Is a Drama—You Are Characters': The Tourist as Fugitive Slave in Conner Prairie's 'Follow the North Star,'" *Theatre Topics* (Spring 2006).

29. Bonnie Sachatello-Sawyer, Robert A. Fellenz, Hanly Burton, Laura Gittings-Carlson, Janet Lewis-Mahony, and Walter Woolbaugh, *Adult Museum Programs: Designing Meaningful Experiences* (Walnut Creek, CA: AltaMira, 2002), 57.

30. David Carr, *The Promise of Cultural Institutions* (Walnut Creek, CA: AltaMira, 2003), xiv, 3–4.

31. Thomas Shaw, assistant site manager, Historic Fort Snelling, personal interview, 13 May 2000.

32. Handler and Gable conducted several interviews with visitors to Colonial Williamsburg, as did Lawson. Greenspan makes heavy use of letters from visitors in the Colonial Williamsburg archives. Peers treated reception theory extensively in her study on Native interpretation at living history sites in the United States and Canada.

33. Maxine Feifer, *Tourism in History: From Imperial Rome to the Present* (New York: Stein & Day, 1985), 270–71.

34. John Urry, *The Tourist Gaze: Leisure and Travel in Contemporary Societies* (London: Sage, 1990), 11.

35. Urry, *Tourist Gaze*, 100–101.

36. See John H. Falk and Lynn D. Dierking, *Lessons without Limit: How Free-Choice Learning Is Transforming Education* (Walnut Creek, CA: AltaMira, 2002) and *Learning from Museums: Visitor Experiences and the Making of Meaning* (Walnut Creek, CA: AltaMira, 2000).

37. Leo Landis, interviewed by Lynn Neary, "Adventures in Re-creating History," *Talk of the Nation*, National Public Radio, 5 July 2004.

38. David A. Fahrenthold, "Living-History Museums Struggle to Draw Visitors: Creativity Drives Changes in Hunt for Attendance," *Washington Post*, 25 December 2005.

39. "Colonial Williamsburg Podcasts Debut," *Colonial Williamsburg: The Journal of the Colonial Williamsburg Foundation* (Autumn 2005): 17.

40. Michel Foucault, *The Archaeology of Knowledge*, trans. A. M. Sheridan Smith (New York: Pantheon, 1972), 124.

~

CHAPTER ONE

The Dilemmas of Contemporary Living Museum Historiography in Theory and Practice

The Progressive Development Narrative
of Living Museum History

History is not a list of names, dates, and events that ought to be remembered because they are more important or have more magnitude than others. History is a practice. It is the arrangement of records by individuals motivated by politics, by bias, or by that which is "knowable." Most often, a history is the end product, or remnant, of a practice or set of practices (sometimes involving great amounts of labor). That product then substitutes for, even erases, the work that went into creating it. It is precisely because of the product that the process becomes unnecessary and does not need to be visible along with the product. However, because the process, politics, or agenda behind a history is no longer visible, it is difficult, if not impossible, for the reader or audience to see why or how this *particular* history has come to exist, rather than another. To put it another way, the reader or audience can see from this history only those events that have been chosen as important, not those that have been deemed inappropriate, unfit, or unworthy of inclusion.

When one reads about the history of the emergence and development of living museums in the United States, there is a certain set of events that stand out as pivotal or essential. One of the major factors motivating the selection of this particular set of events is an understanding, on the part of the historian, that living history museums today are the product of an "evolutionary" development from simple to complex. That is, certain events,

decisions, or changes happened because of the march of progress. By imposing an imaginary, Darwinistic model of development upon the history of living museums, scholars such as Jay Anderson have privileged particular events
in their records that affirm this model, while erasing others. Artur Hazelius's
Skansen, for example, a nineteenth-century Scandinavian outdoor museum,
has been established as the "origin" of the living history "movement."[1] From
there, according to Anderson, the outdoor museum progressed by slow and
consistent degrees, from simple to complex, to arrive at the model of perfection in the first-person, present-tense mode of costumed interpretation, as
exemplified by contemporary living history museums such as Plimoth Plantation in Massachusetts.

The current model of the progressive development of museum display is
detrimental to an understanding of living history museums. Events that Anderson and others choose as the links in such an evolutionary development of
living history become authoritative moments that limit the way these institutions and their recent shifts in programming may be thought about and discussed. By restricting the events to only those that fit into a model of linear
evolution of museum display, other events in the past that lie outside of a linear timeline (especially events that occur chronologically prior to what has
been established as the "origin" of living history development, i.e., Skansen)
are neglected. In so doing, scholars not only engage in a selection process informed by political and intellectual ideologies but also construct the identity of
these events as links in a cause-and-effect chain, rather than as autonomous
moments. Acts, statements, and representational practices always have consequences. It is important, however, to distinguish between causal events (e.g.,
the adoption of first-person interpretation), which have traceable reverberations, and causal patterns or systems that are presumed to "naturally" lead to
the emergence of events (e.g., notions of progress, the "instinct" to perform, or
the American "character") but that exist only in the abstract.

The term *development*, in itself, is also misleading, in that it often implies
an expansion or evolution of something that contains within it the potential
for progress. Thus we talk about the development of land that was formerly
wilderness or the development of a mind from a tabula rasa. In short, to utilize the word *development* implies that the subject of discussion already contains the kernel or code that has a potential for fulfillment in an imaginary
model of perfection—just as an acorn would have, within its makeup, the potential to develop into a perfect oak tree. While the word may be helpful
when discussing oak trees, it is a faulty universalism that would allow the
same model of development to be applied to all subjects. Hazelius's Skansen
was *not* the kernel for Plimoth Plantation. There was no human instinct

within Artur Hazelius toward perfect living history museum display that he could not fully realize due to a shortage of the proper amount of time required for the slow and consistent degrees of evolution to take place. Living history scholars do Skansen a historiographic injustice by assigning it a mythic status of primitive origin. The evolutionary model tempts the museum visitor, interpreter, and curator, as well as the reader and scholar, to favor the present as more advanced—indeed, the pinnacle of evolutionary development to date. This favoritism produces a bias against the past. Thus, discussion of early history museums as well as the subject of their exhibition—the past—is marked by implicit or explicit labels of "primitive" or "naive."

It is necessary to begin chapter 1 of this book by treating the evolutionary model of the development of living history museum interpretation enunciated by those in the scholarly community. Jay Anderson's evolutionary model of living history museums or similar models of the development of museum display have been embraced by other scholars in their work on living history. The model has emerged at numerous intersections in the field of living history, including works by Laura E. Abing, Edward P. Alexander, Jay Anderson, Andrew Baker, Cary Carson, James and Patricia Scott Deetz, Anders Greenspan, H. Holzer, Susan K. Irwin, John D. Krugler, Michael Lang, Warren Leon, Patricia Mandell, Margaret Piatt, Stephen Eddy Snow, Kate F. Stover, and Michael Wallace.[2]

Reexamining the genealogy of living history, suggesting instead a postmodern understanding of the events that allows one to talk about living history in the present, will help to rethink twentieth- and twenty-first-century museum practices. These are not sites or events that tell or teach a latent "history," that is, the events, dates, and individuals in the past that were more important than others. Instead, these are institutions that construct particular "histories" informed by specific events, ideologies, and discourses.

Progressive Histories: Major Works

In his 1984 book *Time Machines: The World of Living History*, Anderson adopts the Darwinian model of evolution as a strategy for placing various events connected to living history museums into an understandable context and thereby giving them meaning. Understood in chronological order, in a movement from simple to complex, Anderson can place a number of events which appear similar—museum display, restoration projects, and performance—into a narrative that provides an identity and history to contemporary living history institutions. This narrative establishes current museum models as the products of progress atop an evolutionary ladder.

Anderson's development narrative is based upon the simultaneous evolution of museum display and a movement toward living interpretation of the past. The latter began, he argues, in 1881 Sweden, with Artur Hazelius's Skansen, which he labels the "prototype" of all open-air museums, a "pocket edition of all the beauty and folklore of Sweden."[3] While this *freilichtmuseen* was the start of many other open-air museums in Europe, Anderson reminds the reader that the "children of Skansen" are not quite what visitors have come to expect at living history museums in the United States. "Visiting most European open-air museums is akin to time-traveling through the past, only to find vacant and silent homes and shops."[4] This statement indicates a bias in favor of contemporary living history museums that populate their sites with costumed interpreters who bring "life" to the environment.

Anderson posits the origins of living display with Skansen, but then needs to make the connection to its development within the United States in order to show that there was a series of natural connections between the origin and contemporary living museums on another continent. He found the link in Hazelius's shipping of six dioramas from Skansen to the Centennial Exhibition in Philadelphia during the summer of 1876. There, the idea was admired and adopted by Henry Ford and John D. Rockefeller Jr., who then created large-scale open-air museums featuring costumed staff and craft demonstrations (Greenfield Village and Colonial Williamsburg, respectively), which, in turn, influenced other regional open-air museums to adopt similar methods of display and interpretation.[5]

From there, Anderson chooses moments that serve as "typical" events that indicate the growing popularity of what had now become a living history "movement," rapidly developing from simple to complex. As the movement grows and expands, Anderson selects organizational and institutional procedures that shape and give authority to the movement in need of control. Already established sites of authority, such as the National Park Service and the Smithsonian Institution, legitimized the development of living history sites by adopting their own living history programs, while new sites of authority, such as ALHFAM (the Association for Living Historical Farms and Agricultural Museums), needed to be created to accommodate living history's new arenas of scholarship and museum work.[6]

Meanwhile, museum display was evolving from "cabinets of curiosities" to formal displays, and then to the addition of costumed interpretation of dioramic exhibits.[7] Plimoth Plantation took the next "logical step" when it moved from static display to living history. With the shift to a more natural environment, the interpreters began to change their mode of presentation from *third-person past* ("They did") to *first-person present* ("we do"), becoming the people they portrayed "without a word being said" by the cura-torial staff.[8]

In using Plimoth Plantation's Pilgrim Village to illustrate the way in which particular living history museums evolved from simple to complex, Anderson does not just give his model a practical application. With the in-sertion of the narrative of Plimoth's development at this moment in the se-quence of his timeline, Anderson engages in a textual strategy that places this specific museum at the apex of living history evolution. Through this maneuver, he monumentalizes Plimoth Plantation. By holding the Pilgrim Village up as an example *par excellence*, Anderson advocates the first-person, present-tense model of interpretation as the model that best allows the ex-ploration of the past—inaccessible through other modes of exhibition. He regards Plimoth, explicitly, as the ultimate form of living museum interpre-tation, saying that it "took visitors as far into a historic culture as it is pos-sible to go," though he adds, "still others would challenge the effectiveness of any living-history museum . . . truly to enliven the past in a truthful manner."[9]

Anderson intends, despite the caveat, to locate Plimoth Plantation and other institutions that adopt first-person costumed interpretation as the far-thest point reached thus far in the linear development of living historical dis-play (and the end of his timeline). Skansen, Colonial Williamsburg in its ini-tial stages, and Plimoth itself, prior to the switch to living history, all contained the *potential* for perfection, but had not yet obtained it to the de-gree found in the contemporary Pilgrim Village at Plimoth Plantation. Sim-ilarly, the early incarnations of "traditional" museum display—the cabinet of curiosities and formal exhibits—are regarded by Anderson as models that could not quite achieve the same kind of visitor interaction found in living museum environments. Therefore, while he canonizes and privileges the for-mer sites, the tendency is to regard them as substandard: at best, near-perfect, at worst primitive.

If Anderson's narrative—with its bias in favor of the present and diminu-tive regard for lower-order evolutionary links that supposedly led to that present—was strictly autonomous or obscure in the field of scholarship on living history, there would not be much at stake. The model offered in *Time Machines*, however, functions within a field of relationships that allows it to intersect and shift various other discourses on living history. The Darwinis-tic model negates, erases, and prevents movements of thought in these dis-courses that might otherwise be allowed to emerge. This erasure happens in the field of scholarship, as can be seen with Stephen Eddy Snow's work on Plimoth Plantation. It happens in studies parallel to Anderson's, such as

Michael Wallace's alternative timeline, and, perhaps where it is the most detrimental, it happens at the curatorial and interpretive levels of the institutions themselves.

Snow's 1993 *Performing the Pilgrims* engages in a similar mode of Darwinian evolution as a strategy to place events of Plimoth Plantation into a progressive development context. Snow outlines the steps in his second chapter, "The Development of a Performative Representation of the Pilgrims at Modern Plimoth Plantation" (see figure 1). He grounds the origins of Pilgrim performance in 1886 with early forms of *tableaux vivants* and pageantry that commemorated the arrival of the colonists, the signing of the Mayflower Compact, and so forth. From these "simple" beginnings, which displayed the first signs of interpretation through performance, the development proceeded by degrees in a movement from simple to complex, from creation of the first Pilgrim house in 1948 to the opening of the Pilgrim Village in 1959. In the 1960s, costumed wax mannequins were added to the interiors, creating static dioramas of typical Pilgrim life. In 1969, Plimoth introduced the living museum concept, discarding the mannequins and putting costumed interpreters in their place. In 1978, the village began to reenact scenes from Pilgrim history, casting "actor/historians" in the roles of the "Pilgrim fathers," which gradually gave way to total first-person living history performance.[10]

Like Anderson, Snow argues that costumed first-person performance was an inherent potential at Plimoth and "had actually been developing all along," so that, by the 1970s, living history was the natural move: "In retrospect, it is easy to see that the step [toward first-person] was inevitable. . . . It was becoming almost impossible for them not to speak in the first person in such a complete simulation of the historical daily lives of the pilgrims."[11] In using the same emphasis on the natural occurrence of first-person interpretation as a result of the milieu and elapse of time that Anderson used to discuss Plimoth, the museum's method of first-person is again inscribed as the top of the evolutionary ladder.

Neither Anderson nor Snow was the first to articulate a Darwinistic model for the evolution of living history museums. Michael Wallace constructed a timeline three years earlier than Anderson that, though not as exhaustive, contained many of the same events Anderson chose. Wallace's timeline was published in an article entitled "Visiting the Past: History Museums in the United States" in the *Radical History Review*.[12] Wallace's intention was neither to sing the praises of rigorous first-person interpretation, as does Anderson, nor to establish performance as the answer to a timeless call for ritualistic retelling of a communal story, as does Snow. Wallace argues

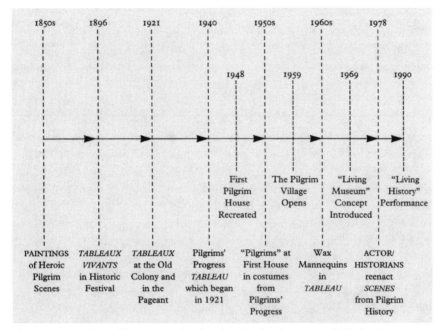

1850s	1896	1921	1940	1950s	1960s	1978
			1948	1959	1969	1990
			First Pilgrim House Recreated	The Pilgrim Village Opens	"Living Museum" Concept Introduced	"Living History" Performance
PAINTINGS of Heroic Pilgrim Scenes	*TABLEAUX VIVANTS* in Historic Festival	*TABLEAUX* at the Old Colony and in the Pageant	Pilgrims' Progress *TABLEAU* which began in 1921	"Pilgrims" at First House in costumes from Pilgrims' Progress	Wax Mannequins in *TABLEAU*	ACTOR/ HISTORIANS reenact *SCENES* from Pilgrim History

Figure 1. Stephen Eddy Snow's timeline for the development of Pilgrim Representation. Reprinted with permission of the University Press of Mississippi.

that living history museums were founded largely in the first half of the twentieth century by members of the dominant class and that they display perspectives on history that reflect and affirm that class's social positions.[13] Unlike Anderson, however, Wallace assigns a role in the development of living history museums to the "historic house museums" that began to emerge with other acts of commemoration of ideals supported by a growing number of conservative elite ancestral societies, such as the Daughters of the American Revolution.[14]

House museums, epitomized by Mount Vernon, affirmed conservative values embodied in the objects of commemoration, namely, antiradicalism, anti-immigration, anticommunism, and "Americanizing the children."[15] Ford's and Rockefeller's open-air museums were expansions of the historic house idea that affirmed similar views on class and politics, idealizing the working class to the point of ineffectiveness. Ford's Greenfield Village was a "precapitalist Eden immune to modern ills," a "*static* utopia" lacking conflict, war, or politics, "and thus helped to inhibit effective political action in the future."[16] Colonial Williamsburg presented an inauthentic and pristine presentation of a gentrified past, a result of the type of elitism emblematized by

Rockefeller and his class. "It is a corporate world," Wallace writes, "planned, orderly, tidy, with no dirt, no smell, no visible signs of exploitation."[17]

Wallace, writing in 1981, concludes that the faults found in modern living history museums lie in the roots of the institutions. The ruling classes had appropriated the past and made it an instrument of their hegemony, deadening any potential for social action in the present. In the face of what he estimated to be a decade of "right-wing offensives" in the 1980s, threatening to undo any gains in living history made by working-class, women's, and black movements, Wallace offers suggestions "for radicals to resist these moves to reappropriate the past."[18] These include looking to nonstate-funded museums, revamping social history programming, and assisting visitors to become "historically informed makers of historiography."[19]

Wallace explicitly recognizes that the past is a product of the arrangement of records in the present. "There is, after all," he reminds the reader, "no such thing as 'the past.' All history is a production—a deliberate selection, ordering, and evaluation of past events, experiences, and processes."[20] Nevertheless, he still uses a linear model of museum display to impose meaning on the events he selects. From his statements, one can see how he carefully places Rockefeller's Williamsburg within a developmental timeline to show the way its past had a clear cause-and-effect relationship not only to the present but also to the future of museum display. From Colonial Williamsburg, Wallace pursues a narrative course of development very similar to that of Anderson, listing first the living historical farms movement, which began in the mid- to late 1960s in the face of revisionism in history, and then the idea that "in the 1970s slavery was discovered at Williamsburg."[21] He arranges his own records along a timeline and adopts the model of a linear development of these museums from their roots. The present identities of the museums, while not more perfect incarnations than their recent ancestors, as Anderson and Snow hold, are still the products of a process from simple to complex, initiated at a point of origin and changing with the elapse of time. Because of this model, and a mode of thinking that posits change as a product of progress and time, Wallace's hopes for more responsible museum display lie in the future, when enough time will pass to allow for the proper arrangement of milieu to let social history come to fruition, despite current barriers. The view is still positivistic and unhelpful.

It is not surprising that Anderson's book and the timeline offered within its first two chapters have been utilized by advocates and supporters of living history museums in scholarship, while Wallace's timeline is often a tool to be used by their detractors (or, more constructively, as a watchdog that keeps living history museum staff vigilant in applying procedures for a more social history and a warning against lapsing in this venture). I chose Anderson's timeline as my starting point for a review of literature because it is more often cited or invoked than Wallace's (in the cases in which the model is attributed to a single author). Whether Anderson can be credited as the originator of the timeline is irrelevant. Regardless of originality, it has become a powerful template for understanding what is referred to as the living history "movement." The template is adopted and reinvented each time it is enunciated from a site of authority. It shifts as it intersects with particular scholars' political or intellectual ideologies.

Jay Anderson is a folklorist and a self-proclaimed "participant-observer" in the living history field, who infuses anecdote and nostalgia into his historiography to promote support and esteem for the living history movement.[22] Stephen Eddy Snow is a veteran Pilgrim interpreter who uses structures from cultural anthropology to impose meaning on living history vis-à-vis human behavior and society. Michael Wallace is a social critic who uses radical tools to indict capitalist systems that deny agency to disenfranchised groups (the working class, minorities, and others).[23] Each scholar selects moments as worthy of remembrance as they fit into a developmental model that affirms their narrative. The moments are conditioned by their ideologies as the narratives force the events to speak the scholars' language of intelligibility. The narratives are not archival repositories of truth. Nor do they exist in a vacuum. The evolutionary models produced by Anderson, Snow, Wallace, and others exist within a field of relationships that structures understandings of living history museums in recent scholarship and practice. They engage and shape how living history museums' curators and staff regard their own operation and identity. They inform the ways visitors to these institutions are encouraged to view the exhibits and participate in the reenactments.

The Progressive Development Narrative in Practice

From research and interviews I conducted between 1998 and 2004, I found that the notions of evolution and progress are inherent *within* the field of living history museums as well as in scholarship. The model of evolution toward progress, in this case, is linked to the move toward an ever more accurate and authentic mode of museum display. When I asked curators and interpreters if the sites they represented were either authentic or accurate, they often responded by saying they were "working on it." I was informed that various plans were under way, even as we spoke, that would allow for greater accuracy. I found that many of the people I interviewed understood their own position as a moment on a line toward future progress. *We may not be as authentic now, but someday, when somebody else is sitting in this chair . . .*

In some cases, the allusion to development toward a more perfect incarnation of living history was no more than a listing of projects currently under way, set into the context of a progressive movement. A third-person costumed interpreter at Yorktown Victory Center in Virginia, for example, shared with me how the institution planned to exhibit the natural progression of a working eighteenth-century farm vis-à-vis its commitment to living history:

> One of the major things here is the living history component. That's why we're expanding. Over in this land to my right—we're gonna start planting orchard trees, and getting into, like, cider press and all this other stuff because there's more of an interest for it. And it was a natural progression as far as it would have been something a farmer at this time would have possibly—Because the farmer's land would be orchards or everything he owned wouldn't necessarily be under cultivation necessarily. I don't consider cultivation orchards. You know, it's basically fruit trees and you pick the fruit when it grows and that's it. You wouldn't have to do much more than that.[24]

Here, the interpreter ties the perceived visitor's agenda, that "there's more of an interest" for the apple production aspect of a working farm, to the agenda of the museum: "One of the major things here is the living history component. That's why we're expanding." Through describing the natural progression of a farm orchard, he links a model of progression to the museum's additions. They will start with the planting of the orchard trees, then add cider presses and other elements of cider production.

Rosemarie McAphee, in the Education Division training program at Colonial Williamsburg, remembers twenty years ago, when visitors were not getting as much of a sense of the lives of the average eighteenth-century citizens of the colonial town as they do currently. However, she says, there is more work to do. She recognizes that Colonial Williamsburg is moving in the direction toward more accurate portrayal of the demographics, but is impatient with the progress.

> Now, I think they [guests of Colonial Williamsburg] are getting more of that reality, that dose of reality. There is more information available about the average person, and the importance of those average people and the poor folks and slaves, and the women, and how they supported the community. And again, we're moving in that direction, especially with the more recent interpretations, but we're still meeting a little resistance. So, I would say, "Okay, stop talking about it and do it!" [laughs] "This is your target date!"[25]

A manager in the Theatrical Productions Department of Colonial Williamsburg spoke to me about the prospect of a more historically accurate production of an eighteenth-century play based upon a rigorous examination of period promptbooks and the physiological model of the humours. While Williamsburg has gathered many sources documenting blocking in eighteenth-century theatre, curators and theatre staff had not yet intentionally worked through these documents looking for "patterns" of style and presentation. She described the early efforts as a "seedbed":

> It's a very new world. . . . There are pockets of people who've done research in eighteenth-century theatre, but there's no institution that I am aware of that has actually studied it and tried to come up with the end result in a presentation. We certainly haven't [laughs]. That's not been our tack. We certainly study style and we certainly study a variety of books on passion and how they learned their techniques. But to really try to put all of that together and then. . . . It's mind-boggling to even think about trying—let alone having the sort of financing—to pull twelve people into a workshop for a year and pull something like that up. So we're hoping that with this seedbed, we will have some downtime in December, January, February, and March, where these sixteen people can really focus on studying these passions and studying these promptbooks, and coming up with a style for a piece, so that's kind of a neat place to go.[26]

Her discussion of efforts at more authentic portrayal seems to hinge upon the collection of the right archival elements, the right individuals, and the proper amount of "downtime" in which to bring these potential elements to fruition. She speaks of the future in spatial terms: "that's kind of a neat place to go" and "it's a very new world." She also locates Colonial Williamsburg as a site of potential for an accurate simulated eighteenth-century production: "There's no institution that I am aware of that has actually studied it and tried to come up with the end result in a presentation. We certainly haven't." This statement suggests that Colonial Williamsburg is at a point further along a developmental line, ready to try something that has never been done before in the past, but also places the institution in relation to other living history museums, perhaps competitively vying for the distinction of being furthest along in development, at least in terms of theatrical production.

Mark Howell, program manager at Colonial Williamsburg, used the metaphor of a turning ball to discuss how various events in the twentieth century were reflected in the programming at the museum. I asked if Colonial Williamsburg could be described as a museum of the twentieth century as well as the eighteenth century. He said it was a good point:

> History is a reflection of the society that's interpreting it. You look at Colonial Williamsburg's history—a lot of our programming in the 1950s was a real

obvious reaction to the Cold War. And then when you get into the seventies. Civil rights and Vietnam created more a sense of the idea of democracy as questioning authority. You get into social history of the later seventies and the eighties where women's rights and civil rights are coming about and inclusive history changes how we take the same facts and look at them. So the ball is constantly turning and being looked at. And twenty-five years from now, I have no doubt that the person who's gonna be sitting probably in this same ugly chair will be basically saying, "Well, that's what that guy Howell did back in the year 2000, but now we've progressed and we'll be doing something totally different." And I think that's pretty cool.[27]

While Howell's description of the way events of the twentieth century informed the curatorial decisions of Colonial Williamsburg is similar to that found in the work of Greenspan, Carson, and Handler and Gable, Howell's model tends toward a seemingly passive stance. Progress occurs outside of the museum, and the curatorial staff changes accordingly. There is a cause-and-effect relationship between world events (e.g., civil rights and Vietnam) and the decisions of the institution (shifting the programming to reflect "a sense of the idea of democracy as questioning authority").

When I asked Jack Larkin, chief historian at Old Sturbridge Village, what he could change at his museum, if anything, he spoke of the future of Sturbridge in terms of building upon, and the expansion of, elements that were already under way. "There are some things I'd like to continue to do and do on a better scale some of the things we have been doing, which is to expand our interpretation of a more inclusive history," he said, listing histories of African Americans, Native Americans, and the Irish as examples. He also expressed hope of eventually supplying every costumed staff member with the dramatic skills that would allow them to make transitions more effectively in their interpretations.

Larkin would "ultimately" like to see a demonstration of a greater range of social class in the museum, perhaps by building and interpreting a "very small house," in which the poorest members of the New England community would have lived. "That's something down the line I'd like to see." He elaborated:

I'd obviously continue to incorporate the best continuing scholarship on our place and region as that does emerge. . . . So we remain a place that's on the cutting edge of interpretation—the program, exhibit, and research reflects the scholarship. . . . I mean I think the revolution [was] to say [we] are a museum of the social history of everyday life—social, material, cultural history of ordinary people in everyday life—I don't think that needs to be done again. I certainly don't want to see it undone. I think that's probably really what we ought to be. That is what makes sense. Ultimately that's the vision that our founders had back in the late 1930s in many ways. . . . It may also be that we may in the long run want to create a more powerful link between what we do as a living history museum and a more extensive presentation of our collections, and that's perhaps another direction, another dimension that we may want to explore.[28]

Larkin's choice to focus on already existing programs may indicate a reluctance or incapacity to look to other models because of the way the museum is understood to be positioned in relation to progress. Larkin also speaks in linear metaphors, referring to the future as "down the line" or "in the long run," firmly grounding Old Sturbridge Village's projects along a temporal, progressive continuum. In citing goals that correspond to the outgrowth of current projects only, and not bringing up other goals that perhaps may not yet have been considered and implemented, Larkin reaffirms the model of the progressive development of elements that start with a potential for evolution. For instance, by "continuing" to engage in scholarship, they can be sure to get the best new information as "that does emerge." Here is perhaps one of the more prevalent models of the accumulation of knowledge: the assumption that there is new information, latent within the field, that remains to be discovered in due time as long as the human effort is made to look for it. Finally, Larkin places current progress and future development within the context of the ideals that were rooted in the very founding of the museum. The "ultimate" goal of fulfilling what the founders set in motion in the 1930s is what "makes sense."

One side note bears mentioning here: despite Larkin's view that Old Sturbridge's programming and displays have fulfilled and continue to fulfill the goals established by the original founders in the 1930s, recent research by Laura E. Abing into documents and correspondence from those years indicates the contrary. In her doctoral dissertation, "Old Sturbridge Village: An Institutional History of a Cultural Artifact," she writes that the museum's founder, A. B. Wells, had little regard for historical accuracy and was more concerned with presenting an environment which showed that "a satisfying, fruitful and well-balanced existence can still be lived by the humblest of us even in a world of change and confusion."[29]

According to Abing, early Old Sturbridge Village structures such as the Fitch House were constructed with historically inaccurate "two-inch by four-inch stud frame walls" instead of the plank framing the original designs featured.[30] Wells's personal correspondence in 1940 expressed some of his sentiments: "I personally don't give a damn whether it was just like this way before. It is the way that will look the best now and suit our purposes, the purpose of the Village and the purpose of the Museum."[31]

Wells did not favor moving historic New England buildings from their original foundations, either. "I would not and do not like the idea of moving old buildings," he wrote in a 1948 correspondence. "A really old building has served its purpose, and by the time you take it down and then rebuild it, it only means a few years when it is entirely gone."[32] Considering that most of the major buildings surrounding Old Sturbridge Village's Common have been relocated from all over New England—the Center Meetinghouse was moved from the town of Sturbridge in 1947, the Fenno House from Canton, Massachusetts, in 1949, the Law Office from Woodstock, Connecticut, in 1965, and the Asa Knight Store from Dummerston, Vermont, in 1972[33]— Wells's position on relocation does not seem to have been honored. It would seem from Abing's work that, rather than consistently maintaining a commitment to Wells's original vision—a community that could reassure visitors that there were simpler, more pleasant alternatives to a modern world filled with industrial and military anxiety—Old Sturbridge Village has reinvented Wells's original vision in order to affirm a progressive view of its own institutional history.

I asked a public relations staff member at Plimoth Plantation what she would consider changing for the better at Plimoth. "I wouldn't want to change as much as I would want to expand," she says, echoing Larkin's plans.[34] This response should not be surprising. After all, Plimoth has continually been described by scholars as the pinnacle of the evolutionary ladder. In terms at least of first-person interpretation, there may not be any progress to be made at this point toward more accurately and authentically giving a sense of everyday life in the seventeenth-century Pilgrim Village. Hobbamock's Homesite, however, presents certain problems, because the Wampanoag interpreters do not speak in first person, as do the Pilgrim interpreters in the 1627 Village. This affects visitor–interpreter interaction, signage, and the attempt to programmatically tie the two sites together for the best visitor experience.

The Plimoth PR worker confirmed my guess that visitors, after spending time in the Pilgrim Village, come to Hobbamock's Homesite expecting to engage in conversation with Native interpreters speaking in a seventeenth-century dialect and that "negative experiences" have occasionally resulted. This is especially the case for visitors who have never been to the museum before and who start with the Village and end their visit with Hobbamock's Homesite. She spoke briefly about a few current ideas for addressing these problems. One is to construct a transitional building that would house exhibit space and an educational center and that would specifically orient visitors to the Wampanoag encampment. Another idea is to pursue first-person interpretation at the Homesite. "It's really vague right now and far away. But it's being talked about." She outlined some of the difficulties with pursuing first-person presentation, language being the primary obstacle: while there is a language reclamation program currently under way in the nearby Wampanoag community in Mashpee, much of the language has been lost.

> So there are a lot of deadlocks to do a strong—well, I don't want to say strong—an *effective* first-person interpretation there. But it definitely can be done, and if anyone can do it, we can do it here. But again, it's a long way off. I don't think it's going to happen in the next five years, even. But from a PR perspective, it is always a balancing act to make sure that when people come here that they realize that there are two cultures represented, because Plymouth, the town, is all about Thanksgiving. The Pilgrims. And really a lot of people [think] only the two cultures are the Pilgrims and the Indians. They don't know what kind of Indians, or the fact that they're native to this area, and how they lived. And so these are the areas that we want them to come away with.

She outlined several ways in which a development toward more "effectively" implementing programming at Hobbamock's Homesite were under way. Because first-person is assumed to be the best model for costumed interpretation, the model is placed over the future of the Wampanoag Interpretation Program as a template for natural progression. First of all, because Plimoth is already the site known for the model of perfection, she is allowed the claim, "if anyone can do it, we can do it here." Second, the results are achievable, but only with the proper amount of time: "But again, it's a long way off. I don't think it's going to happen in the next five years, even." It is not simply a matter of human action. Elapsed time is a necessity for progress.

Judging from the conversations above, it would seem that accuracy in presentation and authenticity achieved through rigor over time are the keys to successful interpretation of the past, and the goals of the "evolution" of living history museums. This assumption leads to several problems.

First, the perpetuation of the model of progress allows for the abdication, or passing on, of responsibility or rigor. It is easy to fall into the trap of believing that not enough time has elapsed to realistically think about changing a problematic status quo. By saying, "We're not there yet, but someday . . . ," the responsibility for change is abdicated to the next person to occupy the site of authority. The current authoritative body becomes complicit with the perpetuation of the status quo.

Second, if the living history practitioners in the field reaffirm the ingrained evolutionary model, which excludes the remembering of events that do not fit the model of development from simple to complex, it is difficult to look outside the events privileged in the timeline for alternative ideas for a performance-based treatment of history. If the only choices for change need to conform to the model idealized in the future—perhaps pure first-person interpretation in all programming or a new visitors' center—then there is no possibility of a radical shift in mode of interpretation that would allow for alternative voicings.

Third, in an increasingly post-tourist world, kitsch-savvy visitors may generally not be disposed to buy into the model of pure first-person interpretive environments. Even for many "traditional" visitors, the irreconcilability of a period environment with the presence of modern-day tourist bodies may simply be too big an obstacle for willing suspension of disbelief. David Lowenthal found himself in this situation upon his visit to Plimoth Plantation in 1981, and apparently so did his fellow visitors:

> Animated re-enactment of the Plimoth type expanded in the late 1970s, after marketing surveys showed that activities attract more people than do artifacts. Yet tourists often seem reluctant to "share a riddle, a joke, a bit of gossip" with these "warm, friendly folk"; beyond technical questions about household skills, crops, and beverages, most moderns seem at a loss. . . . The press of numbers also inhibits a sense of the past: it is hard to suspend disbelief about the seventeenth century with hundreds of twentieth-century folk milling about.[35]

Finally, my venture through the field revealed more criticism of first-person interpretation on the part of living history participants than would be assumed from reading the accounts of Snow and Anderson, suggesting that this "ideal" model breaks down in practice. One of the most difficult issues around which interpreters must negotiate, for instance, is how to make "connections" with the visitor between past and present, which institutions consider a helpful tool in learning. At Greenfield Village in 2003, I asked a group of interpreters sitting down to their midday dinner at the Firestone Farmstead if anyone played character in the village: "We're in third-person here," a young woman answered, "which means we can make comparisons between [the late nineteenth century] and 2003. Some places use first-person, so they can't do that. But there are advantages to both."[36]

Some third-person costumed interpreters I interviewed rued the inability of their site to incorporate some of the same first-person programming that Plimoth and Williamsburg feature. These same individuals, though, often expressed confidence that their third-person mode was ultimately more helpful and accessible to the visitor. A costumed Continental soldier at Yorktown Victory Center told me about his visit to Plimoth Plantation. "It's a neat place—don't get me wrong—it's a neat place," he maintained. "It's well worth the visit. It's just that their charter, their mandate, is a little different than us. . . . They are very, very good." He adds, referring to the use of seventeenth-century dialect, "Kind of hard, sometimes, to understand, though."[37] The interpreter then told me about how his program differs from Plimoth.

> Here we do a lot of compare and contrast, okay? And we can do that because we are third-person. For instance, we can ask folks, "Were you in the military? Did you carry an M16? How much did it weigh?" And if you're doing first-person, you can't do that. It's the compare and contrast. We do a lot of it here. It's a very effective teaching tool. You find something people are comfortable and familiar with. And compare it to the way it was. So you can see the difference. See where we've come. And when you're doing first-person you can't. So it is limited. Good show, though. And they're good, they're very good. To each their own.

Another interpreter at the same site, a woman interpreting eighteenth-century medical procedures, shared some of the same sentiments. Her argument was that it can be easy for visitors to be "turned off" by first-person if their questions cannot be immediately answered. The third-person interpretation at Yorktown, she felt, is better suited to visitors' needs:

> We find that first-person limits you because you can't answer questions. Sometimes people want to know something and if it's not within your little character, you know, "Well, ma'am, I don't know," or something like that. Well, that turns a lot of people off. So we would prefer to do it like this. . . . It just makes it better for our visitors. They get a better perspective, I think, if they can ask anybody any question, and not be put off to somebody else, or "I don't know because I didn't live then" or "I don't live now," that kind of stuff. So we just find this to work better for us.[38]

Guy Peartree, an African-American interpreter in Old Sturbridge Village who adopts both first- and third-person interpretation to talk about black experience in 1830s New England, told me about the problems that can arise when the visitor is unable to make the distinction between the first-person character and the personal views held by the interpreter (or when a transition between the two has not been made explicit), especially when it comes to issues like religion or politics. Much of the time, visitors will often default to an assumption that he is speaking from a current position and consequently are surprised when he voices an attitude or belief in nineteenth-century character. Peartree prefers to be able to go "in and out" to avoid such situations.

> For instance, I'm thinking of some people who were talking to me about religion. . . . I was talking [in character] about being a Universalist, believing in the equality of religions, and I seem to have disrupted someone's feelings about their Christian belief, or made them feel anxious about it. So they had to tell me about what it was like to be a good Christian. Forcefully, they were telling me about that. And they didn't realize that I was talking from the 1830s perspective. . . . There was a couple of other people that said, "Why didn't you—? I thought you were talking about yourself. . . ." But there's ways around that. Sometimes you can just tell people, "I'm pretending. That's who I am now." But talking about religion, no matter what context you are, people always seem to go a little bit overboard in their responses. *They* can't make the switch to the 1830s. Say, "Oh, this is what people believe. These are the issues—their issues."[39]

One of the most difficult issues with first-person interpretation is that when interpreters speak in "pure" first-person present, every injustice, violence, or social movement that occurred *after* the moment of time selected to be the simulated present is automatically erased. Perhaps this is desirable when the visitor's goal is to visit a place that existed before the Industrial Revolution, computers, or other elements of the present from which an individual would seek to escape. But repressing events that have occurred since the time displayed is an act of violence when some of the population, environment, or animals displayed have had atrocities committed against them.

Strictly holding to the 1627 narrative spoken by the Pilgrim interpreters in the village at Plimoth Plantation, for instance, leaves out nearly four hundred years of history in New England. The histories of conflict between Native peoples and colonizers from the late seventeenth century onward, including atrocities committed against indigenous tribes, are absent. Visitors to the Pilgrim Village will not hear about how half of all South New England Indians involved in King Philip's War were killed in battle beginning in 1675.[40] Nor will they hear about the displacement, forced treaty signings, and "humane" conversions of Wampanoag and other tribes accompanying the massive influx of Puritan settlers beginning with the Restoration of the English monarchy in 1660.[41] Least of all will they hear of the southeastern

Massachusetts and Martha's Vineyard Wampanoag communities and culture in the present. The curatorial selection and institutional historiographic practice of focusing on one year in history erases the possibility of focusing on these events, and the willing suspension of disbelief leaves no room for considering them. Nanepashemet, one of the Wampanoag interpreters at Plimoth Plantation, wrote an essay entitled "Wampanoag Cultural Survival: The Dynamics of a Living Culture," which was posted on Plimoth's web site. "We are, sometimes to our embarrassment, often simply known as 'the Indians who met the Pilgrims,'" he writes. "Many historians ignored our continued presence and participation in colonial events right up to the present. Those who grudgingly acknowledged our existence referred to us as some sort of degenerated remnant of our ancestors."[42]

This is part of the reason Plimoth Plantation's Native Wampanoag interpreters at Hobbamock's Homesite, adjacent to the Pilgrim Village, have chosen to remain in the third-person present, so they can answer visitors' questions about events between the seventeenth century and today. "Wampanoag interpreters," writes Nancy Grey Osterud, "are committed to discussing the 1675 war as well as the relatively pacific early period, to comparing Plimoth with other colonies, and to confronting contemporary media stereotypes as they encounter them in visitors' behavior."[43]

When I visited the native encampment in June 2000, I spoke with a young Native woman, in costume, who shared with me not only the everyday practices of seventeenth-century Wampanoag living in the Massachusetts Bay area but also the processes the program goes through in deciding what is appropriate to show to visitors and what should remain private (Elaine Heumann Gurian writes that choices like this signal the emergent "none of your business" concept of interpretation, holding that "the people most intimately connected with and related to the material could determine the access to that material").[44] When I asked if the Wampanoag Interpretation Program included elements of Wampanoag spirituality and practices at Hobbamock's Homesite, she responded:

> We kind of have decided what we're going to share and what we're going to keep with ourselves. . . . We talk about it beforehand. We say a lot of things that we agree upon that should be shared, and then other things that we keep sacred and hold to ourselves. We do share quite a bit, considering we have a lot of things that are done to us in modern day. I don't know why, but a lot of people in other museums think that they can dig up the bones of our ancestors and call them their own. And show them in museums. So I think we do share a fair amount of what we hold spiritual to ourselves.[45]

In the third-person interpretation format, a multiplicity of historical narratives may all exist in the same plane. In this space, the interpreter can share not only seventeenth-century events, as do the Wampanoag Interpretation Program's counterparts in the Pilgrim Village, but also how current fights are taking place over the rights museums have to own and display Native artifacts and remains. In the Pilgrim Village, such conversations are unlikely, since the Pilgrim interpreters will not break character and acknowledge any other present than 1627.[46]

In the same way, the interpreters with Colonial Williamsburg's African-American interpretation programs (formerly known as African-American Interpretations and Presentations or AAIP) use third-person presentation to disrupt the singular narrative of the "just the facts" mode of historiography.[47] When the program's "The Other Half" walking tour stops in front of the Wythe House, the tour leader will often discuss with visitors the possibility of miscegenation between masters and slaves, despite the refusal of the interpreters of the building to broach the subject. Sometimes African-American staff will indirectly bait the white interpreters at the Wythe House by encouraging visitors on the walking tour to return to the Wythe House for an inside tour and ask the white interpreters about miscegenation.[48]

Tactics like these continuously put into question the status quo of a singular narrative comprised only of events provable via factual evidence, delivered through first-person interpretation. They show that there are other possibilities to the trajectory of history established by living museums: we do not have to retain a bent toward exhaustive exhumation of the remnants of history to add to the accumulation of knowledge. Nor do we need to limit our narratives of history to those events that are recorded by authoritative sources. When taking into account the silencing of other voices, the first-person interpretive model simply cannot be held up as the perfect model for living history museums. If this is what is at the end of progress, the model of the linear evolution of living history museums needs to be reexamined.

(In)authentic Revolutions:
Time, Space, and Living History Museums

In what may be the most ambitious of all experiments in re-creation, Old Sturbridge Village has scientists working on the back-breeding of domestic animals so that the hybrid strains of modern, meaty chickens, pigs, cattle, and sheep can work their way back to the condition and appearance of their ancestors in the nineteenth century. Old varieties of plants also have their place in many museum gardens. This is undoing history indeed.

—"Living History:
Getting Closer to Getting It Right," *Early American Life*

Is it real history yet?

—Kate F. Stover,
"Is it *Real* History Yet? An Update on Living History Museums"

Cary Carson includes an anecdote at the beginning of his article "Living Museums of Everyman's History" in which he describes one of his Harvard colleagues "chucking" his studies in the late 1960s to "usher in the revolution at Old Sturbridge Village." The revolution the "Sturbridge dissident" had in mind was the new social history programming that would remove the history from the dominant, white, upper-class individuals and focus on the everyday life of groups in American history.[49]

Coupled with the narrative of a progressive evolution is a tendency to describe major changes in living history programming as "revolutions." On the face of it, *evolution* and *revolution* appear to be contradictory terms: *revolution* implies a complete break with a former trajectory. Indeed, living history museums changed dramatically in the 1960s and 1970s for many different reasons. With the emergence of social history and other modes of historical revisionism, museum institutions recognized and admitted that, up to that point, their subjects were largely clean, unproblematic, and restricted to the accomplishments of powerful white men. Across the spectrum, institutions adopted programs that addressed these oversights, and social historians worked to balance—or even replace—the histories of white men with those of minorities, women, and the middle and lower classes. It soon becomes clear, however, that "revolution" is a misleading designator for these changes in programming, and these very changes are actually perceived in the field as very much in keeping with the legacy of a positivistic model of evolution from simple to complex.

The change Carson describes in his article was *not* a revolution in living history. It was an immense shift in representational practices and subject matter, yes. But the reason it was not a revolution is that the institutional conceptions of time and history remained intact—the same conceptions of time and history, in fact, that are largely responsible for the progressive narrative of museum evolution and its continual reinscription through interpretive practices. In "Time and History: Critique of the Instant and the Continuum," Giorgio Agamben writes that, since culture is first and foremost an experience of time, no culture can be created without a new and different experience of time.[50] Any successful revolution, then, political or intellectual, would need to fundamentally change the notion of time, since without doing so, the new culture that replaces the old one would not be different from that which it replaced. While changes were made at living museums to reflect the diverse histories of those previously left out of the equation, the fundamental notion of time and its relationship to human experience at these sites remains the same: visitors are still encouraged to believe that they are entering an accurate, authentic representation of the past upon crossing the threshold into the living history museum exhibit.

Agamben states that the current notion of time in Western experience is a "vulgar conception" of a "precise and homogeneous continuum of instants,"[51] signifying that time has been popularly conceived, especially in the last hundred years, as a succession of absolute, measurable "nows" in a continuous, abstract progress (the term "vulgar" in Agamben's essay is not used as a derogatory or diminutive value judgment, but as a marker for a conception that is popular and easily disseminated outside of scholarly discourse). This is the conception of time that museums enunciate and reflect in their programming, establishing themselves as authoritative purveyors of history and erasing other possibilities of representation, so that they are allowed to claim an "undoing" of history along a precise continuum of time in order to show a past point the "way it really was." Thus, living history museums become monuments that are thought to protect the events they commemorate from passing into a Hegelian oblivion, while in effect surrogating or standing in for the actual events (and becoming more "real"). Not only that, but they can continue to get better at it by consistently asking themselves the question, as Kate F. Stover put it, "Is it *real* history yet?"

Stover's question frames her analysis of living history programming at the time of research for her article.[52] She introduces criticism of living history museums from many fronts, including Ada Louise Huxtable, who wrote that Colonial Williamsburg was a "stage set" that "'satisfies our craving' for 'educational entertainment'"; David Lowenthal, who wrote that "reconstructed sites alter history through highly selective interpretations of time periods, events and personalities"; and Thomas J. Schlereth, who wrote that living history museums were "peaceable kingdoms" that "did not reflect multiethnic populations or counter cultures."[53] Stover's article goes on to describe how institutions like Conner Prairie, Plimoth Plantation, and Colonial Williamsburg have addressed such criticisms by adopting social history programming and adding social conflict into their portrayal for a "deeper, more comprehensively accurate knowledge of the history they represent."[54] These procedures, however, are informed by an understanding of time as a progressive continuum and delimit the kinds of questions that may be asked about living museum programming. That is, by conditioning the question with the word "yet," Stover and others presume that the possibilities of "real" history lie further down the line with the continuation of the same efforts (i.e., greater accuracy through scientific rigor). The practices of most living museums are deeply entrenched in this mode of inquiry.

For all of their shifts in programming in the last three decades, embracing social history on the one hand and a historio-naturalistic mode of performance on the other, living museums still function with the dominant notion of time as a "precise and vulgar continuum."[55] Plimoth Plantation, Colonial Williamsburg, and Old Sturbridge Village are excellent examples of how a nineteenth-century notion of time has motivated the policies and programming of twentieth- and now twenty-first-century museums and stabilizes particular histories that affirm their institutional goals and ideologies.

Plimoth Plantation

Welcome to the 17th Century

—Sign marking the entrance to the Pilgrim Village

At Plimoth Plantation in 1997, traveling to another age has become as natural as traveling to another town. Once we stroll by a sign marking the line between the 20th and 17th centuries, the past comes alive with vibrant clarity.

—James Baker, *Plimoth Plantation*

The Pilgrim Village at Plimoth Plantation stages the year 1627 every season for visitors. The settlement and plantation, fort and meetinghouse, gardens and pathways, have all been reconstructed according to archaeological evidence, and Pilgrim interpreters dress in seventeenth-century outfits that have been researched to near-perfect accuracy in the minds of the curators. The interpreters that occupy the site speak in varying dialects that have been heavily researched, choosing their words from a vocabulary that has been cleared of any references to events occurring after the mid-1600s. In an effort to make every aspect of the museum as exhaustively accurate as possible, even the rare breeds of animals in the rough-hewn fenced pens have been shipped from as far away as New Zealand to resemble those the settlers would have brought with them to the "New World."

This site is a re-creation of a moment—a year's worth of instants—that passed almost four hundred years ago. The moment has its own remembered past, and a future that is known to the visitors, but not, ostensibly, to the interpreters. The site operates on the assumption that one can pass over a threshold that marks the border between the present instant and a representation of a past instant. The past instant can be represented in a realistic, naturalistic manner precisely because that past instant lay along the linear progression of time through the same space, and the remnants of it have lain latent in the space awaiting rediscovery and reproduction.

The curatorial and research methods at Plimoth Plantation work only with the assumption that the historical evidence they require for an accurate portrayal of this former instant lay archived in art, diaries, records, and so on and require only time and hard work in order to retrieve the information. A 1985 article by Harold Holzer puts the number of "locally excavated Pilgrim artifacts—tools, pieces of clothing, coins, and ceramics" in the Plimoth Plantation library and collection at more than three hundred thousand. These objects are meticulously researched by scholars, who use the empirical evidence in order to portray the time period with the utmost accuracy and authenticity at their disposal.[56]

The director of Plimoth Plantation in 1989, James W. Baker, summed up his stance on the way the museum changes as new knowledge is uncovered: "As soon as anything is discovered that's new, we change. We introduce. We keep our truth by continually moving. By continually keeping things as best as possible."[57] Lorna Kent, Foodways coordinator at Plimoth, offers one such example: "There's always new information coming. Research is always coming up with new things," she says. "It's beginning to look as if we've been using too much English corn, and we're going to have to take that gradually out of the food that we display and introduce a lot more Indian corn . . . , which is going to be quite challenging."[58] A voiceover in a Plimoth promotional video tells us:

> As a visit to Plimoth Plantation reveals, the past is at once a foreign yet familiar place. People who pay a return visit here are likely to discover that tomorrow's past is even closer to the year 1627 than today's. At Plimoth Plantation, the effort to learn more is ongoing. And every historical truth uncovered will find its place in the museum's interpretation.[59]

In the late 1980s and early 1990s, Chief Curator Jeremy Bangs instituted exhibition policies that included portraying every aspect of the village down to the most minute detail. "Everything should be correct," he told Patricia

Mandell in an interview. "I'm trying to get the whole village right."[60] Bangs's staff researched Dutch paintings in order to reproduce seventeenth-century mousetraps to place under the beds of the Plimoth houses—places most visitors will not even think about looking, yet which need as much attention to detail as the more visible aspects.[61] Bangs had received his doctorate in sixteenth-century Dutch art history and decorative arts. He looked beyond the limited collection of evidence exhumed from archaeological digs and documents and looked to art for additional "accurate" material. "The staff now," Mandell writes, "has a wealth of evidence to examine, from Pilgrim court documents and inventories to books on period painting and architecture, archeological digs into early houses in Plymouth, and field research from England and Wales."[62] Bangs's tenure as chief curator roughly coincided with the time that the farm animals began to be imported to more closely resemble what animals looked like in 1627. "A Plimoth Plantation pig, for instance, looks far more like a wild boar than the pigs we are familiar with today, and the museum imports just the right sort of cows from England and Ireland."[63]

Plimoth Plantation, in the last decades, has moved toward a scientific emphasis on social history in order to portray the more quotidian life of the Pilgrims, in the face of accusations that the museum was aestheticizing and simplifying its history of the settlement. Such was Assistant Director James Deetz's call for ethnohistorical rigor in 1969 that the day before the historic reenactment opened for the season, Deetz removed all the antiques that had been amassed in the restored Pilgrim Village from their buildings. The period furniture, Elizabethan glass windows, and oyster-shell walkways, he argued, were not authentic in that they did not coincide with the colonists' economic and social conditions that the new archaeological evidence indicated.[64] Shortly thereafter, Deetz banned repetitive "demonstrations" of crafts and household activities, "since early Americans did not demonstrate crafts in their houses," instead involving the interpreters "in productive activities *when needed.*"[65] "It is significant that demonstrations do not work in this context," writes Deetz, "if demonstration is taken in its usual sense as the constant repetition of a single process. Such repetitive action, whether dipping candles only to melt them again for the next turn, or splitting hundreds of rails, none ever to be used, is damaging to morale."[66] Elsewhere, he writes that it comes as no surprise that demonstrations like this were so pervasive at Plimoth prior to the 1970s, "since three of the museums that served as models for the village in its formative years were Colonial Williamsburg, Old Sturbridge Village, and the Jamestown Festival Park, at the time the leading open-air museums in America, all of which were committed to demonstrations of one or another type of craft activity."[67] Thirty years after Deetz's tenure, no curatorial decision is made at the site without careful research and documentation. According to Mandell, "No one makes so much as a door without looking in a dozen books."[68]

Kate Stover writes that, as a way to gain a "deeper, more comprehensively accurate knowledge" of the past, Plimoth Plantation added social conflict to its representation of the Plymouth Colony story.[69] Such conflict was a tool social historians began to use in the 1980s to answer criticism that living history museums did not portray a *real* history, but only shallow, nostalgic images. In the mid-1980s, Stover writes, in order to dismiss the stereotypical view that the Pilgrims "lived happily ever after" upon arrival to the New World, the staff of Plimoth Plantation chose characters to show the religious differences between the Separatists and the Church of England followers. Master George Soule, an Anglican "Pilgrim," complained to visitors that the Separatists in the majority forced all the colonists to obey strict religious regulations and that his newly born son could not even be baptized.[70] Stover reported that visitors to Plimoth starting that season favorably reflected the new curatorial goals:

> When asked, ten of the twenty visitors interviewed were able to state that the Separatists showed disdain for non-Separatists, and many visitors could cite examples of how the religious restrictions affected the minority colonists. . . . Almost all the visitors interviewed stated that they had found the interpretation of the religious situation at Plimoth interesting and informative. Several people commented that they had received a good understanding of the issues and problems.[71]

In an interview at the Plimoth Plantation research library in June 2000, Carolyn Travers, a staff researcher, told me that one of Plimoth's goals is to deprogram visitors' conception of the Pilgrims that popular culture has so profoundly implanted in their consciousness.[72] Some of the most damaging sources to the "real" Pilgrims, she said, were the books and films that seemed authoritative in the amount of historical information provided, yet gave a very inaccurate view. Historical novels such as *Constance: A Story of Early Plymouth*, Henry Wadsworth Longfellow's *The Courtship of Miles Standish* (readers of this book are mostly familiarized with it in their eighth-grade curriculum and have only "foggy recollections," says Travers), and the 1952 film *The Plymouth Adventure* inform many Pilgrim buffs' conceptions of the time period. The museum keeps these pop culture resources close at hand, so that when visitors bring them up, the staff may recognize what they are referring to and efficiently dismiss the inaccuracies they perpetuate. In contrast to such *illegitimate* sources, Travers continued, the researchers at Plimoth Plantation stick to the "real stuff." By "real stuff," she means behaviors and customs surrounding Separatism, courtship and marriage rites and customs, parentage, military, pottery, and the like.

Travers described some of the recent changes made in light of new research. The *Mayflower II*, formerly painted with bright colors, has been redone with less "flashy" colors. Research revealed the reds, described in accounts of the ship, to be more of a red-ochre versus the "firehouse red" with which visitors had been familiar since the reconstructed ship was launched in the mid-1950s. Clothing took a similar turn toward muted, duller colors, and the workers in the dying department used material that would have been available at the time, such as walnut shells, to get the dyes to look as they would have "for real." On the other hand, she says, some of the colors might be surprising to visitors. There is evidence, for instance, of a color akin to "safety orange" that was favored by some of the colonists.

Visitors, she explained, are often afflicted with what she calls the "Fred Flintstone syndrome," believing that those who lived in the past did not have technology and were not capable of fine detail. Plimoth Plantation exhibits earlier in the museum's history had a similar syndrome. "A while back, they would take lumberyard cut and hack it up" to make it look rougher, for example. "Actually," she says, from what has been determined from archaeological research, "they did some finer work then than we can now."[73] Adding animals to the site allowed Plimoth historians, through reconstructive research, to determine that the decorative fences the site featured previously did not work practically. Nor did the picturesque gardens last, after animals were added.[74] Finally, the museum sold all of its collection of period antiques in order to buy commercial reproductions or make their own, more accurate items.

Travers commented on the importance of looking to the primary documents when researching for exhibits and interpretive programs. Most of the "inaccuracies" that would occur due to looking at transcriptions of documents rather than the originals might not be noticed except by the exceptionally trained eye of an anthropologist or historian. Some discrepancies, though, can dramatically shift a particular vision of 1627. I asked Travers about an African American who had been hired to portray a Pilgrim several years ago, a matter to which Snow alludes in *Performing the Pilgrims*. She explained that the Pilgrim in question, one Abraham Pearse, is documented as having arrived in Plymouth in 1623, and there was no reason to believe he wouldn't have been in the village in 1627, the year portrayed on site. A 1643 document listing names of men able to bear arms contained the entry "Abraham Pearse Blackamoor." In a subsequent transcription, a comma was placed between the words "Pearse," and "Black-amoor," leading future readers to assume that Pearse was black. "Lists are working documents," Travers explained, "not snapshots in time. Names get added in and scratched out, then new [lists] are made to clean them up." Also, in such transcribing, changes need to be made to balance the information in other documents. The curators noticed the name on the list, made a decision to hire the black interpreter, and it became a "flap," said Travers, referring to the ensuing controversy over the "black Pilgrim." The decision was not wise, according to Travers. "A free black up here was interesting, but the decision was made before looking at the original documents. . . . What should have been an academic decision becomes public and a PR thing."[75]

The event was unfortunate, but a learning experience, she continued, and in her view it was "definitely a warning to look at the originals," which are located at the courthouse, fifteen minutes away from the museum. She showed me an example of an original document that Plimoth Plantation researchers had photographed (an activity conducted on an "as needed basis," she told me). There were areas where the ink and handwriting showed that a name had been added after 1627, a detail one would not be able to determine from a typed record. "Until you're as specific as we are, it's not important," she said. "We obsess about details."

Details are significant not only to the curatorial and research staff, but to the interpretive staff as well. Details, as I heard from several interpreters, are a way to make costumed interpretation more "real" for the visitor. Cynthia Gedraitis, a supervisor with the Colonial Interpretation Department as well as one of the Pilgrim interpreters at Plimoth, told me about the details she uses during in-character conversations with visitors in order to make their learning more immediate. "We have several primary sources that we talk from," she told me. "And the meat of our conversations comes right out of our sources." I asked her about the character dossiers I had heard about, issued to Pilgrim interpreters during their training and containing details on the biography and background information needed for the interpretation of their particular individual. "Dossiers most certainly," she confirmed, but added that these are supplemented with several other resources—books by William Bradford and Edward Winslow, for instance. "And there's one called *Three Visitors to Plimoth*. Three people—three different visitors, coming to the town who are writing other stuff—and those letters survived. And they are very informative—not altogether propaganda. . . . Packed with details." She continued:

> I love the details. I love to pick them out. It makes it real, because these guys are talking about daily events that happened in the first seven years that we

represent: 1620 to 1627, basically. But when you talk about your memory of the fire that happened in 1623, you've got a lot of information there that makes it sound very realistic, as if you were really there. A part of it.[76]

The dossiers themselves (four manuals—three for the Pilgrim Village and one for the *Mayflower II*) are reasonably exhaustive in outlining the collected details of daily life and belief systems of the seventeenth-century residents of Plymouth.

> The three [village] manuals cover all kinds of things like worldview of 1627. How do these people think about the sun, and the moon, and the stars? The humours. The humour theory. There's religion chapters, medicine chapters, dialect. It's very well rounded in cooking information, harvesting, brewing beer, baking bread, tending animals, keeping a garden, a kitchen garden. Herbs for medicine. This is all in their manuals.[77]

Gedraitis's description of the stacks of primary evidence, dossiers on Pilgrim biography and genealogy, and anecdotal information is yet another way that the institution can claim historical accuracy through ethnohistorical rigor, despite the fact that the historical "facts" are communicated to the visitors through imaginary encounters with interpreters improvising their daily situations and current relationships.

Plimoth Plantation historians, "obsessing" about details, scour the past to find what has been recorded but forgotten "along the way" in order to remember it as an institutional, curatorial procedure. The museum functions as the embodiment of memories that the "Pilgrim Fathers" had chosen to remember by recording them in diaries, mercantile records, ship logs, and so forth. They exist in the present because they have been marked as worthy of remembering or, as Jean-François Lyotard puts it, "monumentioned."[78]

Colonial Williamsburg

> How to turn your car into a time machine
>
> —Colonial Williamsburg, "Vacation Planner"

> Leaving town? Why not leave the 19th and 20th centuries, too?
>
> —Colonial Williamsburg visitor brochure

John D. Rockefeller Jr., the figurehead and financier of the Colonial Williamsburg restoration project in the 1920s, was apparently a stickler for historic authenticity. He allegedly believed in a completely objective and accurate portrayal of the buildings and grounds as they had actually existed at the time in question. Rockefeller hired his historians accordingly and would not hesitate to stop individual restoration efforts completely and start over again if there was any doubt about being true to the original. In extreme examples, even if a facsimile building was near completion, it would need to be rebuilt if archaeologists discovered that its foundations were six feet off. "No scholar must ever be able to come to us and tell us we made a mistake" was Rockefeller's mantra during the process.

Little did Rockefeller know that the number of scholars who would come and tell Colonial Williamsburg about its inaccuracies would be legion. Many changes have been made to the physical appearance of the historic area since Rockefeller's time, the most significant of which have taken place since social historians in the 1970s focused on a "dirtier, more accurate past." Richard Handler and Eric Gable pinpoint this as the moment when "road apples," the signature artifact of accuracy in living historical environments, began to darken Colonial Williamsburg's streets. This was only the beginning of Williamsburg's revisionist face-lift. Even since the 1990s, things have changed significantly, and a visit to the historic area today is very different than it would have been twenty-five years ago, when Michael Wallace critiqued the museum in the *Radical History Review*.

For one thing, changes were made in the 1980s and 1990s in order to alter the appearance of the buildings on Duke of Gloucester Street. Granted, the street itself is a paved, commercial thoroughfare owned by the city. While Colonial Williamsburg Foundation representatives have worked with the city to mix aggregate into the asphalt in order to give the paved street a more earthy color[79] and have left some of the road apples in plain view, the street lacks the knee-deep mud, ravines caused by water runoff, and garbage that would have littered the street from the College of William and Mary to the Capitol. But the maintenance of the buildings themselves has also been changed in an attempt to achieve a more "accurate" look. Cary Carson told Elisabeth Bumiller in an interview that the foundation stopped painting the buildings every season so that they would have a "less precious" appearance. The result was that some of those houses reconstructed or restored in a $68 million project had the paint peeling off of their clapboard siding: "We used to paint all of the buildings at the same time . . . but nobody now and nobody then painted their property from end to end."[80]

In my research at Williamsburg, I found some of the same commitment to detail and rigor that I found at Plimoth Plantation. Like Plimoth, Williamsburg has its own rare-breeds program, which visitors hear about if they sign up for the "Bits and Bridles" tour. My own experience with this tour in June 2000, led by third-person, noncostumed, volunteer interpreter Victoria West, allowed me to see the backstage area of the colonial reconstruction, including the barns and carriage houses that accommodate the animals responsible for providing Williamsburg with the livestock element of its living history.[81] That summer, the Coach and Livestock Program included thirty-one horses and "countless" chickens. Rare breeds included Red Devon cattle; chickens such as Dominiques, English Game Cocks, and Red Dorkings (apparently brought to England by the Romans at some point in their empire); and Leicester sheep. A "rare breed," I was told, is a term that designates a breed with two hundred or fewer animals in existence. Interestingly, no pigs are allowed at Williamsburg, despite their documented presence in the eighteenth century. The reason for this, explained West, is that pigs were determined to be "mean" and potentially damaging to the historic area.

Anna Logan Lawson writes that the authenticity of the slavery story, and therefore its legitimacy, hinges on historic accuracy at Colonial Williamsburg, as does everything else at the institution. The process of reconstructing the slave quarter at Carter's Grove (a nearby site operated by Williamsburg), for instance, was heavily informed by archaeological rigor, much like that conducted at Plimoth Plantation. Edward Chappell, head of the architectural history department at Colonial Williamsburg and leader of the slave quarter project, "was committed to accuracy in the detail of the museum's objects: the more perfect the details, the more authentic the whole—buildings, furnishings, and thus the closer to a true recreation of the 18th century."[82]

Finally, one of the ways that Colonial Williamsburg directs the consciousness of the visitor to believe he or she is witnessing a precisely reconstructed moment two centuries earlier on the very ground they occupy is the "Days in History" program, adopted in 2000. Through this program, the visit to Williamsburg is not simply a generalized amalgam of late eighteenth-century Virginia. Rather, every day of the week corresponds to a lived day in the years immediately preceding the American Revolution. Throughout each day, all programs, interpretations, and events are focused on a discussion of the events of that day in the given year, such as Lord Dunmore's latest executive decision or the news from Boston regarding British oppression. A 2000 press release from the Public Relations Department described the expansion of the program for that season:

Through new interactive "Days in History," visitors trace the decline of British influence in North America and the dawn of a new nation. Culminating in Virginia's declaration of independence from Great Britain on May 16, 1776, the new seven-day period offers a week full of encounters with "people of the past," daily walking tours and dramatic reenactments that encourage visitors to become part of the events that helped ignite a revolution.[83]

The "Days in History" programming for 2000, for example, centered around the theme of "Taking Possession" and included the events chosen to support a narrative of "the road to revolution," including Lord Dunmore's removal of the gunpowder from the public magazine (April 21, 1775), his declaration of martial law (November 18, 1775), and the Virginia colonists' signing of their declaration of independence (May 15, 1776) and constitution (May 16, 1776).

Bentley Boyd, a Newport News reporter for the *Daily Press*, saw the creation of "Days in History" as an important step toward helping visitors access the history that was presented at Colonial Williamsburg. Between 1992, when he first came to the museum, and when I spoke with him in the summer of 2000, he says he has seen much "progress" in that "they've made the history a lot easier to understand." He used "Days in History" to support his argument:

> When you come to Colonial Williamsburg and you look at the day of the week—today, for example, is Wednesday—you can open up the guide, called the "Visitor's Companion," and it will tell you, "This day, which to you is Wednesday, June 7, 2000, in the Historic Area it is going to be—," and then they give you a date. And every single building and every single person acting in first person is on the same page, they're doing that same date. Which I think is really good. Now, on Thursday, it's going to be a different date, and they're going to move you through time, focusing on the years just before and during the Revolution.[84]

Boyd recalled the format of Colonial Williamsburg's interpretations when he first encountered the museum, describing it as a "hodgepodge," lacking themes or frames of reference to structure visitors' experiences. Adjacent buildings were frequently interpreted by staff using disparate time periods. Often, finding a specific moment in time was a matter of chance: "If you were lucky enough," Boyd said, and "Bill Barker was doing Thomas Jefferson that day, you know he would be talking about the day that the government moved from here up to Richmond. And you sort of had to keep it straight, in your own head, and you sort of picked and chose what you enjoyed." Boyd credits former president Robert Wilburn for the improvements:

> [Wilburn] said, "We have to provide new themes each year, so not only do we have these days, but, for example, one year we're going to focus on slavery. All

of those dates are going to center around the discussion of slavery and people who were slaves and free blacks. . . . Next year, we're going to talk about property. . . . But the idea is that if you have a different theme and you're presenting new programs every year, people will come back." He was battling the idea that most people had, which was, "Well, I came here when I was in middle school, and it's all the same old buildings, so why should I go back?"[85]

The thematic narratives that structure each season, called "storylines," are provided to Colonial Williamsburg staff members in large booklets, much like the "stacks" of sources given to Pilgrim interpreters at Plimoth Plantation at their orientation. The storyline for 1997, for instance, was "Redefining Family," and it took the form of a 352-page document with sections on marriage, child rearing, education, and so forth, along with breakdowns of how these elements would differ based on whether the family was white, Native American, or black. The Redefining Family storyline also included thirty-one biographies of Williamsburg's inhabitants, ranging from Elizabeth Randolph to Lydia Broadnax, a slave in the Wythe household. The thesis of the storyline emphasized the way in which transformations in the eighteenth-century family lives of blacks, whites, and Native Americans led to the way modern American families are structured and behave today:

> During the eighteenth century, customs of family life inherited from Europe underwent alterations that had a profound effect on the way family members defined themselves in relation to one another and to society at large. Gradually, these changes brought the "modern American" family into being.[86]

Each year's storyline is an installment of the overall theme of interpretive programming at Colonial Williamsburg called "Becoming Americans: Our Struggle to Be Both Free and Equal."[87] Instituted in 1994, "Becoming Americans" was intended to provide visitors an overall thematic experience by which they could understand the exhibits and performances they encountered in the historic area and compare them to their own experience. By taking as a given that Americans today are "both free and equal," the thematic interpretation could present the events and people of eighteenth-century Williamsburg as the kernels of potential and determining factors for the results seen in the present.

Colonial Williamsburg's Days in History programming is the nineteenth-century, homogeneous continuum of time epitomized. Not only has history been retraced to late eighteenth-century Virginia, but it has been retraced back to seven days of precise moments. These moments, in a Hegelian understanding, had passed out of existence two hundred years ago, after an instant of being real, but thanks to archaeological research, historical rigor, and curatorial display, they can be restaged in an authoritative air of institutional accuracy. Williamsburg phrases like "the road to Revolution" imply a linear, cause-and-effect process of history. If the events of late eighteenth-century Virginia are understood in light of subsequent events, they are perceived to be links in a chain toward an inevitable outcome, rather than autonomous moments informed by specific possibilities and states of affairs. Thus, the visitor's conception of the events in the Days in History is structured by an imaginary, narrative story, with conflict, rising action, and climax.

Colonial Williamsburg's commitment to archaeological and anthropological rigor, as well as its rare breeds, Days in History, and African-American history programming (and careful publicizing of each), allow the Colonial Williamsburg Foundation to claim authenticity in its presentation. For all of the humbleness on the part of the curators in explaining that 100 percent accuracy can never really be achieved, even for a high-caliber institution such as Colonial Williamsburg, other staff members often express the "frontline" and "party-line" view that is ultimately communicated to the visitors. One of the interpreters who has portrayed George Washington at Colonial Williamsburg stated it directly when I asked him whether or not Williamsburg really made history "come alive" as the brochures claimed:

> Yes, it does make history come alive. We have had comments from visitors, and always right up there at the top, the most enjoyable thing, are the people of history. The character interpreters—you know, the people who will not step out of this time period. And Colonial Williamsburg has a tradition to which I can attest: They are completely dedicated towards historical accuracy, so that you are seeing and feeling exactly what you would see if you were in this city on the day that is being portrayed.[88]

Old Sturbridge Village

> A visit to Old Sturbridge Village is an opportunity to turn the clock back over 160 years and experience the life, work and celebrations of a rural New England community in the early 19th century.
>
> —"Old Sturbridge Village Lodges and Oliver Wight House"

> Each day at Old Sturbridge Village brings another special opportunity to step back in time.
>
> —*Old Sturbridge Village: A Visitor's Guide*

Plimoth Plantation is a total reconstruction of a former site based on rigorous archaeological research, but contains no actual remnants of the time period it portrays. Colonial Williamsburg is comprised of a mixture of new and old, simulated material culture and artifacts (the boundaries often blurring between the two), yet it references a lived site with a documented history—Williamsburg in the late 1770s. Old Sturbridge Village in Massachusetts differs from both in that it is a collection of documented, restored or reconstructed buildings from no singular place, but from all over New England. While the museum does not claim to represent the way a specific site would have appeared in the 1830s, it does promote itself as a museum of everyday life in rural New England, which gives a visitor an "authentic" sense of what any bustling New England community would have been like at that time.[89]

The orientation film informs visitors that the site is a representative landscape typical of an early nineteenth-century rural village, with businesses, meetinghouses, and homes surrounding a common. Started as a museum in the 1930s to display Albert B. Wells's collection of material culture from rural New England, the programming expanded in the 1960s and 1970s to include additional buildings (meetinghouses, printing office, blacksmith shop, bank, school, shops, etc.), as well as Freeman Farm, a working exhibit displaying agricultural practices.

Jack Larkin shared with me the main goals the museum has in portraying the past for visitors:

> We seek to portray the past realistically. We seek to portray it accurately. We seek to portray the past in some terms in its fullness. We seek, obviously, to portray not simply the history of dead white men, but a real inclusive history that deals with a wide range of social movements. And we seek to present it in an engaging way. In a concrete, experiential way. What we tend to focus on—and of course we're not a history of abstractions, but a history of ordinary experience. And how larger historical themes like the history of medicine or politics or presidential elections or whatever impinge on ordinary people's experience. So that's always a lens through which we do things. And in my own writing—I've written some books—and that's basically the approach I try to take.[90]

Sturbridge has been the site of extensive research on the part of social historians. Here, a visitor will not encounter a founding father, a president, or any other personage of great historical import. This is a museum of everyday life in early nineteenth-century New England, and visitors accordingly interact with parsons, bankers, sawyers, and farmers. Upon occasion, one may be treated to a public audience with "the witty and eloquent Lydia Maria Child" (author of books on child rearing and home remedies, but more famous for her poem "Over the River and through the Woods") or abolitionist Abby Kelley, but that is about as famous as the characters get.[91] Sturbridge functions in museum discourse as an ideal model of social history that helped to "revolutionize" the museum industry and American history by focusing on the "everyday," rather than perpetuating the old narrative of great white men.[92]

Like Plimoth Plantation and Colonial Williamsburg, Old Sturbridge Village has made changes over time in the rigor and standards by which it measures historical accuracy and the presentation of the past. In an *Early American Life* article entitled "Living History: Getting Closer to Getting It Right," Old Sturbridge Village is described as having "progressed" in its historic interpretation from museum collection to living history. The article offers the village's furniture exhibits and corrections of its earlier inaccuracies as examples of a growing level of accuracy in museums and historic houses:

> Having progressed through research, study of documents, archaeological digs, and other historical methods to the current level of knowledge, the professionals are continually looking back and discovering anomalies in the way their artifacts have previously been displayed. Old Sturbridge Village, for example, realized that their average house would have contained much less furniture than previously thought, so rooms have been pared down, and excess furnishings relegated to galleries.[93]

While Plimoth Plantation and Colonial Williamsburg have rare-breeds programs to strengthen their historic portrayal, with living animals populating the streets and pens, Old Sturbridge Village goes a step further by creating the breeds it exhibits.[94] The museum's "back-breeding" of plants and animals is cited in the *Early American Life* article as an effective technique in accurate representation of the past:

> In what may be the most ambitious of all experiments in re-creation, Old Sturbridge Village has scientists working on the back-breeding of domestic animals so that the hybrid strains of modern, meaty chickens, pigs, cattle, and sheep can work their way back to the condition and appearance of their ancestors in the nineteenth century. Old varieties of plants also have their place in many museum gardens. This is undoing history indeed.[95]

Larkin was careful to point out to me in our conversation that their back-breeding program's objective was to achieve an accurate phenotype (physical appearance) and not genotype (genetic makeup):

In other words, we're not trying to re-create the DNA of early nineteenth-century dunghill fowl or common sheep or New England common red-and-white lineback cattle. We're basically trying to get back to their appearance. They're larger and healthier, almost in all cases, than the originals would have been. And their actual genotype, their genetic constitutions, is obviously quite different. So, because we're looking for phenotype, not genotype, we're not really—We're looking for color and confirmation, basically.[96]

A costumed farm-worker, milking a back-bred cow at the Freeman Farm area in Old Sturbridge Village, explained to me how the subject of his exhibit, a "lineback," had been back-bred to appear as it would have before the changes brought by the Industrial Revolution. Cows in the nineteenth century were kept for both milk and beef, as well as for leather and tallow for candles, whereas today they are bred for specific, singular purposes. The importance of butterfat and the growing need for milk and cheese for trade prompted the breeding of some cows exclusively for dairy-related purposes, while others were bred for labor to replace horses.[97]

A visitor joined in the conversation and asked how the museum finds out about the way the animals would have changed over time. The interpreter talked about written accounts, such as diaries, that, despite questionable accuracy, were used to make decisions on exhibited breeds. Some of the problems concerned the lack of a standardized system for naming breeds in the 1830s. For instance, there were twenty or more different names for a red cow, depending on the diary account. Definitions for oxen included traits which should be favored in selecting an animal for purchase (bright eyes, multiple coloration) and which should not. He also told us about how during the late 1970s Old Sturbridge Village changed the time period being represented, from generally between the 1790s and 1840s to specifically around the 1830s. By this time, he said, the villagers would have had a lot more solid idea of the types of cows they wanted for butterfat and milk production.

Old Sturbridge Village is a forum in which another problem has been played out. Some scholars found that living history museums, despite the greater degree of accuracy obtained through social history and scientific rigor, did not offer a unified conception to visitors of working, thriving communities as they would have appeared in the past. Facing what he described as a collection of disjointed but highly accurate lectures, Cary Carson wrote that in the late 1970s and early 1980s, museums made a greater effort to unify their sites into a total, social history. He credits Old Sturbridge Village with doing the best job so far. Organizing its history around the three main ideas of work, family, and community, he writes, visitors encounter "central themes," which comment upon and reinforce each other:

> For example, they find family life explained in many of the restored houses. Interpreters at a parsonage discuss religion and reform to call attention to one family's ties with others in the village community. The schoolhouse and the meeting house are used to teach about the community itself, its mores, and its conduct of public business. A restored and restocked general store reminds visitors that a village must have relations with the world outside. And so it goes, through dozens of exhibits, craft shops, farms, and activities that are no less enthralling than those to be found at museums where these are ends in themselves. Indeed they are more so, because a visitor comes away from Sturbridge with his head full of ideas that have been carefully planted and encouraged to grow into a knowledge of the past sufficiently well developed to be called out later and used again. In short, learning worth keeping.[98]

Carson goes on to write that, even with the greater sense of total history, something is missing. The history of society will remain unfulfilled until the institutions place more emphasis on the influence of population and economic growth on these communities and their societal relationships.

Centering interpretation at a living history site around a central theme or themes produces meaning for the visitors and places what they see into an interpretive context they can use to create a unifying narrative about the past in their minds. Susan Irwin writes that, for the benefit of the visitor, living history museums must develop themes that "unite" the sites, for example, "The Golden Age," "Life in the 1830s," or "The War of 1812."[99] Such was Freeman Tilden's argument in *Interpreting Our Heritage*, holding that grouping facts into themes makes them more understandable for the visitor. Barbara Abramoff Levy, Sandra McKenzie Lloyd, and Susan Porter Schreiber similarly advocate thematizing history, offering suggestions for guides on how to tell "people stories" so that visitors remember more about historic sites than just how "pretty" they were.[100]

Andrew Baker and Warren Leon write how Old Sturbridge Village has introduced conflict into its representation of the past through a three-pronged living history program involving reenactments of stormy town meetings (debating such issues as the merits or problems surrounding a proposed poor-farm), volunteer organizations like the Sturbridge Charitable Society (who enact collecting funds to help temperance and abolition movements), and period presidential campaigning (bringing to the fore relevant political issues of the day, such as tariff imposition or revision of the militia system with a national standing army). Such programming and adoption of social history methodologies "dispel the myth of stable, conflict-free communities."[101]

Notions of "undoing" or thematizing history at Old Sturbridge Village and other museums present several problems: the linear view of history does not recognize there are losses, erasures, and marginalizations that make it impossible to simply undo history along the line to a past point. Despite the way thematizing makes history more assimilable for visitors, it also limits what may be thought about a time in history by reducing it to a unifying idea. What is not explicit in the promotion of thematic programming is that the structure of unified narrative, like community conflict, has been imposed upon disparate histories in order to produce meaning for the visitor. Moving through the simulated 1830s environment, the visitor is allowed access to certain histories that affirm and perpetuate this narrative, which in turn motivates their touristic experience to produce an understanding of the period as one that functioned according to a transcendental program. That is, with the certain elements in place (the meetinghouse, the charitable societies, and the right mixture of class and ethnic background), narratives of conflict and community strengthening would play themselves out in a formulaic manner, and these episodes would add to the growing character of the nation.

Storytelling vs. Scientific Discourse

The discipline of history, writes Jacques Rancière in his introduction to *The Names of History*, is faced with a dilemma as to whether it is a soft or hard science. It struggles with both the expectation to proceed with the rigor of sciences and its reputation as a storytelling operation: the relating of a past that has a beginning, middle, and end, themes, characters, and proper names.[102] Because history is a "poor cousin" of science, continues Rancière, the joint condition of scientist and narrator motivated the history discipline to reinvent itself and its reputation by simultaneously entering into three contractual relationships with other discourses:

1. The scientific contract, concerned with finding a "latent" order beneath the manifest order of events with the "substitution of the exact correlations and numbers of a complex process for the scale of the visible weights and sizes of politics"
2. The narrative contract, "which commands the inscription of the structures of this hidden space (the latent order), or of the laws of this complex process, in the readable forms of a story with a beginning and end, with characters and events"

3. The political contract, "which ties what is invisible in science and what is readable in narration to the contradictory constraints of the age of the masses—of the great regularities of common law and the great tumults of democracy, of revolutions and counterrevolutions, of the hidden secret of the multitudes and the narration of a common history readable and teachable to all"[103]

Because "living" history is a historiographic practice that may be discussed in the same manner as written history, Rancière's assessment can exquisitely bring to light the way living museums engage in all three "contracts" in order to construct legitimate histories of their subjects.

Plimoth Plantation, Colonial Williamsburg, and Old Sturbridge Village engage in the scientific contract in order to promote an authoritative view of the past. They use the terminology of scientific rigor to support their authority. To do so, they impose an order upon the events and objects of display, so that meaning is produced. However, as Rancière reminds us, despite its attempts at objectivity in order to counter its reputation as subjective storyteller, the scientific contract of history remains grounded in an assumption of a transcendental order that lies outside of the lived, external order of things. Transcendental notions such as a circle or a line, or a continuum of discreet instants, are precisely what Agamben urges to be challenged with a shift in the perception of written history. They need to be challenged in the realm of living history if museums like Plimoth Plantation are to escape the dilemma of being grounded in an unhelpful and limiting perception of time.

Living museums pursue the scientific contract through reconstructive processes, plumbing archaeological digs and archives to find an order that can organize the accumulated knowledge. One of the best metaphors to illustrate the reconstruction of a past milieu as a total living environment is an ancient clay pot, the remains of which have been exhumed in fragments. If archaeological evidence and period accounts are understood to be pieces of the pot, then the rest of the data (the missing fragments) may be filled in according to the contours determined by the extant shards. Plimoth Plantation, using this metaphor, fills the lacunae of known material culture with, among other things, evidence from Dutch paintings, circa 1627. The operating assumption in this model is that there once was a unified, structured whole to begin with. As is more often the case, however, museums determine the shape of the living history environment (the pot) first, informed by present sensibilities, and then choose the shards that best fit those contours.

In the same manner, these museums engage in the narrative contract in order to fit lived events into a story through which visitors may comprehend those events. Both Plimoth Plantation and Old Sturbridge Village, for in-stance, employ themes of social conflict. In the former, visitors get their facts embedded in stories of the tensions between Separatists and Church of En-gland colonists, or through accounts of tensions with the mercantile compa-nies with which the Pilgrims contracted. In the latter, conflict is emphasized in town meetings or voiced by temperance advocates. A conflict narrative organizes meaning for the museum visitors, through which they may under-stand the disparate events of the 1620s or 1830s. Such themes not only make history more "readable" for visitors but also link the constructed past with an understanding of the present. In the case of Old Sturbridge Village, social conflict becomes the template for the way society works. While conflict is in-deed documented in nineteenth-century New England, its institution as a seasonal program at a living history museum produces the notion that a tra-ditional conflict emerged at town meetings that, through a democratic process that forms the "backbone" of America, brought about change for the better. Thus, conflict builds American character.

Finally, by virtue of the political contract, living history museums produce authoritative facsimiles of the past and link them to prescriptive discourse (what T. H. Breen calls a "forward looking history")[104] by "inventing tradi-tions" that speak to values of the present. Social conflict, for example, is a tradition social historians invented in the late twentieth century that refer-ences lived events of the past but is largely the result of meaning production in the present. This is based on the perception that, with the elapsing of time, social behaviors that have somehow benefited society have survived to be passed down from generation to generation. In a Darwinian "survival of the fittest," those "traditions" that still exist today must have been the most relevant and vital to the community in the past. Museum curators engage in what Eric Hobsbawm calls a maneuver by authoritative bodies to affirm the existing status quo by claiming its elements bear a connection to the past. "Traditions," Hobsbawm writes, "which appear or claim to be old are often quite recent in origin and sometimes invented." These traditions include those that are introduced and instituted formally, like the institution of a na-tional anthem, and those that are less traceable and originate within a brief amount of time. His definition of an invented tradition is "a set of practices, normally governed by overtly or tacitly accepted rules and of a ritual or sym-bolic nature, which seek to inculcate certain values and norms of behaviour by repetition which automatically implies continuity with the past."[105] In other words, while these traditions *reference* the past, their relationship with the *actual* past is tenuous. By locating "traditions" in the present while refer-encing the past, living history museums project an environment backward, down the continuum of instants, to become the kernel of the present status quo.

One of the most ingrained of invented traditions in the United States is the Thanksgiving holiday, nationally instituted by various presidents on specific days in November (most notably by Abraham Lincoln). Though the feast as popular culture envisions it never took place, the tradition has been projected back upon 1620–1621, in order to construct the meaning of the Pilgrims in Plymouth. Plimoth Plantation, in its early years, perpetuated the invented tradition of Thanksgiving, with likenesses of Pilgrims and Indians sharing a meal to give thanks for the harvest after the bitter first winter that killed half of the colonists. Though the Thanksgiving notion has been debased by scholars and disclaimed by Plimoth literature as unlikely to have ever happened, the museum still enacts the "Harvest Home" celebration, for which Plimoth historians and staff have conflated the traditional English autumn festival with accounts of a documented feast that year.

Plimoth Plantation also has a Thanksgiving celebration every year, to which visitors are invited to purchase tickets and which culminates Plimoth's season of operation. The menu includes foods from Victorian English tables in the formal dining area and, as an alternative, a New England Thanksgiving buffet. The museum is careful not to imply that the food served is the same as that enjoyed by the Pilgrims at any mythical "first Thanksgiving" (James Deetz mused at one point that the overwhelming presence of pig bone remains found in archaeological digs of the colony's cellars suggests that the Pilgrims most likely dined on roast pork rather than roast turkey.[106] At any rate, Edward Winslow's 1621 account of the "fowl" eaten at the feast traditionally regarded as the first Thanksgiving suggests the Pilgrims were eating ducks and geese).[107] There is nothing, however, to keep the "museum effect" (the same kind that produces reality out of historical reconstructions for visitors) from legitimizing the Thanksgiving feast served at Plimoth Plantation as that which *really* happened. In other words, if a museum devoted to authentic and accurate portrayal of Pilgrim history serves a Thanksgiving dinner, the feast is curatorially linked to the Pilgrims, despite brochures and signage that declare the contrary.

To use the political contract as a structure to organize past events produces continuity between the displayed past and the present, and a visitor can more easily reconcile the idea that the present is a product of the past—one of the goals of living history museums. Americans, then, become the inheritors of past values that inform the present. As the Colonial Williamsburg "Becoming Americans" training manual puts it, a "new set of beliefs and values . . . were already discernable by the middle of the eighteenth century." It continues:

Some have become fundamental rights that all Americans expect, however diverse their backgrounds and however differently they understand and apply the following ideals:

- This country is a place where a person is free to improve his or her circumstances.
- Every citizen is entitled to pursue a private vision of personal happiness.
- Life and individual liberty are essential to that pursuit.
- These expectations are tempered by one more—equality, which Americans understand to be every person's equal worth with rights to equal justice, equal opportunities, and equal access to the civic enterprise.
- Everyone has a right and a duty to participate in the governing of society.[108]

Linking this organization of knowledge to Agamben's essay, it becomes apparent that, while Plimoth Plantation, Old Sturbridge Village, and Colonial Williamsburg pay special attention to the lives of historical individuals in their programming (e.g., Thomas Jefferson, Myles Standish, Asa Knight), these individuals are not, ultimately, the subject of their history. The real subjects are progress, the building of a national character, and becoming Americans. Through a process of reinscription of these ideals and themes upon the visitors' consciousnesses, the visitors are to understand their own experience of time as a contribution to this march forward.

Even in 1958, Daniel Boorstin noted upon his visit to Williamsburg that the problem with assuming that ideals of the past have survived unchanged to the present is that it denies the "dynamic and federal character of American life, which is actually expressed in the *differences* between what each of these 'concepts' meant to the citizens of Colonial Williamsburg and what they mean to us today." The restoration would serve its patriotic purpose much better, wrote Boorstin, if it dramatized the uniqueness of Southern and colonial political institutions, as opposed to promoting itself as a didactic "abstraction" like "World Freedom."[109]

* * *

Revisionist programming at living museums, beginning in the 1970s, focused on creating a more "accurate" representation of the past by shifting from the "great white men" of history to a more egalitarian, everyday history with an emphasis on women, the working class, and minorities. The accuracy of this history was constructed through the adoption of the narrative and political contracts, as well as through a contract with the legitimate sciences: archaeology, anthropology, and so on. The scientific contract gave the semblance of historiographic validity by suggesting that, through research, specific temporal spaces could be exhumed by "undoing" the time that had elapsed since their occurrence. Such a view perpetuates what Agamben called a vulgar conception of time as a precise and homogenous continuum of instants.

Many living history staff members on the curatorial level at museum institutions will readily admit that accuracy in display is impossible. Barney Barnes, in Interpretive Program Development at Colonial Williamsburg, spoke at length of the various obstacles in the way of achieving accuracy in the portrayal of the eighteenth-century capital, including the paved streets, lack of biographical information on certain segments of society, and the need to generalize from other sources when there are gaps in documentation of characters portrayed by staff. The most obvious inaccuracy, said Barnes, is that Williamsburg has only a small number of African-American interpreters. On any given day, a visitor is unlikely to meet more than ten "slaves," even though the eighteenth-century population of the town was more than half black. "And I don't know if we'll ever get to the point of enough successful recruiting to get half of the interpretive corps to [represent accurately the population of the eighteenth century]," Barnes admitted.[110]

At Plimoth, Cynthia Gedraitis offered examples of inaccuracies that visitors themselves bring up to the interpreters: "It's very difficult sometimes. There are people who will come in and they'll wanna say, 'Your teeth are too good. You're not a seventeenth-century person, your teeth are too good,' or 'I can see the piercings in your ears.'" It's not that these things are impossible to cover up, says Gedraitis, but that there is a threshold of rigor beyond which the staff is unwilling to go. "We're only willing to go so far. . . . I don't think, again, that we're trying to fool people. That isn't the point. We're supposed to be educational."[111]

Plimoth's Carolyn Travers wished aloud that she could get rid of some of the "modern intrusions" that have became an irreversible part of the environment since 1627: English grass, Queen Anne's Lace, the decorative plants that the Hornblowers planted in the Eel River that killed the cattails, invasive species like cardinals and the Japanese beetle that have pushed native species farther north, and so on. "What would a garden look like without modern weeds?" she asked. But if the museum were to take these out, she added, the resulting gaps would need to remain a "blank," since it is not known what would have been in their place. I asked if this dilemma was communicated to the visitors. "It's hard to do," she answered. "It's easier to [pretend] not [to] see an airplane."[112]

At Old Sturbridge Village, Jack Larkin told me that his museum of everyday life is still not accurate regarding the living conditions of the very poor: "Ultimately I'd like to see us demonstrate a greater range of social class by probably building and interpreting a very small house. A house of very poor people."[113]

Yet, despite these attitudes toward accuracy on the curatorial level, the institutional reinscription of time perpetuates the notion in visitors' minds that accuracy is, indeed, possible, and that high-profile museums such as Plimoth Plantation, Colonial Williamsburg, and Old Sturbridge Village are examples of such accuracy. The scientific contract, monumention, and the invention of tradition are all procedures that imply that time can be retraced along a precise and homogeneous continuum to a moment in the past and that that moment can be reconstructed to accurately represent the physicality and social relationships that define the moment as part of a narrative of history. With applied scientific rigor, diligent research, and the passage of time, the needed evidence will eventually be uncovered and will lead to a continually diminishing margin of error or inaccuracy. While curators and programming staff admit that achieving accuracy is impossible, due to limited knowledge, visitor expectations, civic and health issues, and contemporary taste, these limitations are not foregrounded in signage or literature.

I opened this chapter with the notion that the product of a historiographic practice, a "history," stands in for the labor that went into it (much like a signature substitutes for the presence of the real person signing the document). Because we have the product, the process becomes irrelevant. Scholars publish the end products of the historiographic process—the "history"—rather than "the writing of the history." In the same way, living museums hide their own selection processes. Living history museums are not seen as living "making-history" museums, and thus their decisions, agenda, and biases are rendered invisible. Who is the museum's patron? What is its legitimizing institution or society? To whom does the historian report, and whose rules must the historian follow? Moreover, when scholars write about the choices that museums make in interpretive programming, they often leave the institutional authority behind these choices out of the narrative. According to Anderson, for example, Plimoth's decision to choose first-person interpretation evolved naturally, as a product of all the right elements of arrangement of artifacts and costuming came into place. "Without any word" from the curators, Anderson asserts, the Pilgrim interpreters switched to the "we do" mode of discussing the 1620s colony.[114] By stressing the natural arrival at this model of perfection, Anderson reinforces the notion that, if left to its own devices in a suitable environment, and with the proper elapse of time, progress will occur. The structures that privilege this series of events over others are made invisible.

Notes

1. This "origin" has since come into question. See my essay "Performance Practices of (Living) Open-Air Museums (And a New Look at 'Skansen' in American Living Museum Discourse)," *Theatre History Studies* 24 (June 2004).

2. See Laura E. Abing, "Old Sturbridge Village: An Institutional History of a Cultural Artifact" (Ph.D. dissertation, Marquette University, 1997); Edward P. Alexander, *Museums in Motion* (Walnut Creek, CA: American Association for State and Local History, 1996); Jay Anderson, *Time Machines: The World of Living History* (Nashville, TN: American Association for State and Local History, 1984); Andrew Baker and Warren Leon, "Old Sturbridge Village Introduces Social Conflict into Its Interpretive Story," *History News* (March 1986); Cary Carson, "Living Museums of Everyman's History," *Harvard* (Summer 1981); Cary Carson, "Colonial Williamsburg and the Practice of Interpretive Planning in American History Museums," *Public Historian* 20.3 (Summer 1998); James Deetz, "A Sense of Another World: History Museums and Cultural Change," *Museum News* 58.5 (May–June 1980); James Deetz and Patricia Scott Deetz, *The Times of Their Lives: Life, Love, and Death in Plymouth Colony* (New York: Freeman, 2000); Anders Greenspan, *Creating Colonial Williamsburg* (Washington, DC: Smithsonian Institution Press, 2002); H. Holzer, "Turning Back the Calendar to 1627 at Plimoth Plantation," *American History Illustrated* 20.7 (1985); Susan K. Irwin, "Popular History: Living History Sites, Historical Interpretation and the Public" (master's thesis, Bowling Green State University, 1993); John D. Krugler, "Behind the Public Presentations: Research and Scholarship at Living History Museums of Early America," *William and Mary Quarterly* 48.3 (July 1991); Michael Lang, "Marketing Historical Resources" (master's thesis, University of Calgary, 1991); Warren Leon and Margaret Piatt, "Living History Museums," in *History Museums in the United States: A Critical Assessment*, ed. Warren Leon and Roy Rosenzweig (Urbana: University of Illinois Press, 1989); "Living History: Getting Closer to Getting It Right," *Early American Life* 21.3 (June 1990); Patricia Mandell, "Details, Details, Details," *Americana* 17.5 (November–December 1989); Stephen Eddy Snow, *Performing the Pilgrims: A Study of Ethnohistorical Role-Playing at Plimoth Plantation* (Jackson: University Press of Mississippi, 1993); Kate F. Stover, "Is It *Real* History Yet? An Update on Living History Museums," *Journal of American Culture* 12.2 (Summer 1989); Michael Wallace, "Visiting the Past: History Museums in the United States," *Radical History Review* 25 (1981): 63–96.

3. Anderson, *Time Machines*, 17, 19.

4. Anderson, *Time Machines*, 22.

5. Anderson, *Time Machines*, 29–30.

6. Anderson, *Time Machines*, 39.

7. Anderson, *Time Machines*, 45.

8. Anderson, *Time Machines*, 50.

9. Anderson, *Time Machines*, 56.

10. Snow includes a literal timeline of this development: "A progression of the various modes for representing the Pilgrims, from the 1850s to the 1990s" (see figure 1). He starts with the 1850s when the first paintings of "Heroic Pilgrim Scenes" began to visually depict events in the lives of the colonists, and labels the last marker "living history performance," before the continuum terminates in an arrow pointing toward the future. See Snow, *Performing the Pilgrims*, 25.

11. Snow, *Performing the Pilgrims*, 39, 203.

12. Michael Wallace, "Visiting the Past: History Museums in the United States," *Radical History Review* 25 (1981), 63–96. Fifteen years later, he reformatted the essay and published pieces of it throughout his book *Mickey Mouse History and Other Essays on American Memory* (Philadelphia: Temple University Press, 1996).

13. Wallace, "Visiting the Past," 63.

14. Wallace, "Visiting the Past," 66.

15. Wallace, "Visiting the Past," 67.

16. Wallace, "Visiting the Past," 72–73.

17. Wallace, "Visiting the Past," 78.

18. Wallace, "Visiting the Past," 91.

19. Wallace, "Visiting the Past," 91.

20. Wallace, "Visiting the Past," 88.

21. Wallace, "Visiting the Past," 87.

22. Anderson, *Time Machines*, 13. Richard Handler writes: "[Anderson's] enthusiasm is apparently typical of buffs"; see Richard Handler, "Overpowered by Realism: Living History and the Simulation of the Past," review of Anderson's *Time Machines* and *The Living History Sourcebook* (Nashville: American Association for State and Local History, 1985), *Journal of American Folklore*, 100.397 (1987): 338.

23. In his introduction to *Mickey Mouse History*, Wallace positions himself in the field as a scholar and critic, sending "dispatches from the front, mixing reportage with unsolicited advice" (xii). He apologizes: "A full-time history professor in the City University of New York, I have never actually labored in the curatorial trenches, but served instead as a commentator, consultant, cheerleader, and critic. I have taken the liberty of offering suggestions and encouragement from the sidelines, but I have not had responsibility for *doing* anything" (xii–xiii).

24. Third-person costumed interpreter, Yorktown Victory Center, personal interview, 4 June 2000.

25. Rosemarie McAphee, personal interview, 7 June 2000.

26. Manager, Theatrical Productions Department, Colonial Williamsburg, personal interview, 7 June 2000.

27. Mark Howell, personal interview, 7 June 2000.

28. Jack Larkin, personal interview, 21 June 2000.

29. Abing, "Old Sturbridge Village," 42. Here, Abing is quoting from the original guidebook of Old Quinabaug Village, as the museum was called in 1939.

30. Abing, "Old Sturbridge Village," 39.

31. Abing, "Old Sturbridge Village," 40.

32. Abing, "Old Sturbridge Village," 110.

33. *Old Sturbridge Village Visitor's Guide* (Sturbridge, MA: Old Sturbridge, 1999), 21–25.

34. Public relations staff member, Plimoth Plantation, personal interview, 15 June 2000.

35. David Lowenthal, *The Past Is a Foreign Country* (Cambridge, UK: Cambridge University Press, 1985), 298.

36. Third-person interpreter, Greenfield Village, 2 July 2003.

37. Third-person interpreter, Yorktown Victory Center, personal interview, 4 June 2000.

38. Third-person interpreter, Yorktown Victory Center, personal interview, 4 June 2000.

39. Guy Peartree, first-person interpreter (Guy Scott), Old Sturbridge Village, 20 June 2000.

40. Sally Jones, "The First But Not the Last of the Vanishing Indians: Edwin Forrest and the Mythic Re-Creations of Native Population," in *Dressing in Feathers: The Construction of the Indian in American Popular Culture*, ed. S. Elizabeth Bird (London: Routledge, 1996), 13–14. See also Russell Bourne, *The Red King's Rebellion: Racial Politics in New England, 1675–1678* (New York: Atheneum, 1990), and Richard Slotkin and James K. Folsom, eds., *So Dreadfull a Judgement: Puritan Responses to King Philip's War, 1676–1677* (Middletown, CT: Wesleyan University Press, 1978). Accounts of King Philip's War include genocide and burnings at the stake. The signature event was the treatment of Philip's (Metacomet's) body after his capture and death. John Alderman, credited with shooting and killing Philip, was awarded one of his hands as a trophy. Philip's body was beheaded and quartered, and his head was displayed on a pole for twenty-five years at Plymouth. After King Philip's War ended in 1676, the English continued to hunt down Indians involved in the conflicts. Those captured were often sold into slavery (Lee Sultzman, "Wampanoag History," www.tolatsga.org/wampa.html).

41. See Sultzman, "Wampanoag History." See also the introduction to Henry W. Bowden and James P. Ronda, eds., *John Eliot's Indian Dialogues: A Study in Cultural Interaction* (Westport, CT: Greenwood, 1980), and Kawashima Yasuhide, "The Pilgrims and the Wampanoag Indians, 1620–1691: Lethal Encounter," *Oklahoma City University Law Review* 23.1–2 (Spring/Summer 1998).

42. As of 2006, this essay was no longer posted on www.plimoth.org, but was available at http://groups.msn.com/traditions/nativeamerican.msnw?action=get_message &mview=1&id_message=15874.

43. Nancy Grey Osterud, "Living Living History: First-Person Interpretation at Plimoth Plantation, Plymouth, Massachusetts," *Journal of Museum Education* 17.1 (Winter 1992): 20.

44. Elaine Heumann Gurian, "What Is the Object of This Exercise?" in *Reinventing the Museum: Historical and Contemporary Perspectives on the Paradigm Shift*, ed. Gail Anderson (Walnut Creek, CA: AltaMira, 2004), 281.

45. Third-person costumed Native interpreter, Hobbamock's Homesite, personal interview, 17 June 2000.

46. See my essay "Recreation and Re-Creation: On-Site Historical Reenactment as Historiographic Operation at Plimoth Plantation," *Journal of Dramatic Theory and Criticism* (Fall 2002).

47. Rex M. Ellis, "Interpreting the Whole House," in *Interpreting Historic House Museums*, ed. Jessica Foy Donnelly (Walnut Creek, CA: AltaMira, 2002), 69.

48. Richard Handler and Eric Gable, *The New History in an Old Museum: Creating the Past at Colonial Williamsburg* (Durham, NC: Duke University Press, 1999), 86.

49. Carson, "Living Museums," 22.

50. Giorgio Agamben, "Time and History: Critique of the Instant and the Continuum," in *Infancy and History: Essays on the Destruction of Experience*, trans. Liz Heron (London: Verso, 1993), 91.

51. Agamben, "Time and History," 91.

52. Stover, "Is It *Real* History Yet?"

53. Stover, "Is It *Real* History Yet?" 13–14.

54. Stover, "Is It *Real* History Yet?" 14.

55. Social history did not abandon the timeline with cause-and-effect sequencing of events. Rather, it often substituted the singular with multiple timelines. As Lowenthal writes, "Dates and chronology are now out of fashion. Especially since the Second World War, human history has been seen to follow *not one line but those of many different cultures* [my emphasis], impossible or pointless to lump within a common sequence. The Western Civilization course declined along with the ethnocentrism which viewed that civilization as canonically pre-eminent; historians discovered not only the Third World but the West's previously neglected 'minorities'— women, children, Jews, peasants, blacks" (Lowenthal, *Past Is a Foreign Country*, 222).

56. Holzer, "Turning Back the Calendar," 35.

57. *Plimoth Plantation*, VHS (Glastonbury, CT: VideoTours, 1989).

58. *Plimoth Plantation*.

59. *Plimoth Plantation*.

60. Mandell, "Details, Details, Details," 54.

61. Mandell, "Details, Details, Details," 49.

62. Mandell, "Details, Details, Details," 52.

63. Mandell, "Details, Details, Details," 49. See also Michelle Pecoraro, "The Nye Barn: A Rare Breeds Exhibit," Plimoth Plantation press release, 2000.

64. Deetz and Deetz, *Times of Their Lives*, 278–79.

65. Deetz, "Sense of Another World," 45; emphasis in original.

66. Deetz, "Sense of Another World," 45.

67. Deetz and Deetz, *Times of Their Lives*, 276–77.

68. Mandell, "Details, Details, Details," 52.

69. Stover, "Is It *Real* History Yet?" 14.

70. Stover, "Is It *Real* History Yet?" 15.

71. Stover, "Is It *Real* History Yet?" 15.

72. Carolyn Travers, personal interview, 15 June 2000.

73. She added a cautionary note: even though the colonists were adept at technology and craft, some things are just better today. Modern paints do not contain arsenic or lead, and "we don't have twelve-year-olds making lace in a damp cellar until they can't see."

74. Adding the animals also meant that the Pilgrim interpreters could no longer consume the food they prepared on site for demonstration purposes, due to changes in health codes, Travers said.

75. What Travers found ironic was that hiring Pilgrim interpreters of European but not English or Dutch ethnicity was not a problem for visitors. At the time of the interview, for instance, Plimoth Plantation had a Polish interpreter from Gdansk on staff, and no one seemed concerned about it.

76. Cynthia Gedraitis, personal interview, 15 June 2000.

77. Cynthia Gedraitis, personal interview, 15 June 2000.

78. Jean-François Lyotard, "A Monument of Possibles," in *Postmodern Fables*, trans. Georges van den Abeele (Minneapolis: University of Minnesota Press, 1997), 166.

79. Mark Howell, program manager at Colonial Williamsburg, personal interview, 7 June 2000.

80. Elisabeth Bumiller, "Weekend Excursion: Colonial Myth and Reality," *New York Times*, 4 June 1999. I looked for such shabby appearances during my research at Colonial Williamsburg in 2000, but none were to be found. Nor did I see the rough-cut grass that resulted from sheep "mowing" the lawns.

81. *Backstage* is a subjective term, signifying the theatricality of the site, but it is not just my subjectivity. Another tour available to holders of certain passes is called the "Behind the Scenes at Colonial Williamsburg" tour and includes a look at the curatorial buildings, research facilities housed at the former Bruton Heights school, and the John D. Rockefeller Jr. Memorial Library (dedicated in 1995, it is the only building bearing Rockefeller's name). Even though these places are called behind-the-scenes, the tour makes them the stage itself, and not the backstage. The backstage that visitors do not get to see, even with the highest-level passes, are the workaday offices—cubicles with file cabinets, humming computers, and buzzing telephones—behind the eighteenth-century facades in the nonpublic buildings right on Duke of Gloucester Street.

82. Anna Logan Lawson, "'The Other Half': Making African-American History at Colonial Williamsburg" (Ph.D. dissertation, University of Virginia, 1995), 289.

83. "Colonial Williamsburg Expands 'Days in History' in 2000 to Delve Deeper into Virginia's Road to Revolution," Colonial Williamsburg press release, 2000.

84. Bentley Boyd, personal interview, 7 June 2000.

85. Bentley Boyd, personal interview, 7 June 2000.

86. Colonial Williamsburg Foundation, *Redefining Family: Resource Book 1997* (Williamsburg, VA: Colonial Williamsburg Foundation), 1.

87. See Carson, "Colonial Williamsburg," 42–43.

88. First-person costumed interpreter (George Washington), Colonial Williamsburg, personal interview, 5 June 2000.

89. Kent McCallum, ed., *Old Sturbridge Village: A Visitor's Guide* (Sturbridge, MA: Old Sturbridge, 1999), 2.

90. Jack Larkin, personal interview, 21 June 2000.

91. "Welcome to Sturbridge Village," map and guide, 19 June 2000.

92. Carson, "Living Museums," 22.

93. "Living History," 23. The article goes on to cite Jane Nylander, director of Strawbery Banke in New Hampshire: "When accuracy is increased, interpretation is improved" (24).

94. See *Preserving America's Past* (Washington, DC: National Geographic Society, 1983), 48; Scott Magelssen, "Resuscitating the Extinct: The Back-Breeding of Historic Animals at U.S. Living History Museums," *Drama Review* 47.4 (Winter 2004); and Umberto Eco, *Travels in Hyper Reality: Essays*, trans. William Weaver (San Diego: Harcourt Brace Jovanovich, 1983), 11–12.

95. "Living History: Getting Closer to Getting it Right," 24.

96. Jack Larkin, personal interview, 21 June 2000.

97. Third-person costumed farm worker, Old Sturbridge Village, personal interview, 19 June 2000.

98. Carson, "Living Museums," 29.

99. Irwin, "Popular History."

100. Barbara Abramoff Levy, Sandra McKenzie Lloyd, and Susan Porter Schreiber, *Great Tours! Thematic Tours and Guide Training for Historic Sites* (Walnut Creek, CA: AltaMira, 2001), xi.

101. Baker and Leon, "Old Sturbridge Village," 11.

102. Jacques Rancière, *The Names of History: On the Poetics of Knowledge*, trans. Hassan Melehy (Minneapolis: University of Minnesota Press, 1994), 1.

103. Rancière, *Names of History*, 9.

104. T. H. Breen, *Imagining the Past: East Hampton Histories* (Reading, MA: Addison-Wesley, 1984), 7–8.

105. Eric Hobsbawm, introduction to *The Invention of Tradition*, ed. Eric Hobsbawm and Terence Ranger (Cambridge: Cambridge University Press, 1983), 1.

106. James Deetz, *Invitation to Archaeology* (Garden City, NY: National History Press, 1967), 71.

107. Deetz and Deetz, *Times of Their Lives*, 1.

108. Cary Carson, "Becoming Americans: Our Struggle to Be Both Free and Equal; A Plan of Thematic Interpretation," January 1996 Training Edition (Williamsburg, VA: Colonial Williamsburg Foundation, 1996), 6.

109. Daniel Boorstin, "Past and Present in America: A Historian Visits Colonial Williamsburg," *Commentary* 25 (1958): 4–5; emphasis in original.

110. Barney Barnes, personal interview, 8 June 2000.

111. Cynthia Gedraitis, personal interview, 15 June 2000.

112. Carolyn Travers, personal interview, 15 June 2000.

113. Jack Larkin, personal interview, 21 June 2000.

114. Anderson, *Time Machines*, 50.

CHAPTER TWO

~

Toward a New Genealogy
of Living Museum Performance

A Historiography of Immanence

Art imitates life. . . . However, certain conclusions which are not possible in life can happen in Art.

—Aristotle, *Physics*

Gilles Deleuze and Félix Guattari offer a different mode of understanding time and history that is helpful in interrogating both the history of museum performance and the possibilities of museum programming and interpretation. Through Deleuze and Guattari's philosophy of immanence, it is possible to suggest that history is not to be "undone" by digging along an imaginary timeline into the past. Rather, history is found each time it is articulated in the abundance of the present.[1]

Deleuze and Guattari's past is not a line of development but a field or plane that contains all possibilities. History and time, past and present, are all part of a same plane. Thus, a past event does not exist outside of the present— that is, transcendentally—but in the here and now, immanently. Events do not happen as a culmination of cause-and-effect chains, but emerge at spatial "junctures" within the field. In these spatial terms, the event and the state of affairs meet and intersect as two vectors: the vector of the multiplicity of possibilities of events, and the vector of the multiplicity of states of affairs. The states of affairs actualize the event at the space of the juncture between the two vectors and the event, in turn, absorbs the states of affairs.

Neither the event nor the state of affairs can be reduced to itself, apart from its other term in the relation, because "a state of affairs cannot be separated from the potential through which it takes effect and without which it would have no activity or development."[2] The event is like a wound: never emerging on its own, nor the product of a linear progression, a wound is the actualization of a multiplicity of possibles within a state of affairs at a particularly violent or dangerous juncture.

It is the role of modern history, write Deleuze and Guattari, to glean or separate the states of affairs that actualize the event from the chaotic multiplicities of possibility. Once the historical event has been apprehended, the historian's conceit is that its relations can be translated into homogeneous units of measurement and traced back into the past or forward into the future. Historical scientists, by tracing today's material conditions backward through the mathematical calculation of anthropology, can create a system through which they can predict what the material conditions were like at the time of the chronological event. They can then put the conditions into operation—in the abstract. As long as these historical scientists regard time as an objective, chronological passing of measurable, homogeneous instants, Deleuze and Guattari maintain, they can abstractly trace back material conditions into infinity.

Forcing an otherwise chaotic field of states of affairs and planes of possibilities into a concrete and measurable timeline of precise instants, say Deleuze and Guattari, translates the event into a transcendent, objective, scientific fact. Science is concerned with slowing down chaos by imposing limits around portions of it, relinquishing the infinite speed of chaos in order to establish a "plane of reference" or "plane of coordination," like a "freeze-frame."[3] The imagination, however, writes Deleuze elsewhere, is limited by these strict, mathematical procedures and units of measurement. Only by comprehending the set of movements in Nature or the Universe as a whole can one get past such quickly exhausted units and attain a mathematical sublime that surpasses all imagination.[4]

The limitations should sound familiar. The historio-scientific procedure Deleuze and Guattari describe is the same procedure through which historians in Giorgio Agamben's critique retrace history, backward, along a precise and homogeneous continuum. It is how living-history historians are able to trace a line of development back to a point of origin in the nineteenth century or earlier. It is also the notion that allows living museums to claim an undoing of history, through procedures such as back-breeding. The living history museum, in order to better understand the event, slows down the chaos of the virtual in order to construct a plane of reference with which to understand the past. It constructs a history by "ghettoizing" or segregating the event from other references and readings. It carves out a physical space and infuses it with a construction that mirrors a state of affairs at that juncture of the past. By imposing a map upon a spatialized temporality, living history museums establish coordinates which serve as a reference system through which they can claim to understand the past they have created.

All of this labor on the part of living history museums is really an act of constructing monuments to the past—monumention—masking an absence by vainly attempting to stabilize bits of the past. But the monument, write Deleuze and Guattari, is not something that can "commemorate" in the sense that it can remember the past. "The monument's action," they write, "is not memory but fabulation."[5] Living history museums fabulate a past not as memory, but as a production in the present that references and replaces a past event. In these sites, the representation of a past event memorializes one juncture among a multiplicity of possibilities. Living museum monuments are environments constructed out of elements of the present, arrangements of invented objects, ideals, and materiality. These elements are neither salvaged from another time nor do they create windows into the past; instead, they organize a particular collection of present sensibilities and segregate them from others. The term *fabulation* signifies both a fable (something fabulous, imaginary, or difficult to believe) and the Roman *fabulae*, Latin for dramatic literature and representational narrative practices. Living history is a perfect example of fabulation, as it fits squarely with Aristotle's postulate that art contains more possibilities than does life. As an art, living history imitates life, *but its stagings of the past go beyond any lived event.*

Plimoth Plantation, Colonial Williamsburg, and Old Sturbridge Village are monuments that collect a variety of sensations in the present, which, in alignment, give a sense of the past, even though they are not *of* the past. They are extractions of realities, evoking sensations that neither resemble nor were possible in the past.

What follows is a new genealogy of living history museums, not as a progressive development toward a cumulative perfection, but as a genealogy informed by Agamben, Deleuze, and Guattari—a historiography of immanence. That is not to say I offer a new theory of the *origins* of the open-air or living history museum. Tony Bennett has done much in the vein of suggesting a new genealogy of the museum in the eighteenth and nineteenth centuries. In *The Birth of the Museum*, Bennett writes that modern museums developed with political rearrangements of the cultural field, seen concurrently in other public places—amusement parks, fairs, and exhibitions. He argues that the political purpose of museums in the nineteenth century was to bring citizens to a higher cultural consciousness, based on the assumption that well-planned civic additions of libraries, parks, and museums could divert those who would otherwise tend toward drunken idleness.[6] Helpful histories of museum procedures can also be found in Rosemarie Bank's "Meditations upon Opening and Crossing Over: Transgressing the Boundaries of Historiography and Tracking the History of Nineteenth-Century American Theatre" and Barbara Kirshenblatt-Gimblett's *Destination Culture: Tourism, Museums, and Heritage*.[7]

The institutional representation of the past through costumed performance and display, however, did not emerge for the first time in the late nineteenth or early twentieth century. This phenomenon, rather, exists perpetually as a potentiality and emerges at various sites of intersection with particular states of affairs, from ecumenical practices of the medieval Church to royal entries in the late Middle Ages and Renaissance to revolutionary spectacles of eighteenth-century France or twentieth-century Russia. Whether costumed performance at certain major living museums was invented as an answer to internal factors (Plimoth) or resulted from shifts in programming seen at other living museums (Williamsburg), the appearance of living history performance in the cultural landscape of mid-twentieth-century America was another set of particular enunciations of the past, conditioned by certain events, perceptions, and modes of thinking. Shifts in economic and political practices, changes in the language of intelligibility, and specific kinds of discourses about the past allowed living museums as we know them to emerge, while prohibiting alternatives.

Defining an Episteme

At first glance, the milieu in which living history performance emerged in recent times seems incredibly rich in sensitivities for history. David Lowenthal illustrated the degree to which Western culture has been fascinated with the past and has engaged in maneuvers to preserve, restore, evoke, or adapt it to fit present needs. "If the past is a foreign country," he writes, "nostalgia has made it 'the foreign country with the healthiest tourist trade of all.'"[8] Lowenthal cites the admiration of the patina antiquity brings to objects and events, the power of personal and collective memory in defining identity, the function of relics in connecting present values to those of the past, the mourning over the pasts we have lost, and motives for and consequences of changing the past as markers of our seemingly universal desire to preserve and commodify the past. All these, he argues, help us, as individuals and as a culture, to deal with the present. Lowenthal's examples range from the preservation and restoration of art and architecture (such as the Canterbury Cathedral Cloisters in the late 1970s) through the display of aesthetic decay (Knott's Berry Farm's Calico Ghost Town in Buena Park, California) to the relocation of historic monuments (the London Bridge's removal to Arizona) and reenactments at Disneyland, Civil War battlegrounds, and living history museums (Plimoth Plantation). These maneuvers have created a "heritage glut," in Lowenthal's view, which poses a threat to society.[9]

Other scholars have extended Lowenthal's skepticism about the uses of history in popular culture. Alvin Toffler's *Future Shock*, for example, diagnoses a sickness in Americans symptomized by their inability to adapt to rapid change.[10] Richard Slotkin has identified a "frontier myth," which, he argues, motivated American consciousness in movies, literature, and national policy in the twentieth century (John F. Kennedy, for instance, chose the "New Frontier" as the guiding metaphor for his administration), while American cinema engaged historical subjects throughout the twentieth century, from Hollywood images of the Wild West to the historic revisionism of westerns in the 1960s and 1970s.[11]

These shifts in the United States' national "identity," the emergence of a touristic middle class, and changes in politics and museums following World War II, the Cold War, and the civil rights movement have affected the development of operations of living history museums. If, as Michel Foucault suggests, the project of the historiographer is to determine the limits and forms of the "sayable,"[12] what must the mode of existence and the function of discourse be in the twenty-first century to allow for the specific representations of the past found in living history museums? Living history did not develop in a linear succession of evolutionary degrees from simple to complex, motivated from below by some "half silent murmur"[13] of a human instinct for performance and display. Rather, it emerged in response to specific conditions and states of affairs in the field.

An Emergence within a Shifting Field

The concepts of "America" and an "American past" have never been stable. On the contrary, just as those in power labored to continually reestablish definitive notions of "revolution" and the "citizen" in eighteenth-century France, America has been less a nation than a process of realignment of statements. In the mid-twentieth century, the "period" of history that saw much activity in the field of American open-air museums, U.S. national identity was in a particularly turbulent state of flux. If the reverberations of the Cold War functioned as a site of trauma, a *punctum* in the body of America and American identity, then the wound was further aggravated by the Vietnam War, the civil rights movement, and political scandals. In the face of anxiety, certain measures were taken to soothe and stabilize a specific American identity. Museums and emergent tourist attractions contributed to the construction and dissemination of soothing imagery throughout this time. They were one answer, conscious or unconscious, to a sequence of American identity crises in the twentieth century.

During the mid-1950s, McCarthyism labored to define and police a particular American-ness in order for the movement's proponents to establish, locate, and expose that which was un-American. Particular events of the early to mid-1950s blurred the inscribed boundaries between American and un-American. In the infamous 1951 trial of Julius and Ethel Rosenberg, doubts about the couple's supposed guilt, the gruesome public execution, and questions about the future of their two boys added a bitter flavor to the upkeep of national security. Historians still question the probability of the Rosenbergs', particularly Ethel's, involvement in a conspiracy to pass information on the production of atomic weaponry to the Russians. The House Un-American Activities Committee (HUAC) itself soon began to gain disfavor in public perception. The procedures of the committee had included allegations based on flimsy evidence, including friendships with apparent Communist sympathizers, and producing art or literature that was considered to support communist ideals or to present an unfavorable picture of American life or culture. Such allegations resulted in the infamous blacklisting in the film and television industries, and members of faculties and staffs of colleges and universities were required to pledge loyalty to America and prove to be free of association with the Communist Party in order to keep their jobs. McCarthy's committee eventually collapsed after being censured for contempt and misconduct by the Senate in December 1954 when it accused high-ranking officers in the Army and U.S. senators of being Communists.[14]

But the wheels had been set in motion. U.S. citizens engaging in behavior that seemed to threaten a way of life by associating with the "enemy" could not keep their status as Americans. To ascribe the status of "un-American," however, one first needed to firmly establish the notion of American-ness in relation to these activities. This notion, then, needed to be reproduced and disseminated, so that the boundaries could once again be firmly set. The media contributed by producing positive images of "the American," and negative images of "the un-American." Those citizens who did not conform to the ideal were punished, and those who could signify the ideal were displayed as a model. Cold War press strategically conditioned the minds of its readers, radio listeners, and television viewers to accept these particular ideals of American-ness and American heritage.

Concurrently, the developing tourist and entertainment industries were cooperating with the government and media in the production of American culture. Those in power sought to identify and deploy (both domestically and internationally) art and cultural practices that could be identified as partic-ularly American. In the fall of 1954, for example, the José Limón Dance Company was to travel to South America to promote "American art." The tour was originally sponsored by the Performing Arts International Exchange Program administered by the American National Theatre and Academy, which in turn was funded by the U.S. State Department. In the wake of four years of McCarthy's "Red Scare" and the recent executions of Julius and Ethel Rosenberg (and the consequent sense of immediacy felt by the gov-ernment to disseminate American culture), however, President Eisenhower authorized the use of emergency funds in order to speed the process. Ac-cording to Melinda Copel, tours were hastily thrown together and put on the road, in response to a perception of urgency.[15] Herbert Blau, then artistic di-rector of the San Francisco Actors Workshop, recounts his company's invi-tation to represent U.S. regional theatre at the 1958 World's Fair in Brussels, only to wind up in an altercation with the State Department, which some-how found its choice of *Waiting for Godot* un-American.[16]

By this time, of course, the tourism industry had already begun recon-structing, monumentalizing, and inventing sites across the continent in an economic mass-producing venture that formed a part of what both Robert Hewison and Barbara Kirshenblatt-Gimblett have identified as the "heritage industry."[17] Promoting the metonymic reduction of American-ness and its opposite to nostalgic images was a way to soothe the ambivalence fomented by, among other events, the Rosenberg execution. National Park sites, road-side attractions, and historical markers took on the responsibility to condi-tion visitors into accepting those imaginary ideals that were instrumental in shaping the American character.

Living history museums, too, contributed to the construction of the Ameri-can, especially by co-opting signs of the past and using them to signify her-itage.[18] In this state of affairs, living history museums capitalized in part on a di-alectic between Self and Other, constructed and inserted into the narrative. There was, as Lowenthal suggests, an insidious quality to the "othering" of the past. Targeted at older Americans, disturbed by the growing number of incom-ing ethnic groups into formerly white, middle-class enclaves, the past offered solace from uncomfortable change. This was particularly the case with the past linked to the colonial period.

An exclusive WASP heritage, the Colonial past offered a perfect escape. The British heritage was no longer disparaged; early America became an offshoot of Old England, decently Protestant and charmingly quaint, the Revolution a temporary disruption of close fraternal bonds.[19]

Elsewhere, Lowenthal describes the "us" and "them" dichotomy, both capitalized upon and caused by the heritage industry: "The growing worth of heritage aggravates conflicts over whose it is, what it means, and how to use it. Heritage builds collective pride and purpose, but in so doing stresses distinctions between good guys (us) and bad guys (them)."[20] To paraphrase Michel de Certeau, the Self needs the Other in order to articulate its own historicity, a process he calls a "hermeneutics of the other."[21] By allowing tourist visitors to encounter the Otherness of the past, attractions such as living history museums evoked and stabilized a specific view of history—in effect, producing authentic American heritage at a time when the notion of Americanness, unstable and in flux, needed realignment.

So it was that Colonial Williamsburg functioned as a site of nostalgia production, remembering those events that most effectively shaped an American narrative in the 1950s and 1960s. The year 1951 marked the end of twenty-five years of planning and restoration efforts, and in the years following World War II, Colonial Williamsburg had become a major attraction and travel destination for families. As America was getting used to its growing status as a superpower, the attraction served as a symbol of inscribed and institutionalized American values.[22]

Servicemen back from the war, now educated with the help of the GI Bill and raising families, comprised a large segment of the visitors to Colonial Williamsburg. With the growing economic ability for transcontinental vacations, families could come from all over the country to encounter the "American" values the attraction had to offer. One young man wrote, "Of all the sights I have seen, and all the books I have read, and all the speeches I have heard, none ever made me see the greatness of this country with more force and clearness than when I saw Williamsburg slumbering peacefully on its old foundations."[23]

A reporter for the National Geographic Society's publication *America's Historylands* described his movement through the reconstructed town:

> Cocking my tricorn over one eye and giving a tug to my blue velvet coat, I quit my lodgings on Francis Street and strode down the Duke of Gloucester toward Chowning's Tavern. In the yellow glow of the lantern I carried, my brass shoe buckles winked up at me with every step, and from each Yule decked window I passed, a candle shed its hospitable light.[24]

He proceeds to revel in the friendship he found at the tavern, with toasts and tankards of ale, followed by caroling in the streets. In a combination of luxurious attention to material detail (the winking buckles, the Yule-decked windows), the hearkening imagery of Christmas spirit, and lighting the memory for the reader with a yellow glow to set the mood, the author reinscribes Williamsburg as a beacon of goodwill shining toward us from its distant point behind us in the flow of history. The article participates in the perpetuation of the constructed myths informing the memory of Williamsburg by enforcing the romantic views of the past: comfort, good food, and noble ideals of freedom from the British.[25]

These were the ideals to be accessed by visitors in the twentieth century, who would then add to the accumulation of anecdotal accounts. "I like the story of the young G.I. from Fort Eustis who came up with his unit during World War II and got separated," the National Geographic author tells readers. "He was standing before the Peale Portrait of Washington in the Capitol. Suddenly he muttered, 'You got it for us General. And, by God, we're going to keep it.' And he saluted."[26] Richard Handler and Eric Gable also include this anecdote in their account of the shifts Colonial Williamsburg went through in the twentieth century, although in their book, it is attributed to Kenneth Chorley, president of Colonial Williamsburg from 1935 to 1938. Chorley recounted the GI's story to John D. Rockefeller Jr.: "You know, I told that story to Mr. Rockefeller a few weeks later. When I'd finished, he looked up at me, and there were tears in his eyes, and he said quietly, 'Then it was all worth while.'"[27]

The deployment of statements referencing nostalgia for the past designed to comfort America's citizens in the face of change is traceable through travel literature of the time. Indeed, many historians of the twentieth century reinscribe the same formula as a way to understand its events: America, faced with uncomfortable change, consistently returns to the past for solace. Robert Hewison, addressing the (in his perception) alarming rate at which new museums were appearing in England in the 1970s and 1980s, locates nostalgia as the predictable backlash against movements that destabilize social value systems:

> For the individual, nostalgia filters out unpleasant aspects of the past, and of our former selves, creating a self esteem that helps us to rise above the anxieties of the present. Collectively, nostalgia supplies the deep links that identify a particular generation; nationally, it is the source of binding social myths. It secures, and it compensates, serving . . . "as a kind of safety valve for disappointment and frustration suffered over the loss of prized values."[28]

If such generalizations about broad national behavior seem tenuous, at least it may be said that the circulation of statements and discourse perpetuated notions that the past was a remedy for social ills in the present. Another account for National Geographic's *America's Historylands*, this time from Sturbridge, administers a similarly soothing dose of nostalgia:

> Old Sturbridge Village, on the Quinebaug River sixty miles southwest of Boston, recalls these halcyon days of 1800. Its thirty-five buildings house the tools, toys, textiles our ancestors made and used. Visitors flock here all year; in midwinter they spend a "Yankee winter week-end" at the Publick House. They watch artisans mold pottery, dip candles, and make pewter. They dine on venison and bear pie, and sip sillabub before a crackling fire after a sleigh ride through the village.[29]

"Halcyon" is an appropriate metaphor: in lore, the halcyon (kingfisher) builds its nest on the sea, which it has the power to calm. These museums calm the stormy sea of discursive statements about American identity. Recalling Deleuze's *ritornello*, they function as a "soothing refrain" that protects the consciousness from doubt.[30]

These are the statements that were allowed to emerge in the 1950s and 1960s. Others, it would seem, were not possible. Certain remnants of the past were accessible to the historians and public relations staffs working for these museums, yet would not have served the soothing function of nostalgia. Stephen Eddy Snow, for example, lists items that appear in seventeenth-century accounts of Plymouth Colony, yet were never to be represented at Plimoth Plantation in the twentieth century. The officers and board of trustees, "wary of anything that might create public censure or bad press for their institution" endeavored to maintain a "G" rating for family visitors.[31] Items remaining unmentioned included the unsightly muckheaps of excrement behind the Pilgrims' homes and incidents involving questionable sexual practices, such as that of Rev. John Lyford, a "licentious Church of England" minister, accused in 1625 of an affair with a parishioner and "endeavor[ing] to hinder conception." Another example is the bestiality acts and subsequent trial of seventeen-year-old Thomas Granger, who was tried, found guilty, and hanged in 1642, after the mare, cow, and several lesser cattle he had "sodomized" were paraded before him and destroyed.[32] Added to the list of seventeenth-century Plymouth's woes are human suffering, sickness, the rigors of an incredibly difficult life, and the hardship of harsh winters. Not only were these aspects of the past kept out of living reproduction for general reasons of taste, but they were forbidden within the realm of the "sayable," because only those statements about the past that reaffirmed circulating notions of American-ness were possible at this time. Conducting an archaeology of the production of statements linked to events of the twentieth century does tease out the limits of the knowable: there is no way to know for certain how these circulating notions of American identity, nationalism, pride, and ethics were disseminated at living history museums on the quotidian level. It is only possible to identify those statements that have been chosen as worthy of record. Michael Wallace reminds us that there is no conclusive evidence regarding who exactly came to living history and outdoor museums at this time, nor what these visitors got out of them. It is impossible to tell, he suggests, whether themes of American patriotism disseminated by these sites were received in toto and subsequently reproduced or were largely taken with a grain of salt.

> Perhaps the well-off find their world ratified. Perhaps those not so well served by the status quo nevertheless prove susceptible to the museums' messages. But maybe they invest the messages with different meanings. There are, after all, truly radical dimensions to the U.S. tradition, and the shrines might have served as an opportunity to celebrate democratic as well as capitalist values.[33]

Nor, continues Wallace, can we determine why these visitors began to frequent these museums in the first place. It is possible they started coming once they had been separated from the past, similar to the way zoos became popular once civilization had lost connection with animals.[34] At any rate, if we may conclude anything from browsing the discursive formations surrounding U.S. history in the 1950s and 1960s, it is that open-air history museums needed to change and realign the histories they presented vis-à-vis the mounting body of statements connecting the past with values that "made" America a nation worth protecting.

Capitalizing on the Past—Capitalizing on Loss

In Vladimir Nabokov's 1955 *Lolita*, Humbert Humbert and Dolores "Lolita" Haze are the subjects of an intriguing travel narrative. Once Humbert's lust is consummated (after only half the novel) and upon his informing Lolita of her mother's death, the couple begins its cross-country tour of America. They become connoisseurs of the motels, hotels, lodges, "kabins," roadside facilities, and attractions that dot the landscape through which they move, the targets par excellence of the tourism industry's literature. The "must see" clause in brochures and billboards obligates the father/lover to treat his ward to every touristic experience available.

> If a roadside sign said: VISIT OUR GIFT SHOP—we had to visit it, had to buy its Indian curios, dolls, copper jewelry, cactus candy. The words "novelties and souvenirs" simply entranced her by their trochaic lilt. If some café sign proclaimed Icecold Drinks, she was automatically stirred, although all drinks everywhere were ice-cold. She it was to whom the ads were dedicated: the ideal consumer, the subject and object of every foul poster.[35]

The language of necessary consumption (legitimized by Duncan Hines and AAA) served to produce meaning for the travelers. Crisscrossing the continent, the multiplicity of travel "destinations"—"a natural cave in Arkansas converted to a café," "the home of the Wild Bill something Rodeo," a "collection of guns and violins somewhere in Oklahoma," "a replica of the Grotto of Lourdes in Louisiana"—are surrogates for the characters' sense of going somewhere. Indeed, *Lolita* depicts the culmination of several efforts on the part of tourist businesses to insert themselves into a thriving 1950s economy based on travel and consumption. Nabokov describes a tourist milieu in which the United States has become as a network of highways linking together a complex system of emergent Americana.

Economics has as profound a role as politics in delimiting the field in which living history museums could emerge and became tourist destinations in the twentieth century. Tourist attractions capitalized on the travel practices of tourists in twentieth century North America by condensing sites, temporally and geographically, in order for tourists to consume them more readily (museums, writes John A. Jakle, are the most contrived of tourist attractions).[36] Condensing touristic experience to limited areas caused less damage to surrounding areas. Before World War I, efficient thoroughfares and transcontinental automobile travel hardly existed, but in the 1930s, motorists began to demand more and better highways. Depression-era work programs such as the Civilian Conservation Corps helped the North American highway system to expand rapidly. Between 1921 and 1930, 80 percent of federal expenditures went to roads and the number of miles of surfaced highways doubled, doubling again between 1930 and 1940.[37] In the interwar years, travel by car could be taken for granted for the first time (though only by a select group of people), thanks to better cars and smoother roads. Until these highways were in place, it would have been impossible for the now ubiquitous roadside tourist businesses to pop up along them.

While travel and tourism declined sharply during World War II, it was after the war that the "pent-up buying power and increased leisure time" created a boom in the industry.[38] If the emergent highway system allowed the means by which to get to the very travel destinations it spawned, the situation cannot be understood without a discussion of the post–World War II changes in economics variously considered as an emergence of the "mobile" middle class with an unprecedented amount of leisure time. Sightseeing vacations for tourist families in the 1950s were largely made possible by the enormous economic shifts following World War II. The newly established GI Bill allowed more American men than ever before to be eligible for a college education, the graduates of which were to become this new "middle class." Such economic shifts, along with a more prosperous period for white middle-class families, allowed the leisure time and the means of leaving the home to visit the rest of America. Wonders formerly only within the grasp of the rich were now accessible to this class. The "station wagon," a signature vehicle for transporting families to tourist destinations, appeared in greater numbers on the highways.[39] Distance became a commodity for tourist families, who could use the length of a car trip to establish its importance in the scheme of vacations.

An increase in spending money coincided with an increase in leisure time. Work decreased from an average of forty-four hours per week to forty by 1950, and a Department of Commerce survey in 1949 reported that 62 percent of all Americans had taken a vacation. A 1950 survey by the *Saturday Evening Post* showed that means of travel had significantly moved toward the automobile: 80 percent of all long-distance pleasure trips were by car, leaving only a small percentage of vacationers who were using the train, bus, air, or ship transportation.[40] With the surge in car travel came car radios, the "commercial strip," and the roadside service industry.[41]

Such were the circumstances that allowed history to emerge as an "attraction." Jakle compares twentieth-century historical attractions to "fenced-off preserves." Like Lowenthal, he writes that these sites are less products of past events than they are of present-day values. "Instead of remembering exactly what was, the past is made intelligible in the light of present circumstances. Historical attractions are contrived accordingly, often destroying authenticity."[42] Even though Jakle's account reorganizes the events of tourist attraction history in order to counter an evolutionary formula with complex structural models of large-scale changes in the social landscape, statements like this last one evoke nostalgia for the authentic landscape of the past in the face of its impostor.

A second fiscal narrative that links itself to discussion of emergent living history is that describing a shift in civic economies from an initial industry to that of tourism, often accompanying the breakdown or depletion of the former. Boomtowns dotting the continent were largely situated around industries with short life-expectancies. These communities, such as the lumber towns stretching from the East Coast to the Midwest, were created to take advantage of the natural resources around the area and to cater to the laborers that reaped them:

> Dozens of now staid communities in Maine, New York, Pennsylvania, Michigan, Wisconsin and Minnesota were founded mainly to provide saloons, whorehouses and gambling halls to separate lumberjacks and sawmill workers from their earnings with maximum efficiency.[43]

The towns, having no long-range plans for how to continue to operate once the resources were depleted, faced the threat of collapse.

Tourist sites that sprang up in place of the dying industries capitalized both on the new mobility of the middle class and on the history of the areas the sites represented. As Kirshenblatt-Gimblett states, using the example of the transition from mining and forestry to tourism in the region near Cardiff, Wales:

> When a way of life disappears, with the . . . economy that once sustained it . . . tourism is ready to step in. The formula for revitalizing the economy of a depressed region is the resurrection theatre of the heritage industry. . . . While tourist attractions may seem like oases of time out, they are implicated in a larger political economy of transnational flows of money, people and symbolic capital.[44]

These communities, as a way of self-promotion, needed to differentiate their own history from that of other areas. The conscious self-presentation of "otherness" to the rest of the world allowed the tourists to encounter these sites as spaces of alterity, reinforced by the distance traveled from their own familiar homes. Rev. W. A. R. Goodwin responded to the degenerate state of the town of Williamsburg, Virginia, neglected by industry since the Civil War, by dreaming of "restoring Virginia's colonial capital to its former glory."[45] The sleepy town of Plymouth, Massachusetts, made its own bid for touristic attention when it designated a piece of boulder as an original chip of Plymouth Rock and reorganized its town map around the historic harbor.[46]

The notion of a shift from old industry to new imposes upon a location a structure of historical economic change, often painted in broad strokes, which reflects the historian's view of change as a positive means for renewal or as an end to the purity of the old ways. Negative accounts slant toward the idea that tourism is a destructive social or economic force. Susan K. Irwin, for instance, denounces the "quick fix of heritage tourism," which, she says, often causes the destruction rather than the preservation of small towns.[47] This view tends to reflect an unproblematized nostalgia for "unspoiled" small towns and rural communities.

The flip side is the perception of tourism as a salvaging mechanism in the face of other economic movements that threaten to wipe out the heritage of the landscape. In *The Tourist-Historic City*, G. J. Ashworth and J. E. Tunbridge offer relocation and reconstruction as means by which to curb the changes accompanying urbanization and industrialization. Colonial Williamsburg is their example par excellence of an American enunciation of civic preservation:

> Williamsburg is an outstanding, if unusual, example of the tourist-historic city and its marketing in North America. It clearly illustrates the continuum that exists between the New World corporate-enterprise historic gem and the historic theme park . . . since it could be regarded as a hybrid between a Disneyland environment, in which popular entertainment is paramount, and a town seeking to portray the idea of historic authenticity.[48]

In Ashworth and Tunbridge's account of Williamsburg and other "tourist-historic cities," tourism, far from being a destructive force, is effectively used by civic planners to get closer to the ideal model of a town that capitalizes on the past by organically linking itself to its former settlement structure, economy, and society.

It is true that many towns deliberately shifted economic practices to solicit tourist revenue (tourism is, indeed, quite an enormous system—by 1988, according to Richard J. Roddewig, tourism was the second largest industry in the United States and accounted for 54 million jobs),[49] but these individual cases should not be regarded as a wholesale symptom of a universal theme of conversion. Each maneuver toward living history, rather, was a specific act within a field of relationships, a climate fostered by a collection of statements about the viability of one type of business over another that foregrounded tourism-based businesses in the hope of tapping into the widely circulating idea that tourism was the hope of the future.

The advent of disposable income on the part of tourists seeking authentic experiences (and local economies that sought to serve that market) created the demand for heritage Nabokov depicts in *Lolita*. The promotion of a lacuna, particularly a narrative of loss, soon found its way into promotional travel literature—and into accounts of the changes in the structure of American tourism and economics. Several scholars point to the loss of the central town industry as a cause for the emergence of the tourism boom. Others refer to a loss of identity with the growing gap between the worker and labor.

Dean MacCannell writes that, with the growing amount of leisure, there came an alienation from labor as a means of self-identity. The tourism industry, he posits, would be quick to accommodate the consequent social need. He describes the shift between an industrial society and our modern world as one that replaced labor and work as cultural identifiers with what individuals chose to do with their leisure time. In other words, in the postindustrial society, one will more likely describe oneself with "lifestyle" descriptors rather than occupation. The result of this shift, writes MacCannell, has been the transformation of work into the object of touristic curiosity. In this way, labor may still be connected to social meaning, even though it has been distanced from individual psyche.

> It is only by making a fetish of the work of others, by transforming it into an "amusement" ("do-it-yourself"), a spectacle (Grand Coulee), or an attraction (the guided tours of Ford Motor Company), that modern workers, on vacation, can apprehend work as a part of a meaningful totality.[50]

Certainly one could point to the costumed demonstrations of craft and skill as centerpieces of living history museums to bolster this argument: while the musket demonstration seems to be the single most recycled program in all the living history museums I have visited, the martial musket is more often relegated to the background by the focus on everyday activities such as barrel making (coopering), jewelry making, pottery throwing and firing, gardening, wig making, milling, milking, rigging, carding, cooking, brewing, baking, cider pressing, cobbling, shipbuilding, cabinetmaking, glassblowing, bookbinding, wheelwrighting, carpentering, tinkering, printing, plowing, fence building, horseshoeing, weaving, spinning, and, of course, blacksmithing (the blacksmith shop is always a popular crowd pleaser at living history museums and perhaps even a compulsory staple in historic interpretation: the Blacksmith's Forge is one of the sites at Pioneer Village, which depicts the year 1630 in Salem, Massachusetts, even though the first blacksmith may not have arrived until later).[51]

Loss as a means of promoting heritage sites is prevalent in living history brochures. A 1976 guide to living history programming at National Parks particularly stresses this notion. If one wants to be a good and healthy citizen, the guide insists, one needs to seek out touristic experience to reconnect oneself to traditional craft and the outdoors. As was the case with the heritage industry's answer to the changes brought on by politics in the 1950s and 1960s, one of the best and most accessible places to look for solace in the face of present anxiety surrounding economic shifts was, again, the past. Promoting interpretive programs that demonstrated the "historic features" of the parks in this document, the National Park Service posited that U.S. citizens were becoming alienated from "long forgotten" crafts and skills and from a connection with the land.[52] "Farming demonstrations are becoming increasingly popular," the brochure reports.

> In the fast-moving urban world of 20th-century America, fewer people work in agriculture. The unfamiliarity of city dwellers with agricultural practices and problems is complicated by the fact that even farms visible from a car window are inaccessible and far removed from inspection.[53]

To compensate for what has been lost with a movement toward the city, the Park Service offers period farms such as the Oxon Hill Children's Farm in the Washington, D.C., area: "It emphasizes that agriculture is basic to man's existence and is intended primarily for those who have never seen a farm."[54] By situating "man's existence" in the basic farm, the Park Service not only uses a narrative of reconnection as a draw for these attractions but also, by extension, suggests that the problems of the present may indeed stem from the growing disparity with things past. The National Park Service may then insert itself as the mediator of the touristic experience, by choosing which aspects of farmlife and the outdoors are best for demonstration. The guide cautions those who may be cavalier about experiencing the outdoors for the first time:

> For those who have lived most of their lives in the cities, the outdoor life presents an unfamiliar challenge. A few demonstrations have been developed to present some of the simpler and some of the more strenuous opportunities. For all of them, we hope the demonstrations will erase some of the strangeness and encourage people to try new adventures with confidence, safety and a wiser appreciation of the resources they are using.[55]

Elsewhere, the guide complements the narrative of alienation from the land with a separation from the means of production. If living history was informed by a network of anti-Communist sentiment earlier, this passage seems ironically resonant with Marxist ideology:

> Today in highly developed countries, clerical and service occupations employ more and more people. Fewer and fewer people, proportionally, make anything.

Instead, people buy and sell things; they move things around from city to city, and they keep track of inventories and cash balances, and only a very few create tangible goods. Even those who do work in industry seldom see things through. Machinists may well work on equipment they will never see completed and would not know how to use. The detachment of the assembly line is well known. Construction workers commonly never enter finished buildings they have worked on. Even artists and designers are often separated from original works of art by a variety of founders, chemists, printers, and others. Consequently all of our people are both detached and dependent at the same time. Craft demonstrations help greatly to reduce the detachment.[56]

The guide lists parks where visitors may find authentic, traditional practices of glassblowing, basket weaving, blacksmithing, and the like. One may ask if the Park Service offered these demonstrations in order to ease the anxiety accompanying the steadily increasing detachment from the means of production, or if, as a matter of fact, it actually sought to produce a demand for such demonstrations by putting narratives of detachment into circulation. In other words, did the National Park Service guide to living history in the National Parks put its finger on a national sense of loss and alienation and step in to address these problems with living history offerings? Or did it co-opt alienation from other areas and use it for marketing purposes?

Social History and the
Trajectory of Living Museum Performance

One of the most prominent discursive formations defining the limits of how living history museums and their practices may be talked about from the late 1960s to the present is *social history*, the explanation museum historians give for the shift in living history museums from displays of the triumphs of the forefathers to "museums of everyday life." While it is most helpful as a collective term under which to group the miasma of new foci of living historical subjects legitimized by civil rights, workers, and women's movements, it may also be used (as I do) as a densely loaded phrase encompassing the networks of procedures by living history practitioners that allowed different, yet still heavily policed, representations of the past. To unpack the phrase, I will briefly define how I use the term *social history*, then examine the ways it informed living history practices and the way they are discussed.[57]

Olivier Zunz writes that, while the "new" social history was not new to Europe, it profoundly affected historical consciousness in the United States in the 1960s and 1970s. Zunz's reasons for social history's appearance on the American scene are historically, economically, and politically situated. In addition to a "demographic surge" of young historians, the post–World War II discourse between scientists and humanists, and the "timely" appearance of computers and subsequent redefinition of the archive during these decades, the most important factor contributing to the growth of social history was its participation in the new pluralist vision of the 1960s. This allowed historians to treat "groups heretofore ignored or at best misunderstood":[58]

> Pointing to the records of ordinary lives as a source of evidence, social historians called into question the merit of using the acts of elites as a measure of the past and challenged historians in general to reexamine their assumptions, regardless of their ideological commitments.[59]

One of the ways social history revamped the way American pasts were understood was to debunk the large, problematic narratives or myths that organized the history of change in the United States, such as "American Character" or "National Experience," or preordaining events such as "America's Special Destiny," replacing these with meticulous examinations of individual lives. For example, "Instead of debating abstractions that had concerned the previous generation of scholars such as the 'inevitability' of the Civil War," Zunz writes,

> social historians took a closer look at the institution that had for almost 200 years conditioned the outlook of Southerners. They examined the daily reality of slavery and tested its viability as a social system in antebellum America.[60]

Zunz and his colleagues connect social history's appearance with a reaction to Vietnam, the civil rights and women's movements, the "rediscovery of ethnicity," Watergate, and an economic recession after twenty-five years of prosperity. All these things, Zunz believes, "combined to undermine the prevailing atmosphere of consensus and self righteousness. No longer able to understand historical processes through a single formula, most intellectuals of the 1960s and 1970s rejected the very notion of national character."[61]

Living museums engaged in an intense labor to align their history with new notions of ethical and responsible curatorial practices accompanying social history. At Plimoth Plantation, this meant a shift in focus from the "sainted Pilgrim ancestors" to an accurate, ethnohistoric concentration on the everyday life of the "real" Pilgrims. If not a step in the progressive "evolution" of living history practices, the move was a threshold that changed the way history was taught at Plimoth and elsewhere. The culmination of academic and practical literature that uses Plimoth as the ideal model of first person reenactment serves as a testament to this event and its power as narrative coinage in the living history field.

Michael Hall, program interpreter at Plimoth Plantation, spoke to me about the current goals of the organization with regard to the presentation of the Pilgrims, the historical subject and main attraction of the museum. He positioned Plimoth's agenda in relation to those of other public institutions in the surrounding Plymouth area and in the rest of the country. In Hall's words, some Americans "put the Pilgrims on a pedestal" as role-model forefathers, while others "tear them apart, label them, tar and feather them as exploitative colonists" or oppressive invaders of the New World. In contrast, says Hall, Plimoth's goal as a museum is to "present the Pilgrims and the Native culture with, hopefully, some objectivity and allow them the humanity that cultural myth makers deny them. That's something that I'm very conscious of when I'm playing Governor Bradford."[62]

Carolyn Travers describes the way social history in the Pilgrim Village is now seen by visitors, largely through the treatment of wives and children—"in addition to" the patriarchal figures associated with the signing of the Mayflower Compact and the founding of Plymouth Colony. The wives and children are not written about, she informed me. In order to find out about their lives, she says, one must "read against the grain" of historical documents. "All that's written about women is filtered through men," Travers said. "He's writing what he thinks she said. All we have are those words." The choice to interpret the year 1627 rather than the more famous events surrounding 1620 and the founding of the colony is also deliberately geared toward focusing on the everyday life of the Pilgrims, says Travers. "Plimoth Plantation could do a lot of stuff on the founding of the colony, but 1627 isn't a big deal." It is a way to show "ordinary people in extraordinary circumstances. . . . There were fifty people—half of whom were children—in only a few houses. Nothing around but wild people."[63]

Martha Sulya, an interpreter at Plimoth, told me that not only does she help new trainees to understand the museum's striving to get its history "as right as possible" but she also helps trainees understand how the presentation is situated in the historical moment. As she puts it, "It's just very interesting to see how what's happening in society is always reflected in the Pilgrim Village, no matter how hard we try." I mentioned the account in Stephen Eddy Snow's book of how upset the descendants of the original *Mayflower* were at the sight of the Pilgrim interpreters of the early 1970s walking around the grounds in bare feet and bedraggled hair. "It is referred to as the 'Hippie Pilgrim era,'" she explained, and went on to explain how Plimoth has subsequently worked harder to make sure inaccurate decisions that seemed good at the time were not made in the heat of a present historical moment.[64] "To have Pilgrims running around with their hair hanging down isn't really appropriate," she explained, referring to emergent material in manners books and paintings of the seventeenth century.

> So now we try to keep our hair covered with the coifs—the head coverings—as much as possible. In terms of the shoes, certainly, I think, it's as much a health-conscious issue as anything. With not wanting people to step on nails or shards of pottery, and just generally the stuff that's on the ground—rocks and splinters. So, it's interpreter safety as well as showing people . . . what sort of shoes were available back then.

Plimoth Plantation's shift to social history, then, has subjected the museum to a constant tension between maintaining historical accuracy and acknowledging new data and the changing attitudes of historians and archaeologists.

Other institutions were not subject to as radical a shift as that experienced by Plimoth Plantation because they *began* as museums of everyday life, rather than showcasing the founding fathers. Museums founded after the 1970s and the social history surge not only enunciated aspects of historic revisionism in their founding mission statements but were also able to avoid the large programmatic changes older museums faced when encountering social history. Stephen Osman, site manager at Historic Fort Snelling in Minneapolis, for instance, told me that his museum, which began its living history programming in 1971, has always had a social history agenda: "We really started out with life from the bottom up. The story of the enlisted people and common folks here. We've never glorified the great leaders, and probably do it a lot more now than we ever did. . . . But most of our guides down there [in the fort] portray common people."[65]

Old Sturbridge Village, since it began living history programming, has been especially rigorous in promoting itself as a museum of everyday life in New England: the orientation program and slide show in the visitors' center sets the stage for the history the visitors will encounter. This is the story of the colorful characters that one would have found in a rural New England community in the 1830s. Here, one will see families and the ways their lives were shaped by the beginnings of industry, a new emergent economy, and a new political climate. Attention to the themes of social history resonates throughout. "Women's issues," for instance, began to have a high profile in New England communities at this time: the temperance and antislavery movements were made up largely of women.

The bulk of the orientation program, though, comes in the form of the recollections of a gentle-voiced narrator, who describes his life in New England at the time interpreted by Old Sturbridge Village. This fictional character, a twelve-year-old boy in 1832, had just started as an apprentice at his father's printing office. The effects of the Industrial Revolution on the family and town thematically link the memories together for the audience. The printing office just invested in a new iron press—a risk at $350, but one that would help the business grow. Unprecedented goods became available in the stores. Because of these changes, the boy is able to replace his sister's china doll, broken during one of his pranks, at Asa Knight's general store. His mother can decorate the house with new fashions, funded by the influx of money brought by the new printing press. The program emphasizes the daily routines of the working family: the boy is sent to Freeman Farm to collect a crock of butter owed to the family. The mother variously labors at the wash and consults the *Mother's Book*, a common household title in New England, on how to raise her children: "Be careful not to correct your children in anger," is one of the book's precepts.

In the village, the visitor encounters a similarly themed history, organized in terms of everyday working-family life in a farming community. At the Freeman Farm, one woman explains the daily routines in the farmhouse kitchen, the center of the New England woman's domestic realm. For instance, she says, the brick oven is used in a much different way than conventional ovens today. First, she explains, you build a fire right inside the oven, which burns about two hours, until the bricks are "nice and hot." Then you take the fire out and bake the bread in it. "It's a very effective oven," she says. As a third-person interpreter, she is able to make the connection to visitors' lives in the present: "All those trendy pizza places have discovered it makes great baked goods."

A visitor asks how temperature is controlled in such an oven with no dials or controls. "If I had a fire in there for about two hours—a good hot fire with kindling wood," she answers, "the bricks are gonna be white hot." The next steps of the process are enumerated with rehearsed efficiency:

I'll take the whole fire out. I'll take a wet broom, and I'll sweep out any embers and things that are hanging around in there, and I'll test the temperature. Probably when I cleaned it out, it's topping 500 degrees, which is hotter than you need to bake. But in the time it takes to clear it out, the temperature will drop slightly. I'll close the oven for about ten or fifteen minutes, in order to make the hottest spots share with the cooler ones, to even up the oven. Then, I'll test the temperature, just feeling how hot the fire feels, and I'm aiming to start my high-temperature things somewhere around 450. So things like pies go in first. When they're finished, the temperature has dropped down some and gotten to about bread and cakes temperature, so pies come out and bread and cakes go in. [The oven] continues to cool. The bread and cakes come out, the puddings and custards go in. So what you're doing is hitting target temperatures. The oven will drop off at a fairly predictable rate.[66]

This mode of history, foregrounding the daily tasks of individuals to show a "total history" of the period and then making connections for the visitor, is to be found throughout the village's businesses, homes, and farm buildings. In addition, constructions of social themes that lead to change are emphasized in reenactment. Conflict is a driving metaphor in town meetings. Abolitionists, temperance workers, and other members of women's groups with whom visitors can converse in the parsonage are identified as fighters of social ills. In their small way, we are to understand, they helped to change the nation.

If anything, offers David Lowenthal, social history and its emphasis on conflict as an internal factor for change (as compared to external forces such as "national character") make for more exciting, dramatic history. Heritage "customarily bends to market forces," he writes, and its vendors often see nothing wrong with "intensifying" the experience for more entertainment. "Few visited an Indiana pioneer village [Conner Prairie] that featured '1836 Prairietown' as a cohesive neighborhood, because, curators found, 'the past we presented was boring.' So they revamped the Hoosier community as 'controversial'."[67]

I asked Jack Larkin about the social history programming that has been implemented throughout his tenure at Old Sturbridge Village. He explained to me the manner in which social history, since its inception, has been adopted on the site, as well as in the rest of the field of living history. The movement began, he told me, when he was a graduate student, working in history:

> Basically, it was called the "new social history" in the late sixties, early seventies, in the field of American history, which was sort of a rediscovery of the history of families. History of small communities. History of rural people. History of social structure, of social interaction. A movement away from the large-scale themes of politics and policy and presidential elections or state-level political structures, and so forth. That history, which is still powerful in the academy, fit exceedingly well to the mission of history museums, especially in this country. And what that really meant was a major sort of intellectual renaissance for the content of living history museums, as more and more historians were doing history that could feed directly into the mission and interpretation and exhibition and demonstration programs of these museums. And that's been true for Sturbridge Village. It's been true for Colonial Williamsburg. It's been true for Old World Wisconsin, or probably wherever you go.[68]

It is not just that living history museums have "improved," Larkin told me. Other kinds of museums, too, have stressed historical programming with more attention to local and regional foci. Over the last thirty years, he continued, important scholarly work has been done on communities, on families, on regional cultures, and on socioeconomic experiences that has benefited historians. This has especially been the case with history museums: "I think as intellectual institutions, as far as research and learning with a soundly based interpretation, they have all benefited enormously by it."[69]

The reverberations of social history were strongest at Colonial Williamsburg because it was such a bastion of American heritage production and stood to gain or lose the most with a radical shift in its presentation of history. Social history discourse prompted major shifts at Colonial Williamsburg in the 1970s. According to Handler and Gable, this was in part due to the drop in attendance to the museum by Americans. Vietnam, Watergate, and the civil rights movement made for a public that "was no longer willing to buy the old history of consensus and celebration." The shift to social history, and constructionist (relativistic) historiography, then, in Handler and Gable's narrative, was a tactical maneuver to reframe the history offered in a "dirtier" way, refusing to ignore "past injustices and their ramifications in the present."[70]

But the onus on the museum was even greater than a change in how history was coming to be seen: a major shift was being played out in regard to the politics of race and Williamsburg's public relations. Anders Greenspan cites a form letter composed by John D. Rockefeller Jr. that had served to keep inquiring blacks out of Williamsburg's inn and lodge for some time: "The management has not thus far found it practicable to provide for both colored and white guests. I (or we are) am [sic] sorry we cannot accommodate you (or cannot take care of you; or cannot offer you hospitality)."[71] It was up to these visitors to make their own lodging arrangements with local black families in their homes. Black visitors didn't miss the racism in the guise of practicability: "Is it not an irony," wrote George E. Cohron, "that Williamsburg, restored and publicized as the place democracy was founded, should permit discrimination or democracy in reverse?"[72] In the wake of civil rights, Colonial Williamsburg's racial policies could no longer continue to discriminate against African-American families, and the restoration finally took steps to integrate its lodging. Moreover, with more black visitors visiting the historic area, it was getting increasingly hard for Colonial Williamsburg staff to look their audience in the eye and deliver a predominantly WASP history.

Not only was Colonial Williamsburg motivated to shift its emphasis toward social history for political reasons, but social history was also employed as a strategy to combat increasing loss of visitors to its major competitors. Plimoth Plantation and Old Sturbridge Village, which had previously followed Williamsburg's lead in interpretations and demonstrations, were now garnering accolades for their historic revisionism, costumed interpreters, and animals (as opposed to Williamsburg's emphasis on patriotism and an Americanist agenda).[73] Other developments, too, were muddying the perception of Colonial Williamsburg as an institution devoted to accurate portrayals of history: Williamsburg real estate was being sold to developers, who were willing to spend a lot of money for this prime area in which to build upscale residential communities.

In 1969, the foundation sold a large amount of land adjacent to the historic area to Anheuser-Busch for the purposes of a brewery, but also so that the corporation could establish its own tourist attraction, Busch Gardens. A theme park with carnival rides would have been one thing, but the focal point of Busch Gardens in Williamsburg was four of its own "historical hamlets"—England, Germany, Italy, and France—which also simulated bygone days associated with particular communities.[74] With a theme-park historical display right next to one devoted to educational purposes, it is no wonder that visitors often conflated Colonial Williamsburg with the same type of theme park atmosphere that the curators were trying to avoid.

Within Colonial Williamsburg, other trends were departing from historical accuracy. The "Christmas at Williamsburg" pageantry, devoted to nostalgic holiday season sentimentality, had far more inaccuracies than accuracies, but had become such an entrenched tradition among visitors that removing it would have risked offending many potential return visitors. Social history in Williamsburg's main programming could buttress the museum against critics' claims that it was catering to a demand for kitsch rather than to historical accuracy.

Thus it was that after a particular moment in the 1970s, for the first time since the museum was put into operation, "road apples" could be found in the street. The by-products of the "authentic" horse carriages, which had formerly been so carefully and tastefully hidden from view, were now left in the open for visitors to encounter. Handler and Gable, with tongue in cheek, emblematize the road apple as a marker of Williamsburg's move to a more authentic, organic—and dirty—past.

The change to a "social history" at Williamsburg was not without its detractors, both within its own ranks and on the part of visitors.[75] By 1977, however, the social history agenda had largely replaced an objective model of history based on traditional values, that is, to "teach of the patriotism, purpose, and unselfish devotion of our forefathers to the common good."[76] The orientation film *Williamsburg: The Story of a Patriot* had, up until then, been in keeping with Colonial Williamsburg's agenda. The film, which had welcomed every visitor coming through the gate since 1957, emphasized a Revolutionary history based on the idea that the colonists affirmed a particular set of timeless values and principles when they chose to take up arms and challenge the corrupt British, who taxed them without representation. Viewers were encouraged to "dedicate themselves to those principles."[77] In 1977, however, a curriculum committee prepared a plan to change the history of the Revolution as it had been presented thus far at Colonial Williamsburg. Instead of the Revolution being a product of those traditional, timeless values that stewed in a pressure cooker until they reached critical mass, the new history suggested that the colonists' choice for revolution was prompted by economic self-interest.[78]

Within two years, the first three black costumed interpreters were hired.[79] By far the most political of changes to Colonial Williamsburg programming has been an emphasis on portraying the histories of black inhabitants of eighteenth-century Virginia, whether slaves or "free Negroes." "Continuing to omit the impact of black people on the 18th century was no longer acceptable to CWF's leadership," writes Christy Coleman Matthews. "They also knew that they had to tread carefully because this was the first known attempt by a mainstream ('white') museum to deal with slavery on such a scale."[80] Handler and Gable call the treatment of African-American history the "linchpin of historical revisionism" at Williamsburg.[81] Jim Bradley, Colonial Williamsburg Foundation's public relations manager, couched black history in terms of the narrative of the *building of the nation*:

> Certainly, you can learn about the founding fathers, but you can also learn about the other people that contributed. You have to realize that half of the population of this town, at the time of the Revolution, was African American. Few Americans are aware of the contributions that African Americans made to the development of this country. Granted, many of those contributions were done under the bonds of slavery, but still it was done. Those contributions can't be denied.[82]

The change most visible to visitors today is that there are many more black interpreters on the grounds. There are also several programs dedicated to illuminating for the visitors the lives of Williamsburg's slaves, advertised in the foundation's literature as the "other half" of Colonial Williamsburg (the *New York Times* has placed the black population at 52 percent, while Colonial Williamsburg currently holds that 52.4 percent of the city's population was enslaved. The rural Tidewater region surrounding the city was more than 70 percent black).[83]

While African-American interpreters have been employed at the site since its early years of operation, the staging of slavery has been touchy for several reasons. In the beginning, the harsh aspects of slavery would not have fit with the pristine city of Rockefeller's utopian vision. Later, it was hard to visualize an enactment that did not threaten to rob the interpreter and blacks in general of their dignity. Upon the idea of founding a black experience interpretation program, some vocalized their fears that it would make workers vulnerable and might open up the possibility of "racist slurs from visitors and to more subtle forms of racial discrimination from some of their white colleagues."[84]

The "Other Half" walking tour, created by what was then the African-American Interpretations and Presentations program (AAIP), is the most thorough way for visitors to access revisionist history at Williamsburg. The tour differs spatially and conceptually from other tours of the historic area in that the visitors enter the historic and reconstructed buildings not through the main door (as would the upper-class colonial visitor) but through the rear door, which slaves would have used. Rex Ellis describes the reasons for this arrangement:

> The goal was to challenge visitors—on various levels and planes and by various juxtapositions of ideas and objects—to see the town from the point of view of the Africans and African Americans who lived and worked there. The setting of the tour was not new, but the way visitors saw it created an entirely different perspective and level of understanding.[85]

Robert Jackson, my guide in the summer of 2000, told me that the aim of the Other Half tour program was to emphasize to visitors that black slaves and "free Negroes" were not "equal to" but "as important as" a founding father when placed historically next to each other. In one and a half hours, Jackson covered not only the history of Virginia's institution of slavery and an overview of the slaves' space in the city (from kitchen outbuildings and taverns to the fashionable right hand of the founding fathers—you don't want to touch these valuable slaves or you'd be sued by their masters and Lloyds of London) but also a demographic breakdown of the community. Two percent of the population was made up of Williamsburg's "top-notch" gentry: the Hollywood Boulevard of Colonial Virginia. "The middling sort," that is, the shopkeepers and clerks and their families, made up 18 percent. The other 80 percent were the poor folk, pronounced "po"—"so po' they can't afford the '-o-r,'" Jackson joked. The disparity led to animosity between poor white people and the house slaves of the wealthy, who generally lived much better lives. In one case, a lawsuit was brought against Surry County in 1692 charging that allowing house slaves to wear white linen shirts "increased their foolish Negro pride." This led to a law that said the linen could no longer be worn; instead, slaves were restricted to wearing coarse, blue material. Such events, according to Jackson, signaled the beginnings of a deep racism in the South.[86]

Other programs developed by the AAIP focused on little-treated aspects of African-American history such as the presence of free Negroes—those black townspeople who had either descended from free black colonists who arrived before slavery was instituted or recodified, or had been freed by their deceased masters in their wills. Some of the free Negroes owned slaves themselves—a surprising and oftentimes touchy subject for visitors. Black townspeople have also been portrayed in a light contrary to the themes of American founding values. In June 2000, the Colonial Williamsburg Foundation was preparing for "Brothers in Arms," a retrospective of Americans of African descent who had served in the military. One of the historic units to be represented was Lord Dunmore's Ethiopian Regiment. In 1775, Dunmore, the British governor of the Virginia Colony, offered freedom to any slave who would willingly flee from his master and take up arms against those colonists who advocated separation from Great Britain.

It appears that social historians at Williamsburg made several strides toward telling a larger story within the first years of incorporating the new programming in the historic area. It was not long, however, before a change in administration at Williamsburg maneuvered the programming back toward the more traditional scope of colonial history. Colonial Williamsburg today is not the museum envisioned by its social historians. Class exploitation and social conflict are downplayed, perpetuating a myth of America as a land of opportunity, and "corporately managed and disciplined front-line employees are a poor conduit for complex historiographical narratives."[87] *The Story of a Patriot* is still shown (with certain racist scenes omitted),[88] and as can be expected, the pristine Williamsburg landscape peopled with individuals dedicated to patriotic values depicted in the film does little to prepare visitors for the contemporary historic area infused with disparate social history and traditionalist narratives.[89]

Upon my June 2000 visit to the historic area, I found a return to showcasing the forefathers that visitors had come to expect prior to the shift in emphasis to the lives of everyday people. I was not the only one to notice. Bentley Boyd covered Williamsburg and its programmatic changes during Robert Wilburn's tenure as president in the 1990s for the *Daily Press* of Newport News, Virginia. Boyd's diagnosis was that the shift back to an emphasis on the forefathers was a result of economic and political influences:

Wilburn . . . came from the Carnegie, and his idea was to return somewhat to the "great men" theory of history. In the late seventies and most of the eighties, the emphasis here followed the emphasis in most historiography, which was to go towards this broad approach to history: Let's look at all the statistics, let's talk about the common people. You know, let's find out, what were housewives doing in 1775? What were slaves doing? Now, Wilburn didn't get rid of that, but he said, "Look, we're going to get more people here, and it's going to be more lively if we mix the story of the common person with George Washington, Thomas Jefferson, Patrick Henry. We've got to keep those guys in the forefront.[90]

Boyd observed that the return to emphasizing Williamsburg's famous white patriots was accompanied by a shift in the appearance of the historic area from a distressed, lived-in feel that it had presented in the late 1980s to the more pristine look of the museum's first decades. Buildings and houses that were looking dilapidated (but more historically accurate), due to less frequent whitewashings, were cleaned up and freshly painted. Social history had gone so far that it was "starting to eat into their image." As Boyd put it, "Wilburn said, 'Look, you know, we can still do some of that [social history], but we really gotta keep looking nice, because the white upper-middle-class people don't really want to pay all this money for a high-priced ticket to come and see a dingy town.'"[91]

I asked Boyd about the commitment of Colonial Williamsburg historians to the 98 percent of the population that were not the founding fathers, as prescribed by social history. He replied:

The study of the common people was a new paradigm. And they've held on to it, I think. They've done a good job talking about those people, because the records for Williamsburg are pretty good. Most Southern communities lost a lot in the Civil War—records being burned, lots of things being destroyed. But Williamsburg survived pretty well, because it was under Union occupation for most of the Civil War, and they took good care of it. It was not a battleground after 1862. So they're able to pick out these little individuals from the other 98 percent. They can say, "This person owned this store, and here are the records, and this person owned that tavern, and this person was a freed black," and so they can pull these people out and make them real.[92]

Visitors to Colonial Williamsburg are able to engage these personae in the historic area, but, says Boyd, what the visitors *really* want to see are the Thomas Jeffersons, Patrick Henrys, and George Washingtons of the town. "If you go to Thomas Jefferson today," he told me, "you'll just see dozens and dozens and dozens of people standing around him, and it's riveting." This is not a bad thing, says Boyd, who admits to enjoying both kinds of characters: "I do believe that great people make a difference. You know there are some people that have gone so far as to say, 'Well, the times make the people and their greatness has been thrust upon them.' Well, I don't think that's true."[93]

I mentioned to one of the program managers at Colonial Williamsburg that it seemed to be general knowledge that the museum had, in the previous ten or fifteen years, improved greatly in terms of focusing on more than just the founding fathers, adding lower classes, ethnic "minorities," and women to the programming. "It has definitely filtered down the social strata," he agreed, but hinted that, at least in the category of gender, there is now *too* much of a female presence for historical accuracy. In the military programs, he said, visitors will now see women portraying men, which would not have been the case in eighteenth-century Virginia. The museum has found ways to justify the choice, he says, and he works and deals with the situation. But, if he could change anything about the historic programming, he told me, that is what he would change—although he added that, "at the end of the day, the women are actually the military program's biggest supporters."[94]

Just as political and economic conditions limited the enunciation of American narratives at Colonial Williamsburg in the 1950s, so a network of governing factors has prevented many subjects of social history from being presented. As far as Handler and Gable are concerned, while the programs at Colonial Williamsburg have changed in the past twenty years to inculcate greater awareness of the slavery issues of the time period in Virginia, the site as a whole still maintains a sanitized and anesthetizing image of the slaves' history. "The more widely disseminated story still is an upbeat one, in which slaves, like other immigrants, establish themselves in a new land and work hard to improve their lot," they write.

> Moreover, black history remains secondary at Colonial Williamsburg. It is still easy for visitors to tour the entire site without hearing anything about African Americans other than how much they cost their owners and how many lived and worked in a particular white person's residence.[95]

Anna Logan Lawson, a colleague and fellow researcher of Handler and Gable's, goes further than their critique that black history remains secondary and merely reaffirms traditional "land of opportunity" narratives of America. Unfortunately, writes Lawson, while the Other Half walking tour most likely guarantees the average visitor that at least 25 percent of his or her day will be devoted to hearing black history delivered by an African-American interpreter, the tour is attended on a voluntary basis and is often the only venue in which to hear a historical account of African-American life in eighteenth-century Virginia. The small number of black interpreters and the limited availability of the tour during her two summers of research restricted the number of participants to no more than seventy per day.

> By contrast, during the same two summers, Patriot's tours, which came free with the purchase of the Patriot's Pass admission ticket to the museum, were offered hourly between 10 am and 3 pm seven days a week, with a group maximum of twenty-five. . . . Although there were vast differences between the more general Patriot's Tour and the specialized Other Half Tour, it could be argued that in a museum where the administration's stated commitment was to telling the story of the African-American "half" of the 18th-century population, there was an imbalance between seventy people a day, five days a week, on Other Half tours and three hundred people a day, seven days a week, on Patriot's Tours—350 versus 2100.[96]

Furthermore, through the framing of interpretive maneuvers, Lawson maintains, African Americans at Colonial Williamsburg become ethnographic objects themselves, reinscribing racial stereotypes. "In its presentations of relationships, stereotypes, and images involving African Americans," she writes, "Colonial Williamsburg, despite its best intentions, reproduced racist situations which helped maintain one of the hegemonic attitudes it sought to change."[97]

Social history, while fomenting an incredible shift in multiple aspects of living history programming, was not a "revolution," in that it did not articulate a new understanding of time. Nor was it a progressive step in evolution, a developmental move forward in a march toward perfection. It was a consequence, rather, of a rapidly shifting state of affairs in U.S. political climate, competition with other museums, and emergent historiographic discourse. Social history has not had the success envisioned by its first proponents.

The "bottom line" for Handler and Gable is that, while social history is currently the dominant paradigm among Colonial Williamsburg historians, and though social history programming has been widely encouraged, the philosophy of it has been lost in the transfer from the "planning documents and programs" to the museum's daily practices:

> Colonial Williamsburg [is] perhaps a dirtier and more democratic place than it had once been. . . . But despite the manure that signaled dramatic "change" in comparison with the earlier clean streets, Colonial Williamsburg, it seemed to us, was still a Republican Disneyland.[98]

They cite the "just-the-facts" mentality that governs frontline interpreters' regard for legitimate history, the "good vibes" mandate that conditions how visitors are to experience Colonial Williamsburg's presentation of the past (as exemplified in the backstage phrase "smile free or die"),[99] and the relationship between Colonial Williamsburg's identities as a corporate entity and an educational facility, with the former facet often overshadowing the latter—hospitality and courtesy are more emphasized than history.[100]

Peter Novick suggests that the more revisionist and controversial historiographic practices throughout the twentieth century were hamstrung by being adopted and tempered by the dominant, conservative hegemony of the American history profession. He calls this strategy "restriction through incorporation," a kind of insidious move that accepts radical historians as "legitimate participants in a pluralistic professional discourse," then depoliticizes and dilutes their major arguments so that they may more easily and palatably fit into the mainstream.[101] This may be what has happened with social history at living museums. At Colonial Williamsburg, however, it seems more likely that the middle-ground, safe course pursued by the administration in its programming, seeking to both offer the best in history scholarship and please the crowds, is more to blame for compromising the politics of social history than a shadowy cabal of conservative historians.

The Naturalistic Ideal

The visiting public has the right to expect that what they are seeing and hearing at a historic site is the truth.

—William T. Alderson and Shirley Payne Low,
Interpretation of Historic Sites

Once we stroll by a sign marking the line between the 20th and 17th centuries, the past comes alive with vibrant clarity.

—James W. Baker, *Plimoth Plantation*

Step over the threshold of history to live in New Hampshire's oldest seacoast neighborhood.

—Strawbery Banke Museum website

The emergence of large-scale, costumed, first-person role-playing as an interpretive strategy attracted more visitors to open-air museums in the late 1970s than did artifacts.[102] This section examines the ways costumed performance became the "ideal" model of interpretation in the last decades of the twentieth century (and why living museums enshrined it as the goal toward which they had been heading since Hazelius's Skansen a hundred years earlier).

* * *

In June 2000, I stepped out of the bright and cool morning air of the Plymouth Colony common, surrounded by the rough-hewn palisade walls of the colony, and into the dark home of Mistress Fuller. I had been invited in by this woman, in her coif, apron, and skirts, who then bade me sit down on a wooden bench while she prepared for the day. As Mistress Fuller conducted her chores, she told me about the arrival of her fellow saints in the New World aboard the *Mayflower* seven years ago, about how half of her companions failed to survive the first harsh winter, and about how hard it was to meet the requirements of the contracts signed with the merchants in order to procure this land for their new home.

It was hard to believe that this simulated 1627 environment had, only a few minutes earlier, been bustling with grounds crews with plastic rakes and huddled groups of costumed interpreters, busily preparing for the twentieth-century visitors who would arrive at 9:30. I caught this last scene accidentally, by forgoing the half-hour orientation program in the Visitor Center, which formed the buffer between when the museum opened at 9:00 and the opening of the Pilgrim Village at 9:30.

Stumbling into the village a quarter of an hour early, I was approached by a plainclothes staff member, who, in a friendly tone, asked if I was lost, or a part of a group, and explained to me that the interpreters had to get ready and have a meeting, and that they'd be ready for visitors in about fifteen minutes. After browsing in the Carriage House Craft Center and Museum Store, I returned to the village a few minutes later to find the site transformed into a seventeenth-century environment, with none of the modern intrusions—twentieth-century staff uniforms or plastic rakes—I had seen before. It was in this environment that I could willingly suspend my disbelief and speak with Mistress Fuller as if she were a seventeenth-century Pilgrim at home in her daub-and-wattle surroundings.

The total representation of a three-dimensional milieu with first-person interpretation is a fairly recent genre of simulated setting. Changes in representational practices and conceptions of time have informed the ways individuals are able to willingly suspend their disbelief and perceive certain geographically bounded spaces as having a different temporal quality than the surrounding area. While this concept of the audience's acceptance of the-atrical illusion has been incorporated into "mainstream" dramatic presenta-tion for more than a hundred years, its transfer to living history environ-ments was not possible without the changes to museum historiography prompted by the emergence of social history and ethnohistorical approaches in the 1960s and 1970s.

Before then, open-air museums used a presentational approach in which costumed docents used lecture-style demonstrations in front of, or within, historical buildings, but did not impersonate the character of an individual from the time period on display. They stood at right angles to their historical display backdrops, much like the nonrealistic acting style August Strindberg condemned in his preface to Miss Julie.[103] Objects were arranged in the his-toric buildings in a manner similar to a museum of decorative art—preserved in place and not to be touched. The shift to a totally re-created, "living" en-vironment is usually pinpointed today as occurring before Plimoth Planta-tion's 1969 season, when James Deetz removed the wax mannequins, signage, and inaccurate antiques from the Pilgrim Village and subsequently encour-aged the interpreters to do the Pilgrim's chores and crafts, rather than demon-strate them.[104]

Now, Plimoth, Colonial Williamsburg, and Old Sturbridge Village strive to use the same rigor in creating the illusion of a historical environment as did the naturalists in their late nineteenth-century independent theatres.[105] A visitor to Plimoth Plantation today, for instance, would not find artifacts displayed in a traditional museum format within the Pilgrim Village, but would see the costumed interpreters living with the objects, working with them, and using them to create a believable slice of 1627 life in the Plymouth Colony. Handler and Gable dub a similar commitment to this naturalistic mode of historic interpretation at Colonial Williamsburg "mimetic" or "pro-gressive realism."[106]

What conditions allowed this emphasis on total re-created environment and the encouragement of visitors' suspension of disbelief to emerge in the museum industry by the time it had already become passé in the avant garde theatre? After all, Surrealism, Dada, Futurism, and Expressionism with their shattering of the idea of naturalistic re-creation of everyday life all emerged within the first two decades of the twentieth century, less than forty years af-ter the early naturalist productions of Antoine, Émile Zola, and Strind-berg.[107] Strindberg himself departed from strictures of naturalism in his later work, and even within Miss Julie.[108] With Bertold Brecht's work in theatre, it has become far more acceptable for an actor to break character and address the audience directly, or for mainstream theatre productions to make visible the staging elements like lighting instruments or wires, such as those which suspend the angel that descends through Prior's bedroom ceiling at the end of Tony Kushner's *Angels in America: Millennium Approaches*.[109] Productions such as these tend to celebrate and indulge in the possibilities offered by theatricality, rather than limiting themselves to a passable illusion of real life based on observable data. So, what events or modes of thinking prompted living history institutions' curatorial goals in the late 1960s and early 1970s to advocate naturalistic settings?

It is not the case that, before the late 1960s, visitors were unable to imagine the environments at outdoor history museums as a walk into a past era. Bert O. States cites an account by the biographer of Aeschylus of such a convincingly terrifying performance of *The Eumenides* in the fifth century B.C. that children in the audience died and women suffered miscarriages. Though hard to believe, writes States, the account reminds us that "'the suspension of disbelief' does not depend in the least on what we would today call a photographic likeness of the image to reality. It depends only on the power of the image to serve as a channel for what of reality is of immediate interest to the audience."[110] Hence, the reverent and immediate image of the distant past in the musings of Dr. W. A. R. Goodwin, who initially suggested the restoration of Williamsburg, Virginia, to its colonial appearance, writing in 1907 (before restoration):

> If you have ever walked around Williamsburg lake on a moonlight night, when most of the people . . . are fast asleep, and felt the presence and companionship of the people who used to live here in the long gone years, and remembered the things that they did and the things they stood for, and pictured them going into or coming out of the old houses . . . you would then know what an interesting place Williamsburg is.[111]

Statements like these enunciate a willful suspension of disbelief even when physical reminders of the present would otherwise logically interrupt a believable experience of the past. When I spoke with him in 2000, Jim Bradley allowed that imagination is still required by the visitor to access the feel of Williamsburg's historic area, now restored in near accordance with Goodwin's vision:

> I think it requires on the part of the visitor a little imagination. . . . It doesn't take too much to be walking down the street and let your mind sort of go with the flow and [wistfully say,] "This is the same street that Jefferson walked. This is the same street that Washington walked. I wonder what Jefferson thought about while walking to George Wythe's house. Was he thinking about the law

books that he was reading at the time? What kind of bill to write?" It doesn't take a lot of imagination. You just have to be willing to imagine it . . . to think about it. There's something almost magical about having the opportunity to walk down the same streets as some of these people, where history was made.[112]

Living history programming beginning in the late 1960s was a strategy for meeting the visitors' suspension of disbelief halfway, in a similar manner to the procedures of the naturalists at the end of the nineteenth century. One way in which this mode of seeing is conditioned for the spectator is the use of first-person, costumed interpretation. A greater emphasis on this mode of presentation accompanied Deetz's move to ethnohistorical rigor and production of a total living environment at Plimoth Plantation in the summers following 1969. Deetz's principle, outlined for the general public in a 1980 *Museum News* article, is still a major tenet of living interpretation at Plimoth:

> Involve the interpretive staff in as many [historical] tasks as possible in a genuinely productive way. If the interpreters have done most of the things they are supposed to discuss, they will automatically employ first-person interpretation in a natural way. After all, if one has been riving shingles to attach to the roof of a house, it is more natural to say "*we do* it this way" than "*they did* it that way." The shift from third-person past to first-person present, if done well, goes a long way toward making the interpretation convincing to the visitor. After all, if the visitor is given to believe that the houses are the way they were, why shouldn't the interpreters also fit into this plan?[113]

While these moves were initially criticized among some museum professionals and Pilgrim-reverent *Mayflower* descendants, James Baker sees the tension happily ending as early as 1978:

> The new [ethnohistorical accuracy] approach did meet with an enthusiastic response from many visitors. It was exciting, different, and dynamic, a far remove from the virtuous pedagogy usually found in historical museums. The introduction of first-person interpretation in 1978, in which the costumed personnel assume character roles and become living artifacts, completed the logical move to reproducing the 17th century Plymouth community. In time, even the majority of the 1969 critics admitted that the living history, first-person Plantation was an interesting and entertaining place.[114]

Cynthia Gedraitis, a supervisor with the Colonial Interpretation Department at Plimoth, shared with me the way she and others prepare for their roles as Pilgrim interpreters when on site in the village. Even though she hesitates to call costumed interpretation "theatre," she describes a sort of transformation into a seventeenth-century person through the visceral act of putting on the period clothing:

> When I'm down on the *Mayflower* doing third-person interpretation and some-
> one will ask me, "Say something in dialect," . . . I can't do it. And I'm not
> alone, and other people say that, too. It comes with whatever happens to you
> as you're getting ready in the morning, or you're down on site. We jokingly
> used to say that it's when you change in the morning and get into your clothes.
> Because the clothes are *so* different. . . . You're tying your neck. You're tying
> your garters, you're tying your shoes, you're tying your skirts, your hooks, your
> buttons, and, you know, twenty minutes later, you're ready to go. You're wear-
> ing a corset, a coif on your head. That's where the transformation happens.
> And even when there aren't visitors around, they're not talking in dialect to
> each other about the latest *Seinfeld* episode, or "the car broke down on the way
> to work." We're not talking to each other like that, but it's instantaneous,
> when a visitor comes around, or you can hear footfalls coming under the win-
> dow, and you just know. I don't know. That's the characterization part to me.[115]

From Gedraitis's account, it would seem that the techniques actors started using in the late nineteenth and early twentieth centuries to psychologically
immerse themselves into their roles now allow living history interpreters to
"embody" their characters and not simply present them as cultural artifacts
on display.

Another way in which living history programming and curatorial practices encourage visitors to suspend their disbelief is their emphasis on scientific accuracy in the re-creation of the environments. Through scientific
methodology like archaeological digs, examination of period artifacts, ge-
nealogies, and documents, museum literature and public relations can pro-
claim accurate re-creation of living environments. As Zola and Strindberg
encouraged in their naturalist writings,[116] the curators of Plimoth Plantation
employ an incredible amount of historiographic research and archaeological
rigor ensuring that the Pilgrim Village approximates the actual Plymouth
Colony of 1627 according to documents and archived evidence. Walt Woodward, director of education resources at Plimoth Plantation, told me that
Plimoth is looking toward what he described as "psychohistory," that is, interpreting and decoding historical documents for the psychology of their authors and translating this psychology into performance for museum visitors.
A 1985 "Guide to Developing Characterizations" by Donna DeFabio, used
in training at Plimoth Plantation, encourages interpreters to analyze their

subjects in order to determine appropriate emotions and thoughts to complete their performance:

> As you immerse yourself in reading your training materials, remember that you
> will be portraying a person that did once actually live and breathe upon this
> earth, a person that *thought* and *felt*. Trying to discover what thoughts and feel-
> ings your character might appropriately express is a delicate process.[117]

The training manual evokes the type of building of a character based on observable data and one's own psyche that Konstantin Stanislavsky advocated
in his methodology.

Finally, the spectators of living history environments may suspend their
disbelief by virtue of the power and authority of the institution itself. The attractions take advantage of a "museum effect," capable of altering the
tourists' perception. Barbara Kirshenblatt-Gimblett describes the museum effect as the phenomenon in which the setting changes the standards for experiencing objects. When a museum separates certain objects from the quotidian as worthy of display, they take on a special significance.[118] The
artifacts arranged in these museums are not important because they create a
different time, but because of the very fact that a curatorial institution has
chosen to display them. It is the power of the institution that places living
history museums up and over other living historical practices, such as rendezvous or battle reenactment activities, in which the participants are usually amateurs or buffs rather than museum professionals. Though these
"weekend warriors" may indeed employ an enormous amount of research and
rigor into their historical personages, without the power of a legitimate educational institution supporting them, they may never achieve the perceived
status of "real" historians.

Living History as Pleasure

Under the influence of the natural sciences, "development" and
"progress," which merely translate the idea of a chronologically orien-
tated process, become the guiding categories of historical knowledge.
Such a concept of time and history necessarily expropriates man from
the human dimension and impedes access to authentic historicity.

—Giorgio Agamben, "Time and History"

Historical interpretation at living museums organizes past events by categorizing them according to cause-and-effect patterns, narratives of progress or

social cycles (i.e., conflict, redressive action, resolution), and allowing the missing links to be filled in with hypothetical models. An analysis of discursive formations is no less a strategy of organization, but it rejects defaulting to transcendental systems (to notions of progress or social cycles, for example) in favor of seeking the statements and strategies in the field which give events specificity.

This historiography, rather than offering a new grand scheme for living history in the twenty-first century, has interrogated the elements that allowed a particular enunciation of history to emerge, while disallowing other possibilities. Concepts such as "America," "progress," or even "living history" were not ideal entities that spurred the development of living history museums. Rather, these are discursive formations—networks of statements—that were invented and reinvented at specific times through a realignment of various relationships for political or economic gain and stability—or, in the case of social history, as a reaction to the gaps in history (real or imaginary) made visible by political and economic changes. Soothing narratives of the past that countered anxieties of mid-twentieth-century America, like Deleuze's *ritornello*, offered comforting refrains to protect the nation's consciousness from doubt. What remains unclear, however, is whether these were "actual" feelings of anxiety or were produced and disseminated in light of domestic and international policies or goals.

Existing rationalizations that speak to economic shifts in the twentieth century—the development of highways, for instance—allowed tourists to access sites formerly restricted by distance. Tourist destinations rose to meet the occasion. Again, certain themes in living history studies and documents, such as loss of or disconnection with the land that historical sites sought to redress, fueled the transformation of communities into tourist destinations. We cannot know if the narratives developed by these tourist sites spoke to a "real" sense of loss felt by the American people or if, in capitalistic fashion, the loss was an imaginary idea circulated to produce demand for the goods and services tourism had to offer.

Social history programming, too—far from being a perfect solution to critiques of living history's bias toward rich, white forefathers—contributed to the production of a new collection of political, racial, and social tensions. Living museums of everyday life are still relatively free of workers' strikes and social action.[119] The horrible images of slavery, as noted by Handler, Gable, and Lawson, are not to be seen at Colonial Williamsburg—doubly silenced by curatorial intervention and by economic/cultural factors. To market the Other Half tour in the same way as the more popular Patriot's Tour is neither viable nor does it answer perceived visitor desire. The number of African-American interpreters employed by the Colonial Williamsburg Foundation in no way approaches the 50-plus percent of the actual eighteenth-century African-American population. Similar situations have been encountered at Plimoth Plantation and Old Sturbridge Village.

The combination of authoritative site, an explicit focus on scientific accuracy, and the naturalistic ideal of first-person interpretation produces an environment of trust. Here, visitors are encouraged to suspend their disbelief without the peripheral doubt that what they see is anything but total scientific accuracy. William T. Alderson and Shirley Payne Low, in *Interpretation of Historic Sites*, their manual for creating sound and ethical simulations of past environments, exhort current and potential curators to present the "straight story" of history, reminding them that "the visiting public has the right to expect that what they are seeing and hearing at a historic site is the truth." They continue, "Usually there is an abundance of true details that can enliven an interpretation without sacrificing the truth," and conclude that good interpretation "tells the story as it was."[120] When institutions respect this right, and remind visitors that they do so in their brochures and travel literature, these visitors are free, if they so choose, to "tumble in" to the living environment.

What remains to be acknowledged are those shifts in museum performance genealogy that emerged in ways that cannot be discursively grouped with economic, political, or performative narratives. In the end, a desire to produce history at living museum sites on the part of many participants themselves is motivated by neither a political agenda to shore up American heritage against threatening elements nor a nostalgic scientific inquiry into creating an exact replica past. The commitment to voice untold stories will always be cited by participants as a reason for spending their summers in historic costume, but this could only go so far were it not for the fact that reenactment is a *pleasurable experience* for both the interpreter and the museum visitor. Paradoxically, it is the pleasure of the moment that liberates history from servitude to the vulgar notion of a precise and homogeneous continuum of instants.

At the end of his essay "Time and History," Giorgio Agamben offers his own notion of time as broken by moments of pleasure—instants that erase any real notion of time as a mere passing of measurable, quantifiable instants. He draws upon the Stoics' curative notion of time as an abrupt, sudden decision of grasping opportunity and life: a *Cairós*. For Agamben, authenticity is not that which actually happened as measurable by material evidence. It is the *cairological* experience of joy that allows the individual to *become* historical in order to take control of his or her own history and get around alienation from history based on the state's precise continuum. In authentic rev-olutions, history is no longer that of the *state*, alienating the individual, but of the *individual*.

Wendy Erisman taps into this conception of authenticity in her work on living history. Erisman has done much to investigate the assumptions under-pinning living history scholars' narratives of the causal factors that lead to the broad spectrum of popular living history attractions in the contemporary United States. She takes issue with Jay Anderson's definition of *authenticity* as misguidedly emphasizing a correspondence between the actual past and its rigorous representation through which living history participants can get a "true experience of the past."[121] Erisman likewise finds fault with living his-tory critics like Richard Handler, who find that "living history is a funda-mentally flawed activity which actually reproduces the inauthentic life its participants are trying to escape."[122] For Erisman, a living history participant herself, both modernist scholars like Anderson and his more recent post-modern detractors overgeneralize the complex psychological and emotional space into which living history enthusiasts enter when they perform the past. They fail to take into account the participants' personal searches for mean-ing and identity. In the end, she writes, "accuracy" or "authenticity," defined as an exact correlation to the actual or lived past, does not matter to partic-ipants as much as what they get out of their participation.[123] In other words, authenticity is radical, personal fulfillment as praxis and is fundamentally ahistorical, or in Nietzsche's terms, *unhistorical*.

Friedrich Nietzsche held that the human mind is capable of being over-whelmed—"oversaturated"—with history. Such an oversaturation "leads an age into a dangerous mood of irony in regard to itself and subsequently into the even more dangerous mood of cynicism, rendering individuals incapable of action, that is, "making history themselves."[124] History is a malady, an ex-cess that has attacked life's plastic powers. Nietzsche calls upon youth to for-get enough until it can conduct itself and its making of history in a healthy way once again. The consequent moment of happiness, the ability to forget the past, allows one to feel "unhistorically." This ability to forget, in mo-ments of pleasure, is essential to life. The one who is unable to sink into the "threshold of the moment" and forget the accumulated past will never know what happiness is: "worse, he will never do anything to make others happy."[125]

Unhistory, a radical forgetting, is a mode of resistance to history, outside of taxonomic time, but the very space, according to Nietzsche, in which events are able to happen.[126] Such a forgetting can be found on Thanksgiv-ing Day in 1970, in Plymouth, Massachusetts. When Native Americans took over the *Mayflower II* and cast sand upon Plymouth Rock in a performative act of protest, the deliberate forgetting sought to erase that which had been chosen by authoritative institutions as worthy of monumentalizing. A commemorative act, it did not reference an event of the lived past, but instead brought to light what Deleuze and Guattari would call a "meanwhile": "When time passes and takes the instant away, there is always a meanwhile to restore the event."[127] The meanwhile is the becoming which is not tied to the instant, but which "has the privilege of beginning again when the time is past."[128]

Time, when viewed as interruptible, or variable, by moments of pleasure, or pure revolution, is no longer homogeneous, Deleuze writes, and allows the mind to understand time as a unified whole in order to gain comprehension of time, "no longer as a succession of movements and of their units, but time as a simultaneism and simultaneity."[129] The takeover at Plymouth turned time into an infinite simultaneity and reintroduced the notions that time could be understood as a whole and that an understanding of history could pass beyond the mere comprehension of successive units of measurable time. The *Mayflower II* takeover was a cairological moment. It did not cease to exist after passing into oblivion with the coming into being of the next instant. Rather, it continued to exist as a "meanwhile." Dwelling in the plane of immanence, it continually reemerges in the plane of immanence again and again, most visibly at each subsequent Day of Mourning on Thanksgiving Day at Plymouth Rock, and likewise at Plimoth Plantation's Hobbamock's Homesite, where the Wampanoag interpreters do not *commemorate* a singular past event, but open space to the multiplicity of past and present enunciations.

Deleuze and Guattari's philosophy of immanence offers different conceptions of the understanding of time and space that allow the perception of multiplicities of possibilities. The final chapter will look at the kinds of performance that are going on at present in living museums, how interpreters regard their craft, and how museums and history are already being rethought by participants in the field.

Notes

1. Gilles Deleuze and Félix Guattari, *What Is Philosophy?*, trans. Hugh Tomlinson and Graham Burchell (New York: Columbia University Press, 1994), 153, 155–60.

2. Deleuze and Guattari, *What Is Philosophy?*, 153.

3. Deleuze and Guattari, *What Is Philosophy?*, 118.

4. Gilles Deleuze, *Cinema* (Minneapolis: University of Minnesota Press, 1986–1989), 1:46.

5. Deleuze and Guattari, *What Is Philosophy?*, 167–68.

6. Tony Bennett, *The Birth of the Museum: History, Theory, Politics* (London: Routledge, 1995).

7. Rosemarie Bank, "Meditations upon Opening and Crossing Over: Transgressing the Boundaries of Historiography and Tracking the History of Nineteenth-Century American Theatre," in *Of Borders and Thresholds: Theatre History, Practice, and Theory*, ed. Michal Kobialka (Minneapolis: University of Minnesota Press, 1999); Barbara Kirshenblatt-Gimblett, *Destination Culture: Tourism, Museums, and Heritage* (Berkeley: University of California Press, 1998).

8. David Lowenthal, *The Past Is a Foreign Country* (Cambridge: Cambridge University Press, 1985), 4.

9. David Lowenthal, *Possessed by the Past: The Heritage Crusade and the Spoils of History* (New York: Free Press, 1996), 11.

10. Alvin Toffler, *Future Shock* (New York: Random House, 1970).

11. Richard Slotkin, *Gunfighter Nation: The Myth of the Frontier in Twentieth-Century America* (New York: Atheneum, 1992), 2.

12. Michel Foucault, "Politics and the Study of Discourse," in *The Foucault Effect: Studies in Governmentality*, ed. Graham Burchell, Colin Gordon, and Peter Miller (London: Harvester, 1981), 28.

13. Foucault, "Politics," 28.

14. Laurence Urdang, *The Timetables of American History* (New York: Simon & Schuster, 1981), 360. See also Michael O'Brian, *McCarthy and McCarthyism in Wisconsin* (Columbia: University of Missouri Press, 1980).

15. Melinda Copel, "The 1954 Limón Company Tour to South America: Goodwill Tour or Cold War Cultural Propaganda?" in *José Limón*, ed. June Dunbar (New York: Routledge, 2000), 97–98.

16. Herbert Blau, "Notes from the Underground," in *Sails of the Herring Fleet: Essays on Beckett* (Ann Arbor: University of Michigan Press, 2000), 37–38. The State Department placed a ban on the production's stage manager "for unspecified reasons," but the company decided to go regardless, and more meaningfully now, because it was "under protest" (38).

17. See Kirshenblatt-Gimblett, *Destination Culture*, and Robert Hewison, *The Heritage Industry: Britain in a Climate of Decline* (London: Methuen, 1987).

18. Charles Edward Merriam's 1931 manifesto *The Making of Citizens: A Comparative Study of Methods of Civic Training* linked good citizenship with historical interpretation. The healthfulness of the nation and its people depended on the citizen to walk with his ancestors, "whose blood is in his veins and whose domain and reputation he proudly bears." Freeman Tilden makes heavy use of Merriam's work in his *Interpreting Our Heritage* (3rd ed., Chapel Hill: University of North Carolina Press, 1977). See also Henry Wiencek, *An Imperfect God: George Washington, His Slaves, and the Creation of America* (New York: Farrar, Straus and Giroux, 2003), 173. The quote about the ancestors' blood is found in Tilden, 12.

19. Lowenthal, *Past Is a Foreign Country*, 122.

20. Lowenthal, *Possessed by the Past*, 248–49.

21. Michel de Certeau, *The Writing of History*, trans. Tom Conley (New York: Columbia University Press, 1988), 221.

22. *Colonial Williamsburg Interpreter*, cited in Jay Anderson, *Time Machines: The World of Living History* (Nashville, TN: American Association for State and Local History, 1984), 35. "Right-minded" visitors went as far as reporting on their fellow visitors to the Rockefellers if they appeared insincere or critical of the Americanist agenda promoted on the grounds (Anders Greenspan, *Creating Colonial Williamsburg* [Washington, D.C.: Smithsonian Institution Press, 2002], 79).

23. Kenneth Chorley, citing a young soldier in "Only Tomorrow" (Williamsburg, 1947), 21; quote reprinted in Caroll Van West and Mary S. Hoffschwelle, "'Slumbering on Its Old Foundations': Interpretation at Colonial Williamsburg," *South Atlantic Quarterly* 83 (Spring 1984): 162.

24. *America's Historylands: Touring Our Landmarks of Liberty* (Washington, DC: National Geographic Society, 1967), 121.

25. The Taverns, in particular, are continuously resituated as the sites where the "United States of America" was born at Colonial Williamsburg. Most notably, when the governor of Virginia dissolved the House of Burgesses upon reports of anti-British talk, its members reconvened in private at the Raleigh Tavern. Callers placed on hold when phoning Williamsburg for visitor information may hear an advertisement encouraging them to make a reservation for dinner in one of the many Williamsburg taverns, where they can "enjoy the food the Founding Fathers savored as they contemplated revolution."

26. *America's Historylands*, 136.

27. Richard Handler and Eric Gable, *The New History in an Old Museum: Creating the Past at Colonial Williamsburg* (Durham, NC: Duke University Press, 1999), 63, quoting from *Colonial Williamsburg News* 28.9 (18 February 1976).

28. Hewison, *Heritage Industry*, 46, quoting Fred Davis's *Yearning for Yesterday: A Sociology of Nostalgia* (New York: Free Press, 1979).

29. *America's Historylands*, 294–95.

30. Gilles Deleuze, "Music and Ritornello," in *The Deleuze Reader*, ed. Constantin V. Boundas (New York: Columbia University Press, 1993), 201–3. The phrase "protecting consciousness from doubt" is from Jean-François Lyotard's essay, "Answer to the Question, 'What Is the Postmodern?'" (trans. Don Barry, in *The Postmodern Explained*, ed. Julian Pefanis and Morgan Thomas [Minneapolis: University of Minnesota Press, 1992], 5); it refers to "the task academicism had assigned to realism."

31. Stephen Eddy Snow, *Performing the Pilgrims: A Study of Ethnohistorical Role-Playing at Plimoth Plantation* (Jackson: University Press of Mississippi, 1993), 114–15.

32. Snow, *Performing the Pilgrims*, 116. See also James Deetz and Patricia Scott Deetz, *The Times of Their Lives: Life, Love, and Death in Plymouth Colony* (New York: Freeman, 2000), 135–38.

33. Michael Wallace, "Visiting the Past: History Museums in the United States," *Radical History Review* 25 (1981): 90.

34. Wallace, "Visiting the Past," 90.

35. Vladimir Nabokov, *The Annotated Lolita*, ed. Alfred Appel Jr. (New York: McGraw-Hill, 1970), 150.

36. John A. Jakle, *The Tourist: Travel in Twentieth Century North America* (Lincoln: University of Nebraska Press, 1985), 26–27.

37. Jakle, *Tourist*, 126–27.

38. Jakle, *Tourist*, 185.

39. For a history of the station wagon, see Steve Manning's "A Short History of Station Wagons in the USA" at www.stationwagon.com/history.html.

40. Jakle, *Tourist*, 186.

41. Jakle, *Tourist*, 191ff.

42. Jakle, *Tourist*, 289.

43. Robert B. Wells, *Daylight in the Swamp* (Ashland, WI: Northwood, 1987), 15.

44. Barbara Kirshenblatt-Gimblett, "Afterlives," *Performance Research* 2.2 (Summer 1997), 2.

45. Michael Omert, *Official Guide to Colonial Williamsburg* (Williamsburg, VA: Colonial Williamsburg Foundation, 1998), 22.

46. *America's Historylands*, 68; informational sign, Plymouth Rock (1968).

47. Susan K. Irwin, "Popular History: Living History Sites, Historical Interpretation and the Public" (master's thesis, Bowling Green State University, 1993), 50.

48. G. J. Ashworth and J. E. Tunbridge, *The Tourist-Historic City* (London: Belhaven Press, 1990), 142.

49. Richard J. Roddewig, "Selling America's Heritage," *Preservation Forum* 2 (Fall 1988), 10.

50. Dean MacCannell, *The Tourist: A New Theory of the Leisure Class* (Berkeley: University of California Press, 1999), 6.

51. Pioneer Village map/guide, 2000.

52. "Living History in the National Park Service," brochure (Washington, DC: National Park Service, 1976).

53. "Living History in the National Park Service," 2.

54. "Living History in the National Park Service," 2.

55. "Living History in the National Park Service," 15.

56. "Living History in the National Park Service," 11.

57. For other accounts of the historical emergence and problems of social history, see Geoff Eley and Keith Nield, "Why Does Social History Ignore Politics?" *Social History* 5 (May 1980); Jack P. Greene, "The New History: From Top to Bottom," *New York Times*, 8 January 1975; Raphael Samuel and Gareth Stedman Jones, eds., *Culture, Ideology and Politics* (London: Routledge, 1982); Walter T. K. Nugent, *Structures of American Social History* (Bloomington: Indiana University Press, 1981); James B. Gardner and George Rollie Adams, eds., *Ordinary People and Everyday Life: Perspectives on the New Social History* (Nashville, TN: American Association for State and Local History, 1983); and Miles Fairburn, *Social History: Problems, Strategies and Methods* (New York: St. Martin's, 1999).

58. Olivier Zunz, introduction to *Reliving the Past: The Worlds of Social History*, ed. Olivier Zunz (Chapel Hill: University of North Carolina Press, 1985), 4.

59. Zunz, *Reliving the Past*, 3.

60. Zunz, "The Synthesis of Social Change: Reflections on American Social History," in Zunz, *Reliving the Past*, 54.

61. Zunz, "Synthesis of Social Change," 56.

62. Michael Hall, personal interview, 13 June 2000.

63. Carolyn Travers, personal interview, 15 June 2000.

64. Martha Sulya, personal interview, 15 June 2000.

65. Stephen Osman, personal interview, 13 May 2000.

66. Costumed interpreter, Old Sturbridge Village, 19 June 2000.

67. Lowenthal, *Possessed by the Past*, citing John Patterson's "Conner Prairie Refocuses Its Interpretive Message to Include Controversial Subjects," *History News* 41.2 (March 1986), 98.

68. Jack Larkin, personal interview, 21 June 2000.

69. Jack Larkin, personal interview, 21 June 2000.

70. Handler and Gable, *New History in an Old Museum*, 4.

71. Greenspan, *Creating Colonial Williamsburg*, 72. Jewish visitors were also barred from the Williamsburg Inn and Hotels before the changes brought by the civil rights movement (Wiencek, *Imperfect God*, 177).

72. Greenspan, *Creating Colonial Williamsburg*, 89.

73. Deetz and Deetz, *Times of Their Lives*, 276–77, 143.

74. Handler and Gable, *New History in an Old Museum*, 41.

75. See Handler and Gable, *New History in an Old Museum*; Christy Coleman Matthews, "Twenty Years Interpreting African American History: A Colonial Williamsburg Revolution," *History News* 54 (Spring 1999): 6; Greenspan, *Creating Colonial Williamsburg*, 168; Deetz and Deetz, *Times of Their Lives*, 281; and Cary Carson, "Colonial Williamsburg and the Practice of Interpretive Planning in American History Museums," *Public Historian* 20.3 (Summer 1998), 41.

76. John D. Rockefeller Jr., quoted in Donald Garfield, "Too Real for Comfort," *Museum News* 74.1 (January–February 1995): 8.

77. Handler and Gable, *New History in an Old Museum*, 69.

78. Handler and Gable, *New History in an Old Museum*, 69.

79. Greenspan, *Creating Colonial Williamsburg*, 151.

80. Matthews, "Twenty Years Interpreting," 7. CWF stands for Colonial Williamsburg Foundation, the name given to the museum operation in 1969 upon the mergers of its two divisions, Colonial Williamsburg, Inc., and Williamsburg Restoration, Inc.

81. Handler and Gable, *New History in an Old Museum*, 23.

82. Jim Bradley, personal interview, 8 June 2000.

83. Elisabeth Bumiller, "Weekend Excursion: Colonial Myth and Reality," *New York Times*, 4 June 1999; Joel Garcia, noncostumed third-person interpreter at "Enslaving Virginia," at the Secretary's House, 3 June 2000.

84. Eric Gable, Richard Handler, and Anna Lawson, "On the Uses of Relativism: Fact, Conjecture, and Black and White Histories at Colonial Williamsburg," *American Ethnologist* 19.4 (November 1992): 794.

85. Rex M. Ellis, "Interpreting the Whole House," in *Interpreting Historic House Museums*, ed. Jessica Foy Donnelly (Walnut Creek, CA: AltaMira, 2002), 69.

86. Robert Jackson, guide, Other Half tour, Colonial Williamsburg, 7 June 2000.

87. Handler and Gable, *New History in an Old Museum*, 121, quote on 207.

88. Greenspan, *Creating Colonial Williamsburg*, 137.

89. John D. Krugler, "Stepping Outside of the Classroom: History and the Outdoor Museum," *Journal of American Culture* 12.2 (Summer 1989): 84n.

90. Bentley Boyd, personal interview, 7 June 2000.

91. Bentley Boyd, personal interview, 7 June 2000.

92. Bentley Boyd, personal interview, 7 June 2000.

93. Bentley Boyd, personal interview, 7 June 2000.

94. Program manager, Colonial Williamsburg, personal interview, 6 June 2000.

95. Eric Gable and Richard Handler, "In Colonial Williamsburg, the New History Meets the Old," *Chronicle of Higher Education*, 30 October 1998.

96. Anna Logan Lawson, "'The Other Half': Making African-American History at Colonial Williamsburg" (Ph.D. dissertation, University of Virginia, 1995), 135.

97. Lawson, "Other Half," 57.

98. Handler and Gable, *New History in an Old Museum*, 220.

99. Handler and Gable, *New History in an Old Museum*, 226.

100. Handler and Gable, *New History in an Old Museum*, 228.

101. Peter Novick, *That Noble Dream: "The Objectivity Question" and the American Historical Profession* (Cambridge, UK: Cambridge University Press, 1988), 459.

102. Lowenthal, *The Past Is a Foreign Country*, 298.

103. August Strindberg, "Preface to *Miss Julie*," trans. E. M. Sprinchorn, in *Dramatic Theory and Criticism: Greeks to Grotowski*, ed. Bernard E. Dukore (Fort Worth, TX: Harcourt, 1976), 572. For a description of interpretive styles, see Anderson, *Time Machines*, and Snow, *Performing the Pilgrims*. See also Stacy F. Roth, *Past into Present: Effective Techniques for First-Person Historical Interpretation* (Chapel Hill: University of North Carolina Press, 1998); James Deetz, "A Sense of Another World: History Museums and Cultural Change," *Museum News* 58.5 (May–June 1980); and Deetz and Deetz, *Times of Their Lives*.

104. Deetz and Deetz, *Times of Their Lives*, 278–79, 289–90. Cf. Anderson, *Time Machines*, 51, and Snow, *Performing the Pilgrims*, 39–40.

105. See my essay "Stepping Back in Time: The Construction of Different Temporal Spaces at Living History Museums in the United States," *Theatre Annual* 57 (2004).

106. Handler and Gable, *New History in an Old Museum*, 70.

107. See Roselee Goldberg, *Performance Art: From Futurism to the Present* (New York: Abrams, 1979); Mel Gordon, ed., *Expressionist Texts* (New York: PAJ, 1986) and *Dada Performance* (New York: PAJ, 1987); John A. Henderson, *The First Avant-Garde,*

1887–1894: Sources of the Modern French Theatre (London: George G. Harrap, 1971); Michael Kirby and Victoria Nes Kirby, eds., *Futurist Performance* (New York: PAJ, 1986); and Annabelle Melzer, *Latest Rage the Big Drum: Dada and Surrealist Performance* (Ann Arbor, MI: UMI Research Press, 1980).

108. In his introduction to *A Dream Play*, Strindberg elaborates on how the play departs from traditional drama governed by order and logic: "Everything can happen. Everything is possible and probable. Time and Space do not exist; on an insignificant basis of reality, the imagination spins, weaving new patterns; a mixture of memories, experiences, free fancies, incongruities, and improvisations. The characters split, double, multiply, evaporate, condense, disperse, and assemble." See *Strindberg: Five Plays*, trans. Harry G. Carlson (Berkeley: University of California Press, 1983), 205–6.

109. An advocate of Brechtian technique, Kushner writes that *Angels in America* "benefits from a pared-down style of presentation, with minimal scenery and scene shifts done rapidly (no blackouts!) employing the cast as well as stagehands—which makes for an actor-driven event, as this must be. The moments of magic—the appearance and disappearance of Mr. Lies and the ghosts, the Book hallucination, and the ending—are to be fully realized, as bits of wonderful *theatrical* illusion—which means it's OK if the wires show, and maybe it's good that they do, but the magic should at the same time be thoroughly amazing" ("Playwright's Notes," in *Angels in America: Millennium Approaches* [New York: Theatre Communications Group, 1992], 5).

110. Bert O. States, "The Actor's Presence," *Acting (Re)Considered: Theories and Practices*, ed. Phillip B. Zarrilli (London: Routledge, 1995), 36–37.

111. W. A. R. Goodwin, *Bruton Parish Church Restored and Its Historic Environment*, quoted in Anderson, *Time Machines*, 30.

112. Jim Bradley, personal interview, 8 June 2000.

113. Deetz, "Sense of Another World," 44; emphasis in original.

114. James Baker, "Haunted by the Pilgrims," in *The Art and Mystery of Historical Archaeology: Essays in Honor of James Deetz*, ed. Anne Elizabeth Yentsch and Mary C. Beaudry (Boca Raton, FL: CRC Press, 1992), 355.

115. Cynthia Gedraitis, personal interview, 15 June 2000.

116. See Strindberg, "Preface," and Émile Zola, "Naturalism and the Stage," in *The Experimental Novel, and Other Essays*, trans. Belle M. Sherman (New York: Cassell, 1893), 719.

117. Snow, *Performing the Pilgrims*, 128.

118. Kirshenblatt-Gimblett, *Destination Culture*, 51.

119. Wallace, "Visiting the Past," 72.

120. William T. Alderson and Shirley Payne Low, *Interpretation of Historic Sites*, 2nd ed., rev. (Nashville: American Association for State and Local History, 1985), 31.

121. Wendy Erisman, "Forward into the Past: The Poetics and Politics of Community in Two Historical Re-Creation Groups" (Ph.D. dissertation, University of Texas at Austin, 1998), 60.

122. Erisman, "Forward into the Past," 61.

123. Erisman, "Forward into the Past," 63.

124. Friedrich Nietzsche, "On the Uses and Disadvantages of History for Life," in *Untimely Meditations*, ed. Daniel Breazeale, trans. R. J. Hollingdale (Cambridge, UK: Cambridge University Press, 1997), 62.

125. Nietzsche, "On the Uses and Disadvantages," 83.

126. For an example of an "unhistory" museum, consider the Museum of Jurassic Technology in Los Angeles, which "remembers" and "monumentalizes" things that never existed; see Lawrence Weschler, "Inhaling the Spore: Field Trip to a Museum of Natural (Un)history," *Harper's* (September 1994); Lawrence Weschler, *Mr. Wilson's Cabinet of Wonder* (New York: Pantheon, 1995); and Scott Magelssen, "The Vulgar Representation of Time: Time Space and Living History Museums," *California State University, Stanislaus, Journal of Research* (Fall 2001).

127. Deleuze and Guattari, *What Is Philosophy?*, 158.

128. Deleuze and Guattari, *What Is Philosophy?*, 159.

129. Deleuze, *Cinema*, 1:46.

A first-person interpreter talks about her garden in the 1627 Pilgrim Village, Plimoth Plantation, June 2000.

A conversation with Thomas Jefferson at the DeWitt Wallace Art Gallery, Colonial Williamsburg, June 2000.

Guy Peartree, a costumed interpreter at Old Sturbridge Village, June 2000.

A third-person costumed interpreter at Hobbamock's Homesite, Plimoth Plantation, June 2000.

The 1627 Pilgrim Village at Plimoth Plantation, as seen from the fort/meetinghouse, June 2000.

A first-person interpreter at Plimoth Plantation's 1627 Pilgrim Village, June 2000.

The sign welcoming visitors to the 1627 Pilgrim Village, Plimoth Plantation, June 2003.

A public audience with Thomas Jefferson, Palace Gardens, Colonial Williamsburg, June 2000.

A public audience with George Washington, Palace Gardens, Colonial Williamsburg, June 2000.

A costumed interpreter milks a cow at Freeman Farm, Old Sturbridge Village, June 2000.

A blacksmith at Jamestown Settlement, June 2000.

An interpreter demonstrates the customs of the American flag at Old Sturbridge Village as costumed participants at the summer day camp look on, June 2003.

Grotelueschen Blacksmith Shop, Old World Wisconsin, July 2001.

A first-person costumed interpreter aboard the Mayflower II, June 2003.

A reenactment of the 1875 funeral of William C. Daum at Living History Farms, June 2001.

An 1875 funeral reenactment at Living History Farms, June 2001.

Historically accurate "road apples" on Duke of Gloucester Street, Colonial Williamsburg, June 2000.

Costumed interpreters portray an eighteenth-century slave, Nero, and a Baptist preacher, Gowan Pamphlet, at a special program at the Robert Carter House, Colonial Williamsburg, June 2000.

A costumed interpreter at Conner Prairie's 1816 Lenape Camp, April 2004.

A costumed hostess demonstrates "long milk" at Skansen, July 2002.

Musket fire at the "Virginia Prepares for War" program, Colonial Williamsburg, June 2000.

A colonial constable, portrayed by historical interpreter John Mitchell, keeps a group of slaves together prior to a reenactment of a slave auction at Colonial Williamsburg on October 15, 1994. Photo by Steve Helber, courtesy AP Photo.

Baseball at Conner Prairie, April 2004.

CHAPTER THREE

~

Performance as Historiography at Living History Museums

The Historiography of Performance

Authenticity and accuracy at living museums are not far-off targets to be gradually approached with continued historiographic rigor, but are produced by living history interpreters each day the museums are open for business. History, it would seem, becomes "real" when it involves costumed characters. Because of an inculcated trust in living interpretation to convey a truthful and accurate picture of life in another time (informed by notions of progress), visitors may temporarily suspend disbelief and cross a threshold into a different time. Living history museums provide for this perception by heavily grounding their performance practices in nineteenth-century modes of naturalism. Naturalism, though, is limited in its potential, and, as I showed in chapter 1, despite being touted by Jay Anderson and others as the epitome of living museum interpretation, there is substantial criticism of first-person interpretation circulating in the field.

Currently, there are several divergent performative practices at living history sites that tactically deviate from the naturalistic ideal by inserting counternarratives into the story. At Plimoth Plantation, the Wampanoag Native interpreters wear seventeenth-century costumes, but speak to visitors about Native issues in the present tense. At Colonial Williamsburg, African-American interpreters discuss events in black history that are absent from the written accounts of the eighteenth century. These and other alternative practices allow a fuller range of pasts and presents at living history sites than is possible by using only the first-person interpretive model. But these practices remain on the margin of living museum interpretation.

Aristotle stressed that art is an imitation of life but that, because it is *not* life, art has the potential to create conclusions that were not or would not otherwise be possible. Living museum environments are uniquely positioned because the spatial dimensions and relationships offered by their environments differ so dramatically from stage theatre. As such, they are the custodians of a tremendous potential to create alternative possibilities and conclusions to those offered by traditional modes of theatre and historiography. These performative institutions already disrupt traditional actor–spectator relationships shaped by the proscenium arch that separates the performance from the viewer and renders passive the latter. The proscenium theatre is what Gilles Deleuze would call an optic, or striated, space:

> Striated space . . . is defined by the requirements of long-distance vision: constancy of orientation, invariance of distance through an interchange of inertial points of reference, interlinkage by immersion in an ambient milieu, constitution of a central perspective.[1]

The image of a historical event behind the arch is a mirror representation of a past moment, reconstructed for view. The spectator is constantly aware of the exact distance between his or her temporal position in the theatre seat and that of the performers on stage. This distance grants the privilege of optically constructing the past from a determined, set viewpoint.

The removal of the proscenium arch in living history performance, though, erases the normal rules of theatre perception. With the absence of the arch, the objective viewpoint is erased and the spectator may become immersed in the milieu without the separating, objective distance. Such a space allows for a different mode of perception—no longer a mirror of reality on the other side of the picture frame, but a total surface, in which a multiplicity of realities may exist. Here, because of the erasure of the boundary between two distinct times, several histories could exist alongside one another: the narrative of the spiritual journey of the Puritans to the New World at Plimoth Plantation may engage and interact with a narrative of ethnic violence committed against Native peoples by the Pilgrims and their descendants, for example.

But museums do not foreground this possibility. They seek to direct the visitor's gaze and condition it with singular narratives, imposed meaning, and scientific contracts. Despite its three-dimentionality, the total living history environment replicates the audience–spectator relationship of the proscenium theatre. Herbert Blau put a finger precisely on the problem. In a talk at the University of Minnesota, he posed a question to the audience: "You want to know where the proscenium is?" he asked, standing on the thrust stage of the auditorium. "It's here, in our own heads," he answered, gripping the sides of his temples and forehead. "It took a long time to establish [the proscenium arch] as a convention of the theatre, and it's going to take a long time to get rid of it."[2]

What is keeping these living history museums from exploring performative possibilities available to them now that the constraints of the proscenium arch have been lifted? Why is it that they are reluctant to break from strict modes of naturalism and realism? Much of the reason lies in what I discussed in chapter 1. Because museum curators and staff place their own work on a trajectory of positivistic development, they stick to their current tack, assuming that, with the discovery of more data, their institutions will progress in a timely manner, getting better, more mature, and more accurate in their presentation of history. Another impeding factor, though, is the living history museum's perception of itself as something *other* than theatre or performance, instead categorizing itself as an outgrowth of history or a mode of pedagogy that, if anything, *borrows* techniques from theatre and performance.

This perception is not, by any means, unanimous. In fact, Stephen Eddy Snow's work has done much to allow living museum professionals to see what they do as theatre. Snow devotes the bulk of *Performing the Pilgrims*, the lengthiest work on the subject of living history performance to date, to arguing that the living interpretation conducted at Plimoth Plantation is a "Theatre of the Pilgrims." He uses specific textual methodologies in order to make a convincing argument that the practices of interpreting the past conducted by Pilgrim interpreters are forms of theatre. These methodologies include a heavy use of late nineteenth-century theatre forms and definitions of acting grounded in Stanislavsky (i.e., inner characterization, beats and units, the stage task, emotion memory, and super-objective), in addition to later theories of Michael Chekhov ("psychological gesture") and Viola Spolin ("space substance exploration").[3] Snow also includes a systematic interrogation of the way outside media discuss Plimoth Plantation using traditional theatre vocabulary, and an anthropological model of theatre based on the social aspects of performance (Schechner, Turner, Goffman, et al.).[4]

Snow often steeps his own narratives in theatrical metaphors to stylistically bolster the hard data of his argument. In his description of the process of becoming a Pilgrim interpreter, he writes of the detail given to trainees through biographical materials, dialect training, and historic accounts as

"Shavian" descriptions of the dramatis personae.[5] In an illustrative anecdote, he equates an interpreter preparing for his day to an actor preparing a role: "Today, just as an actor preparing for a Shakespearean play would do, the interpreter must master a specific seventeenth-century English vernacular, with all its strange and sometimes difficult vowel sounds and diphthongs."[6] Snow, though, fails to historicize realism and naturalism as forms that emerged in the nineteenth century because of specific material conditions. He sees the performative mode at Plimoth not in terms of harking back to nineteenth-century naturalism, but simply the status quo: where we have arrived after getting rid of the elements restricting it from its state of highest fulfillment.

It is clear to theatre theorists and practitioners that Plimoth's interpretive programming *is* theatre. The question remains, if the definition of theatre is broadened to include forms of theatre *outside* of realism and naturalism, such as performance art or happenings, would their validity as theatre be *as* guaranteed? If the nineteenth-century definitions of theatre and performance used by Snow *were* broadened, then perhaps it would be possible to discuss costumed interpretation as mode of representation with a fuller look at the ways in which it intersects with performative practices that have occurred after the turn of the last century. Before that can be addressed, however, we ought to tease out exactly how interpreters believe their work relates to theatre.

The Field

In addition to theatre scholars, many cultural theorists and academics in performance studies, anthropology, and museum studies recognize living history performance as a form of theatre. Outside Snow's work on Plimoth Plantation, however (and even within Plimoth today), this assertion becomes quickly contestable. It is imperative that, in order to determine the limitations of current living history performance practices, we grasp just how *curators* and *interpreters* see what it is they do.

I set out to answer this question by visiting living history museums and asking the participants whether or not they viewed their occupation as theatre. Though I regard the terms as interchangeable, I purposefully chose the word *theatre* instead of *performance* when questioning people in my interviews and deliberately left the term undefined and open-ended. *Theatre* has a more fixed discursive meaning than *performance*, which can cover any human interaction. With the emergence of performance studies as a legitimate scholarly field and the relative vagueness of its definition, it is much easier for individuals to at least agree that living interpretation is "performance," even if not "theatrical." This may be why Snow, when publishing his dissertation in book form, changed the original title from *Theatre of the Pilgrims* to the much safer *Performing the Pilgrims*. As he explains in his introduction:

> My analysis is undertaken from the perspective of performance studies, a new scholarly discipline that widens the definition of performance, focuses on the complexities of cultural performances, and aims to provide some answers. The emergence of this field and the developing theatricality at Plimoth are both manifestations of what anthropologist Clifford Geertz, at the beginning of the 1980s, identified as the "blurring of genres" in the social sciences and the humanities.[7]

As Snow indicates, "performance" is a more appropriate designation, since many people can agree, at least, that there are performance elements to living interpretation at museums like Plimoth Plantation. In my research, however, I sought to avoid agreement, as it tends to mitigate or water down the specific delimitations I was out to ascertain. Anne Bogart holds that uniform agreement is ultimately unhelpful in the movement of thought. She cites work in theatre as an example: "Americans are plagued with the disease of agreement," she argues. "In theatre, we often presume that collaboration means agreement. I believe that too much agreement creates productions with no vitality, no dialectic, no truth."[8] The use of the word *theatre* in my interview questions deliberately provoked a firm stance and prompted disagreement, and it is in the space of disagreement where one can see the inadequacies of traditional understandings of theatre in discussing the performative possibilities in *both* theatre and living history museums.

Naming living history "theatre," or refusing to do so, has material consequences in conditioning how we think about both living history and theatre, and practitioners' definitions of theatre and performance very much inform their perceptions and procedures of living history. I found that *theatre* has a very narrow meaning for participants in the field of living history, even when defined by individuals with a background in theatre. One of the most frequently expressed notions, for instance, is the idea that living history interpretation is not acting or theatre because it doesn't use a script. (This is even the distinction offered in some museum literature in defining the types of interpretation visitors will find in their sites. The 1990 "Visitor's Companion" at Colonial Williamsburg included the following claim: "Character interpreters are not actors; they have no script. Every character is prepared to converse freely on a variety of topics from politics to childbearing. A visit with these character interpreters provides the opportunity to learn about the past from the personal viewpoints of the people who lived it. It is a way for the visitor to talk with the past.")[9]

The absence of a script was the distinction most often cited by the living history participants with whom I spoke. One of the members of the Theatrical Productions Department at Colonial Williamsburg is a case in point. This department's job is to produce the period plays that are performed during the evenings at the museum. She carefully differentiates between the theatrical productions and the first-person interpretation in the historic area. "Theatre is a pretty consistent thing," she says.

> There is a script, there are actors, there is a director, there is a setting and there is a rehearsal process and every time you come to see this presentation, this theatrical presentation, it should be what the audience saw before, and the audience before that. . . . There is a preplanned, rehearsed dialogue that the actors learn, and there is a director saying, "you will do this" and "you'll do that" and "you'll do that." Living history, on the other hand, is just that: it's living, it's breathing, it's free-form. Not that there isn't free-form theatre in avant-garde theatre. But I'm saying the traditional theatrical sense. . . . The actors wouldn't know their lines—they're not actors. . . . It's more of a role-playing, classroom technique than it is a staged theatrical presentation.[10]

Here, the staff member articulates the reasons living history cannot be called theatre: it lacks a script, a director, and repeatability. (Implicit in her response, though, is the suggestion that perhaps living history is much closer to alternative or "avant-garde" forms of theatre than the more traditional mimetic realism it appears to emulate. It is living history's "free-form" nature—its very unrepeatablity—that offers its boldest performative potential.)

For interpreters, the use of a script is, and has been, a persistent gauge for determining whether or not interpretation can be considered theatre. Richard Handler and Eric Gable cite accounts of early costumed hostesses at Colonial Williamsburg describing their roles. When asked in 1946 whether she and her colleagues were actors, Mrs. Albert M. Sneed responded, "Oh no, we don't have any set speech. We just talk as we please more or less."[11] (Sneed's choice of words in describing her performance, *sans* script, as lacking a "set speech" links itself to an age-old distinction: one of the qualitative differences that Aristotle cites between *ritual* and *performance* is the "set speech" Thespis gave the actor when he stepped out of the chorus—thus converting the Dionysian dithyramb into "tragedy" for the first time.)

Carolyn Travers, at Plimoth Plantation, expressed the danger of relying upon a "set speech" when interpreting in the first person: "God help you if you interrupt them!" She continued:

> It's got to sound real here. If something comes up you've never thought of before, you need to think of what you know, what your character would know, how to work it, in the time it takes to answer a question.[12]

Emily James says living historical interpretation goes far beyond what she sees as the limitations of "mastering a script." James, a Jamaican woman who portrays a black slave at Colonial Williamsburg, cited personal responsibility to one's ancestors, which may be fulfilled through costumed interpretation but not, in her perspective, through theatre:

> I wouldn't call it a theatre. It's actually not being in the body of these people, but actually reliving their life or trying to show people what their life was really like, and oftentime I sit by myself and I'm wondering, you know, "I wonder how the ancestors feel. I wonder if I'm representing them well." And the money's important, but it's more than money. What we do here is more than money. Trust me, it's more than money. And American history's not just African history, European history. You have to bring Native American history, African history, and all these together to make it an American story. You know, because it's all linked together. It's interwoven together. . . . It's an important story that needs to be told. And no, I don't really look upon it as theatre. I don't look upon myself as an actor, because after you give the actor the script and they master the script, and that's it. This is more than a script.[13]

James's notion of a personal responsibility toward voicing the history of one's ancestors was echoed by one of the Wampanoag interpreters I spoke with at Hobbamock's Homesite at Plimoth Plantation. I asked her if she would regard the type of interpretation conducted by the Wampanoag Interpretation Program (WIP) as a form of theatre, specifically in relation to the first-person interpretation in the Pilgrim Village. "To a degree," she answered.

> I mean, we do the same things that our ancestors would have throughout the season, and we get a different perspective on life, because of it. So, we kind of, in a way, are being brought back into that time, even though we talk from a modern-day perspective, and we're talking in public, in that manner. So, [it is] in a way, but not as much as them [the Pilgrim interpreters], where we can't get into character as much as they can. Which would be interesting, too.[14]

For Native interpreters, portraying ancestors bears a lot more weight than simply portraying a historical time period. Laura Peers, in her dissertation on Native interpretation at living history museums in the United States and Canada, argues that interpretation of ancestors goes beyond historical interpretation or storytelling because, politically and ethnographically, visitors often perceive Native performers as "playing themselves" versus playing a historical persona. Peers offers a different notion of what it means to perform in a living history museum, especially for Native interpreters. She asks, "To what extent does the work of Native Interpreters, and the addition of their unique perspective on the past, challenge and counteract the hegemonic processes that traditional historical narratives serve?"[15] Peers takes special care in using the phrase "playing one's self" in reference to the performance of Native personae by Native interpreters in the informants she interviewed. "Despite the word 'playing,' they were not exactly acting—and certainly were not 'play-acting'—when they donned historic costume, but . . . they were representing themselves in the present as well as their ancestors in the past."[16]

James Deetz saw many examples of visitors' confusion regarding the Native interpreters' performance (rarely a problem in the 1627 Pilgrim Village with the white interpreters), during his tenure at Plimoth Plantation. One Native interpreter, Steve Figueroa, was asked by a visitor if he was "allowed" to go home at night, to which Figueroa, in order to impress upon this visitor the distinction between his museum job and his outside life, replied, "Yes. I own a car. I go home, have a beer, and watch T.V." On another occasion, writes Deetz, a missionary from India visiting Plimoth Plantation was found trying to convert two of the Native interpreters to Christianity, "believing that he had found, finally, some unreached tribal Indians, suitable subjects for conversion. He was promptly, and firmly, told not to continue and to leave."[17]

Marge Bruchac, who plays Molly Geet, an "Indian doctress" based on an amalgam of historical persons at Old Sturbridge Village, is a consultant with Plimoth Plantation's WIP, as well as at other museums with Native programs, on how to deal with third-person costumed interpretation. She told me that, whereas white interpreters can remove their costume when they are done working and become a twentieth-century white person, distinct from their historical role, the Native interpreters are "at the end of the day . . . still Indian and have to deal with how their friends and neighbors view them." Bruchac told me the story of the son of one of the interpreters at Plimoth who refuses to get involved with the WIP, because "as soon as his school friends got one look at him in a loincloth, he'd never hear the end of it." Interpreters vary in the way they approach their role, Bruchac continued. "Some interpreters put on the costume and deal with it as an interpreter. Others become the costume and become the people they portray." (Bruchac, incidentally, categorically insists that living interpretation is a form of theatre. "I regard this whole place as a big theatre," she told me. "Everybody here is an actor—even the visitors.")[18]

Others with whom I spoke related stories in which new interpreters came to the sites with a theatre background and had a difficult time making the transition to living interpretation, or in extreme cases ended up leaving within a few weeks, because they were so dependent upon a script or stage direction. One individual told me that she found actors to be the *worst* interpreters:

> I've been in this business for fourteen years, and every time I hire an actor, it kills me. I just can't get 'em to get beyond needy, you know? Because their whole training is based on getting a director's direction. I mean, even if you are a theatre major, all of your classes are directed. I mean, you take Acting 101— it's all about doing scenes and directing. It's not about self-motivation and creating off the seat of your pants. I mean, you may do some improvisation to loosen you up, but the reality is actors become so coached that they need coaching, and living history isn't about coaching. Living history is about you being the teacher—just in a different form.[19]

A staff member in Interpretive Program Development at Colonial Williamsburg described a similar situation to me. While a theatrical background is often very useful to an interpreter, he said, "there are actors who are dependent upon having a script." These individuals cannot deal with living interpretation, he says.

> I mean they're really, "Oh my God, I don't have a prepared response for that. I don't know how to handle that." So they really depend on that kind of distance that a proscenium kind of presentation offers. That "the audience is out there, and I'm up here, and I don't have to deal with them. I only have to deal with this and I've got a script to tell me how to deal with it."[20]

Cynthia Gedraitis, a supervisor with the Colonial Interpretation Department at Plimoth Plantation, recalled a recent example of someone who could not make the transition between scripted theatre and first-person interpretation in the Pilgrim Village: "We had a young woman who I hired last fall. She had a very strong theatre background. We were so excited to get her. And she lasted two days, I think." Gedraitis explained what happened.

It was just so different from what she had thought it was. It was completely out of her realm, beyond what she was willing to attempt. And it was a shame to lose her, but we all understood why. It just wasn't for her.[21]

Kate Hill, a third-person interpreter at Old Sturbridge Village, expressed yet another similar sentiment when telling me about new interpreters that join her staff. It's a "rare person" that can make the leap from director-dependent acting to living history, she told me. "We have a few on staff like that, and they're some of the worst. They have to have a script and they can't—It needs to be spontaneous." Hill added, though, that experience with improvisation is beneficial to an interpreter. "I think an improv background is very helpful. That's a wonderful background to have for this, but a traditional theatrical background can be a liability."[22]

Hill, who has a theatre background as a "professional actress," further elaborated the differences she saw between living interpretation and theatre. At Sturbridge, the interpretation is primarily in the third person (though there are some programs, like the Parsonage drawing room and the Parsonage Barn stage presentations, that use first-person interpretation). Primarily, living interpretation at Sturbridge is not theatre, according to Hill, though it *is* a form of acting:

> It's a totally different type of acting. It's more improvisation, which I like, because that's most of my background. The role-playing here has to be a lot more subtle, because, as I always emphasize with the staff, you're depicting real-life characters, not real-life people, but you're trying to show a slice of real life from the 1830s and '40s, and you're trying to show the average person, not the extraordinary. . . . And visitors should be able to come in feeling as if they can talk to you and they're just having a conversation with a real nineteenth-century person.[23]

Hill works with interpreters on their interaction methods and actively discourages them from thinking of what they do as theatrical. In some cases, this is to avoid any discomfort an interpreter might have if they do not bring a performance background to their job: "We're dealing with people who don't have any theatrical experience, and they're petrified of that." But even when interpreters do have theatre experience, she discourages them from applying their craft to their interpretive roles: "We did, in the past, have people that tried to make it more theatrical, and it just fell flat. Because it was too overpowering for most visitors, and it rang too false." Hill clarified the exceptions at the Parsonage Barn Theatre. There is a "performance staff," she explained, which offers seven performances throughout the day's schedule.

These include musical programs, storytelling, and monologues by historic characters. Hill herself is a member of this staff. But, "that's a whole different thing," she argues.

> That's pure acting. The performer is working from a script, whether written down or an outline, and the audience is passive. There is a time limit to a performance, whereas the Parsonage [drawing room] type of role-playing is more fluid.[24]

Alternatively, though in fewer instances, a lack of a script may be a caveat to certain interpreters' belief that living history *is* theatre—that is, for the most part, that costumed interpretation is a form of theatre *despite* not having a script. A staff member at Colonial Williamsburg told me that, while living interpretation at Colonial Williamsburg was a lot like theatre in many ways, it was *unlike* theatre in that it did not have a script. If theatre means "that you're somebody other than you actually are," he reasoned, "then it's clearly theatrical in that sense." But, he continued, it's unlike theatre in some ways: "I mean, very little of what we do is scripted. . . . We just don't have the ability, probably, at this point, to write eight-hour-long scripts covering ten days."[25]

I asked Toni Brennan, a first-person costumed interpreter at Colonial Williamsburg, whether she felt character interpretation at Colonial Williamsburg was theatre. "*I* do," she answered.

> I think some people back away a little bit when you say it's acting and it's theatre. But you're portraying a person that's not yourself. You're wearing clothing of that person and of that time period. You're in a different setting. You're saying words that aren't really your own. You don't have a script, but in a sense, it's theatre.[26]

Finally, there are those practitioners who see no problem with calling living history theatre and do not regard a script as the slightest requisite for the designation (or the lack thereof as being an exception to the rule). Bill Barker, who portrays Thomas Jefferson at Colonial Williamsburg, believes, like his colleague Brennan, that character interpretation is theatre. "No question about it," he responded.

> I don't think there's any question that putting on a costume and portraying a character is theatre. We're becoming someone other than ourselves and speaking lines that we might know they have written. . . . We cannot know exactly what Nero, say, who was Pendleton's slave, wrote, or Billy Lee, Washington's

slave, but we have an idea from the writings of other slaves, from the oral his-tory of other slaves, what they would have thought and what they would have written, so that in itself is very much an element of theatre.[27]

Barker admitted that he started out with "somewhat of a script" when he first came to Williamsburg fifteen years earlier. "And they did give me guide-lines," he added, "and I certainly was allowed to wander off of that, but in the last several years, no, there certainly has been no script."[28]

A first-person interpreter playing Lydia Maria Child at Old Sturbridge Village told me that, while she had no theatre background before coming to work at Sturbridge sixteen years earlier, she has developed as a "historic ham" since she began. "When you're on a stage and performing, that is a form of theatre. . . . And what a stage you have!" When I told her that many indi-viduals responded negatively to the same question, citing the lack of a script, she caviled. "It is in my case, because I'm in a role, and I'm talking to people and bringing them in to it. And that's what you hope that theatre will do."[29]

Though most of the individuals who talked to me referred to a script with very literal connotations, it bears mentioning that there are also broader con-notations to the term *script* or *scripted* in the living history field that go be-yond the mere idea of a document upon which previously determined dia-logue has been recorded for one-time or multiple recitations. A third-person costumed interpreter at Pioneer Village in Salem, Massachusetts, stationed at the Governor's Faire House, criticized museums like Plimoth that use first-person for not focusing as much on education as do third-person sites.

It's like a Disney World for kids, because everything is scripted, and they can't get their questions answered unless it's referring to 1627. Here at Pioneer Vil-lage, we are able to balance education with entertainment for kids. Here, they can do a lot more with education, unlike the type of drama they do at Plimoth Plantation.[30]

Despite Plimoth interpreters' own insistence that Pilgrim role-playing differs from theatre in its lack of script, the Pioneer Village interpreter perceived Plimoth's rigidly structured programming as a scripted mode of performance.

As in the example above, interpreters would often draw distinctions be-tween actor and educator when discussing whether living history was the-atre. The interpreter I spoke with who portrayed George Washington at Colonial Williamsburg described first-person interpretation as a combination of both. "For me it's a mixture of theatrical and educational," he explained, though he shared that many of his colleagues made a definite distinction:

There seems to be a little bit of a line drawn here for some people, [in that] they consider themselves historical interpreters, and, in some small way, resent the people who have theatrical or acting backgrounds. But hey! I'm playing George Washington. It's gotta be convincing, you know? One of the guys with the biggest mouth against the actors here, who wanted to play Washington here, I could never see him doing this.[31]

He added that, though there was a difference in approach and interpretive philosophy at Colonial Williamsburg, which in some cases led to a form of contempt, he would not go as far as to say that this caused any outward conflict:

Everybody here gets along. I don't know of any problem, but there is that little line between actor and historical interpreter. For me, you know, you can be somebody maybe in one of the trades who's a historical interpreter, who explains their trade in a very naturalistic way, and that is the best way to explain that and understand that, you know? But if George Washington or Thomas Jefferson has to get up there, and they have no sense of drama, how interesting is it going to be? That's just the way I feel because I'm coming to it from a theatrical background.[32]

Many third-person interpreters do not regard what they do as theatre, but *do* consider first-person interpretation as theatre. An interpreter at Pioneer Village (an exclusively third-person living history museum) told me his site was not theatre:

Not so much what we do here, since we're not first-person. And my background isn't theatre. My background is as an electrician, so you're probably asking the wrong person, but if it were first-person, along the lines of Plimoth, then I'd say yeah, without hesitation. . . . I mean, in one sense of the word we're just tour guides who hang around in one building all day, just work all summer with projects going on, usually whatever needs doing, as close to 1600-style as possible. But I wouldn't say it's exactly a form of performance. We're certainly in the spotlight, but I wouldn't put it in the same boat.[33]

For that interpreter, and many others, whether interpretation is theatre hinges on the issue of first-person versus third-person. This is not always the case, though, as I learned from another interpreter at the same site, who just as firmly held that third-person can be considered theatre as well:

I mean, obviously, when you're doing first-person, it is [theatre], much more than this. I think [third-person] can be, because even though you're not really talking in their accents or maybe their language, you're trying to maybe act the way they act. You definitely want to know what was going on in their minds, and what they were doing in their lives, so even if you're not talking like them, you can at least give people a very accurate sense of what their lives were like and what they were doing on a daily basis. I think that's how we make up for it, as best as we can.[34]

It was not rare to find that interpreters on the same staff and in the same interpretive positions differed widely in their regard for the theatricality of their role. The range of responses from coworkers at Williamsburg and Sturbridge, above, bears this out. I was therefore not surprised to find a similar divergence in the accounts of hosts and hostesses costumed as nineteenth-century Swedish folk at Skansen in Stockholm.[35] "Do you think this is a type of theatre?" I asked a hostess interpreting an 1860s representation of Oktorps-Gården. "No, no," she responded. "Even with the costumes and historical chores?" I pressed. "No, it isn't."[36] But the very next hostess, at adjacent Ekshärads-Gården, had a very different response to the same question. "Oh, yes, absolutely," she said. "We dress in nice clothes, and we try to make it as real as possible. But I don't think that you necessarily have to act all the time to make it valuable for people who come in here."[37]

The strongest line of reasoning voiced by those opposed or hesitant to calling living interpretation theatre, as indicated above in several of the responses by both curatorial and interpretive staff members, is that interpreters are *educators*, rather than actors. In a promotional video, role-player Kathleen Rawlins discusses what she feels is the function of the interpreter at Plimoth Plantation (again finding it necessary to mention the absence of a script): "I think an interpreter is an educator. In some ways you're an actor. But you are an actor who's been put into an enormous set without a script. . . . But I think much more than an actor it's an educator."[38]

Several practitioners with whom I spoke would not call living history a kind of theatre, but did allow that living museum interpretation was a form of education that uses a number of "theatrical techniques" in order to achieve educational goals. Mark Howell, program manager at Colonial Williamsburg, for instance, says, "I don't see it as theatre as much as an educational technique which just happens to borrow a lot of the technique as an educational process." For Howell, first-person character interpretation is one of many techniques museum educators may use to teach history. In this case, the technique happens to be perceived as a more "cutting-edge" interpretive style—so cutting-edge, in fact, that Williamsburg management works to ensure that the third-person interpreters are not left feeling "pushed out" or un-appreciated.

> We're making sure that they understand that theatrical technique is not sup-planting them, but rather is just another technique. They may use interactive rhetorical questions, for example, as a technique. But theatrical presentation is just another technique to get at the same objective, getting another perspective.[39]

Those who practiced third-person interpretation often distinguished be-tween educator and actor in order to *undermine* the effectiveness of the lat-ter. At the simulation of James Fort at Jamestown Settlement in Virginia, a third-person interpreter in the guardhouse contrasted the techniques he and his fellow staff members used with those of Plimoth Plantation. "You're ac-tually playing the role of one person at that place," he said. "Here, we're in third-person, so we can talk in depth, and I don't have to use King James English or Shakespearean, which is [limiting] because you can't intergage [*sic*] with the person as well. Here, I'm only representing, not acting."[40]

Another Jamestown staff member, interpreting a facsimile of a seventeenth-century ship, the *Discovery*, made a similar observation in connection with nearby Colonial Williamsburg:

> Nobody [here at Jamestown] tries to feign an accent. The people that do that well in Williamsburg are well paid for it. Thomas Jefferson, James Madison, and those folks, Mrs. Southhall—the ones that speak with a British accent. They're trained actors. You know the guy that opens the door for you and counts tickets and so on, he's getting paid $6.50 an hour.[41]

In this instance, the interpreter draws a distinction along meritocratic and economic lines. In his analysis, first-person "character interpreters" are more highly valued, and therefore better remunerated, than third-person inter-preters or other staff members at living history museums.

Esteem is not an uncommon distinction among well-known first-person in-terpreters when it comes to distinguishing between their position and that of other kinds of costumed reenactors: William Sommerfield, who portrays George Washington at Mount Vernon, told NPR's Lynn Neary how he splits up "the business of interpretation." Responding to a caller's confusion between battle reenactors and living history museum interpreters, he explained:

> There are reenactors, the people who are in costume and have weapons and march about, but most often they are not *superlative* presenters. And then we

have people who are generic living history people who do people that are not actually well known. But I would say, with modesty, at the top of the heap we have what I call notable historical interpreters, and all of them are easily recognized by the public.[42]

One can see from this complex range of responses that the question of whether living historical interpretation is theatre prompts confident assertions about the nature of both, even though these same assertions might differ dramatically with those of another interpreter in the building or vegetable garden next-door. For many interpreters, it is clear that, while they do not consider what they do to be theatre, they do believe it constitutes performance, representation, or even "acting," and in this regard "theatre" becomes not so much an inaccurate designator as an *inadequate* one. "Theatre," for these interpreters, denotes scripts, directors, rehearsed lines, and a preprogrammed format; it requires rote memorization skills, collaboration with a director, and little of the personal creativity or improvisational abilities required for living history. In these cases, being "theatrical" retains all of the stereotypical connotations that we associate with the term in common usage: big, emotive, nonrealistic, and something that "rings false" with visitors who want to interact with *real people. Theatrical* means "scripted," "Disney World," and "entertainment."

It would be fair to conclude from the negative feelings about *theatre*—which many interpreters are not shy about expressing—that the term has acquired a connotation in circulation as a dirty word. A Colonial Williamsburg Theatrical Productions staff member spoke to this sentiment. "I think in the field you'll find that people who feel they are true living historians do not want to be associated with theatre—that somehow theatre invalidates . . . what they're doing. And that theatre makes it play. Pretend. Not real."[43] Surprisingly, though, the idea of theatre rendering historic interpretation *less* real was not cited by my interview subjects more than a handful of times. Considering the value living museums place on an authentic simulated environment, it would reasonably follow that the question of the real would be more frequently cited. Much more often, though, it was a matter of efficacy in transmitting a sense of history, or even simply providing good, solid visitor interaction. For theatre's detractors, it just doesn't *work* as well: historians should be educators, not actors.

It is clear, though, that some interpreters are *both*, and they will tell you so. How does one begin to tease out the relationship between acting and educating? Snow uses the term "actor-historian spectrum" when discussing how Plimoth's Pilgrim interpreters understand their roles. Various individuals occupy different sites along a line with pure actor on one end and educator/ historian on the other.[44] He cites examples on either end of the spectrum, but also discusses how some interpreters can synthesize elements of both. A spectrum, however, implies a strict line with a gradual development of one extreme quality with the gradual disappearance of its opposing quality as one moves from one end to the other. To synthesize elements from multiple points on the spectrum would be to simultaneously occupy several points along the line—a situation which begs a less limiting structure.

* * *

The main mode of visitor–interpreter engagement at living history museums—question-and-answer sessions initiated by the visitor—by necessity precludes the use of a script and thus, on a superficial level, differs from the kinds of theatre with which most individuals are familiar (prompting many to conclude that these interpreters are not actors). Another staple of living interpretation, however, is the "presentation." This is when there is a pause in the regular routine visitor–interpreter interaction for the living history staff to stage a "moment" in history, whether conjectural or based on documents of the time. Depending on the institution, these moments can be loosely based around scenarios with a handful of teaching objectives (such as when the colonists periodically "muster" for militia drills in Plimoth's 1627 Village), or they can be just as scripted as a traditional drama.

The 1994 *Publick Times* Estate Auction at Colonial Williamsburg, staged by Christy Coleman and the African-American Interpretations and Presentations program (AAIP), serves as an excellent example and brings out some complex performative issues. The reenactment, one of the most controversial events in Colonial Williamsburg history, recalled a 1773 auction that put up for sale, in addition to land and miscellaneous farming equipment, four black slaves.[45] In the course of the program, two slaves, Lucy and Daniel—married to each other and Lucy expecting a child—were sold to different owners, breaking up the family. This was a facet of slavery that had remained largely untouched by Colonial Williamsburg's interpretive programming.[46] The event was an experiment and had never before been done, for reasons including taste and the offensive subject matter.

According to Anders Greenspan, "Such programs were vital if Colonial Williamsburg was to live up to its social responsibility to present the past as accurately as possible and to demonstrate the ways in which past events influenced modern-day issues such as race relations."[47] In the words of Barbara Kirshenblatt-Gimblett, here was a "respected historic site" that

> tested the threshold of virtuality. Its aim was . . . to mobilize moral outrage and stimulate critical reflection on a shameful aspect of national history. But there was fear that "education could be trivialized into entertainment" or that "the re-creation might be inaccurate or sensationalized for entertainment."[48]

More than two thousand visitors attended the Estate Auction event, in addition to several protesters from civil rights groups, including the National Association for the Advancement of Colored People (NAACP), Southern Christian Leadership Conference, and others who objected to what they viewed as a demoralization of human dignity. Colonial Williamsburg program organizers claimed that the project was meant to give "the tragedy of slavery a human face" and to "remove it from the abstraction of words in a history book."[49] Yet its opponents claimed that the reenactment degraded and trivialized its subject. One Baptist pastor, Dr. Milton A. Reid, felt that displaying "this kind of anguish" for entertainment was "despicable and disgusting."[50] Such a remark highlights the confusion of the community over whether the historic reenactment offered at Colonial Williamsburg fell under the heading of "education" or "entertainment." For Dr. Reid, the answer was the latter. One wonders if his attitude would have changed if there had been more of an effort to promote the slave auction as an educational enterprise (though news of the upcoming auction traveled much faster through word-of-mouth and media commentary than by Williamsburg press releases, often causing widely disparate expectations and considerable misunderstandings, including the rumor that visitors would be able to buy slaves at the auction block and use them for their family vacations).[51] The educational aspects became clear to some of the protesters by the end of the performance: after the show, many of the former antagonists had been converted. Jack Gravely, an NAACP member and one of the most outspoken against the auction, admitted he was wrong about the issue and said that the program had profoundly impacted him.[52]

In a telephone conversation, Christy Coleman (now Matthews), who was chair of the AAIP in 1994 and is now president of the Charles H. Wright Museum of African-American History in Detroit, spoke to me of how extremely difficult it was for her fellow AAIP interpreters trained in first-person interpretation to shift to a more "traditional" theatrical approach. The interpreters experienced extreme emotional exhaustion, said Matthews, much of which was caused by the need to internalize the characters' emotions in the performance, since historically the slaves on the auctioning block were not allowed to speak.[53] When living history programs such as the AAIP move toward embracing traditional theatre practices, the interpreters find the experience of immersing themselves in characters to be psychologically and emotionally more draining than their regular job, because realistically playing a historical character means surrendering most of the agency they maintain in first-person interaction (where there is more room to meta-theatrically comment on the historical situation and moment). In the auction, Matthews said, the slave characters "couldn't wear their interpreter hat. They were used to relying on both theatrical tricks, for suspension of disbelief, and the story told as an interpreter. [During the auction,] they had to dig into their personal psyche. That was a new experience for these people."[54]

Matthews cited this phenomenon as the reason the estate auction was performed only once. Despite perceptions, Matthews stressed, the AAIP did not stop staging the auction for political reasons. On the contrary, many supporters wanted them to restage it. The interpreters at Williamsburg have not returned to the auction, she says, because it was so hard the first time. "The staff didn't want to do it," she replied, "because it was too emotionally draining." This was true for herself, as well. "It took me a year before I could even watch it on tape," said Matthews. She described the reactions of the spectators and public, both positive and negative, as "epiphanous moments," which were also intense for the white interpreters involved in putting on the auction. The participants were taken aback by the emotional responses and by their own emotions. "This was intense," she said. "Past, present, and future all slammed together in one intense moment."[55]

The estate auction was quite powerful and is still a topic of discussion by living history participants today. Its emotional impact was due to the subject matter and the volatile environment in which it was staged, but also because it was firmly grounded in the naturalistic ideal, drawing upon the rules of spectator empathy, conflict, and climax. It is not surprising, notes Bruce McConachie in "Slavery and Authenticity: Performing a Slave Auction at Colonial Williamsburg," that Colonial Williamsburg made this choice. As James Clifford has noted, McConachie reminds us, "Most museums are imbedded in modernist notions of authenticity" and will more than likely default to realistic techniques to "legitimate the 'authenticity' of their performances."[56] McConachie holds, however, that realism is not the most appropriate choice, especially in treating narratives of slave history. Realism tends to disempower spectators' ability to critically question whether what is put before them is the full scope of the historical narrative, rendering them passive.[57]

That is not to say that a different mode of historical interpretation would be less emotionally exhausting. African-American history, say its interpreters, is frequently the most painful and, at times, frustrating subject to treat at historical sites. "It is difficult at best to introduce a topic as controversial as slavery and have people view the exhibits, hear the interpretation and leave the museum with smiles on their faces," writes Rex Ellis. "If they leave the museum laughing and joking, it is possible that the message has not been delivered or that the museum has been in some way misguided or mistaken in the implementation of its interpretive plan."[58]

Missed Opportunities

It is fair to say that the definition into which theatre has been pigeonholed by living history has been around for only a little over one hundred years: naturalistic environments with close attention to observed data, fourth-wall realism, and psychological analysis of character all emerged at the end of the nineteenth century. But symbolism, futurism, Dada, surrealism, absurdism, Epic, and Brechtian practices put the effectiveness and responsibility of realism into question before it was twenty years old. Absent from analysis in the living history field is a broad range of other forms of theatre or acting that could perhaps more appropriately be used to discuss the types of performance used at living history museums. That participants need to look outside these strict definitions for descriptions of what they do, however, is unmistakable.

Stephen Eddy Snow does briefly treat what he posits as a form of Brechtian alienation at Plimoth Plantation. He credits Richard Schechner[59] with pointing out the Brechtian aspects of Pilgrim performance in the way that the visitors are always aware of the interpreters' liminality: both modern-day performers *and* the characters they portray. Pilgrim interpreters, writes Snow, "frequently use visual cues to let the audience know that the performance is, indeed, not real life, but a play."[60] Snow's understanding of Brecht's *Verfremdungseffekt* is to "disallow the audience's suspension of disbelief, so that they would not empathetically engage in the performance but instead, consciously think about it."[61] *Unlike* Brechtian performance, however, writes Snow, the alienation effects come from outside sources penetrating the Pilgrim Village, rather than a willfully employed strategy by the performer. The performers are alienated from their roles by the intrusion of modern elements into their performance space. In Snow's terms, the acting at Plimoth Plantation is an "amateur form of improvisational, naturalistic acting in which the actors are never fully able to identify with their characters because of the alienating influence of the audience and because of their own awareness of educational objectives."[62]

Cary Carson, somewhat awkwardly, has called first-person interpretation at Colonial Williamsburg "performance art."[63] He is right that living history is ill-served by the traditional connotation of the word *theatre*, but to call it *performance art* is a similar misnomer. Performance artists—for example, Robbie McCauley, Karen Finley, Tim Miller, Yoko Ono, and Guillermo Gomez-Peña, to name a few—continually challenge audiences' modes of perception and the comfortable relationship between spectator and performer, often inducing audience anxiety or discomfort by pushing the boundaries of taste, breaking social mores, or not allowing the spectator to fall back on traditional rules of passive observation. Performance art almost always stresses the subjectivity of the performance artist, relegating the presented material to a secondary level while foregrounding the performer's creative act. Living history performance subjugates the performer's history and subjectivity to the background. The subjectivity is not supposed to emerge for visitors, save in an ironic wink to let the audience know he or she is making a connection to the present.

The field's often-cited stipulations of what theatre includes (scripts, director, repeatability) are often based on misperceptions, as they deal largely with a select number of theatre forms associated with the late nineteenth through mid-twentieth centuries. As far as the use of a script is concerned, the amount of time that actors have used scripts, historically, is relatively short and generally confined to Western, text-based theatre. Much of theatre history has pursued the search for "playtexts" that document legitimate theatrical performance. For example, historians regard the origins of Egyptian drama differently depending on whether they consider the hieroglyphics recorded upon the Ikhernofret Stone (c. 1868 B.C.) as the so-called Abydos Passion Play.[64] Michal Kobialka has shown how medieval scholars' readings of monastic documents such as the *Regularis Concordia* (970–73) are informed by a search for the birth of medieval drama in the tenth century.[65] Despite an association between "real" theatre and written dramatic evidence, and an equally formidable "canon" of dramatic literature beginning with Aeschylus, however, Western modes of representation cannot be confined to only those that rely upon a playtext or script. Popular theatre forms such as ancient Roman pantomimes and the Italian commedia dell'arte in the Renaissance were based on loosely constructed scenarios rather than scripted plays,[66] and "street theatre" of the twentieth century (for example, El Teatro Campesino, led by Luis Valdez, in the mid-1960s and Augusto Boal's Theater of the Oppressed in Peru, Argentina, and

Brazil) often improvises.[67] Similarly, stage directors also emerged in the nineteenth century, partly in response to the staging conventions of realism.

When theatre is stabilized as naturalism, it becomes deadened, and the possibilities of thinking about it become quite restricted. In order for theatre not to be considered a "dirty word," its definition must be broadened to include other possibilities besides reliance on a script, director, and fourth-wall acting styles. Until living history interpreters and curators see what they do as theatre and performance *as well as* education and embrace the possibilities allowed by this admission, living museums will continue to follow the path they set for themselves, grounded in conservative, naturalistic practices that prohibit alternative narratives. Living history will continue to be "science" or "teaching," but not art, in Aristotle's generative sense. To paraphrase African-American playwright Suzan-Lori Parks, theatre is a tool to make new realities, in the absence of those that have been erased.

In the currently striated, proscenium mode that living history museums offer as their main form of performance programming, first-person interpreters remain in their fixed time period. The visitors remain in the present and are discouraged from getting caught up in the action and pretending to be of the past themselves. A consistent temporal distance is maintained between performer and spectator, granting the latter the optic privilege of an objective vantage point. Thus, while programming at living history museums does encourage more active learning in the forms of hands-on experimentation, dialogue with interpreters, and visceral immersion in re-created environments, tourist realism still enforces a mode of seeing and consumption of information that more directly echoes the realism of the nineteenth-century proscenium theatre. Holding to the naturalistic ideal prevents the presentation of dynamic temporal spaces at living history sites, spaces where all events are in a state of potential becoming, and in which tourists may move through a *haptic* milieu with "close range" vision.[68]

The singular mode of seeing is perpetuated by the reluctance on the part of museum staff to treat any subject not documented by "reliable sources." This just-the-facts approach to legitimate subjects of interpretation at living history museums leaves out the potential for discourse treating racial oppression, unfair labor practices, and the like.[69] This is especially the case when dealing with undocumented black history at Colonial Williamsburg. In this fabricated environment, the boundary between reality and fiction is so blurred that it would seem that the discussion of other possibilities of history would remain fair game. However, with mimetic realism, there is still an insistence on telling only those stories that may be backed up by material, factual, recorded evidence. Inside George Wythe's restored house at Williamsburg, the white interpreters' reluctance to broach the subject of the undocumented yet widely circulating history of Wythe's affair and "miscegenation" with one of his slaves, Lydia Broadnax, resulting in the birth of a child, prevents discussion of the relationships between master and slave, sexual politics, and deconstruction of the idea of ethical American forefather, not to mention the discussion of what facts are chosen to record in the history books. Was this particular case of eighteenth-century miscegenation an example of a violent, power-laden relationship between a master and slave or a suggestion of a love relationship that supersedes law and breaks the artificially imposed boundaries between blacks and whites in colonial America? These prove to be compelling questions, which is why the black interpreters on the "Other Half" tour bring them up, circumventing the just-the-facts rule maintained by the interpreters inside the house.[70]

In a situation similar to that inside the Wythe House at Williamsburg, Michael Lang cites a 1990 interview with Sara Carnham, supervisor of museum education at Old Sturbridge Village, saying that third-person interpretation is a way to guarantee that staff are discussing only things that are based on documented evidence, rather than making things up: "We refer to our interpretation as third-person interpretation," Carnham says. "We do some specific role playing, but we tell the visitor what they're going to encounter. Our research department is very uncomfortable about having people talking as if they are people from the 1830s on a continual basis. They just don't feel we've got the evidence to support everything that they would say, so it's a fairly controlled situation." Carnham points to the anxiety curators face even in employing more than limited first-person interpretation at Old Sturbridge Village, as they feel that doing so would involve compromising the idea that everything spoken in the village should be backed up by documented evidence.[71]

Therefore, while living history museums physically incorporate staging models that break the performer–spectator relationship of the proscenium theatre, much knowledge remains on the periphery of museum interpretation. The authoritative, institutional voice that constructs the space as one of authentic history manipulates the willing suspension of disbelief of the spectator and allows for only *certain* histories to be voiced. The audience, though no longer constrained to tiered rows of theatre seats, is nonetheless guided into a passive acceptance of specific narratives of America. This is compounded by grouping historical facts into singular, accessible themes, such as social conflict building American character, as emphasized at Old Sturbridge Village, or "The Road to Revolution" at Colonial Williamsburg.

Though thematizing makes history more assimilable for visitors, it limits what may be thought about a time in history by reducing it to a unifying idea that inhibits counternarratives (such as the relationship between George Wythe and Lydia Broadnax). In a procrustean manner, forcing history into predetermined "storylines" (i.e., Colonial Williamsburg's "Becoming Americans" theme) even disallows the voicings of *documented* elements that do not fit into the themes emphasized by museums. For example, the corporal punishment practiced by the Pilgrims to encourage proper behavior by their children will not be found at Plimoth Plantation's Pilgrim Village, even though Plimoth's interpreters are well aware of recorded instances of such practices.[72]

Nor will one find accounts of racial violence in New England at Old Sturbridge Village. Guy Peartree, an African-American interpreter at Old Sturbridge Village, can list several accounts of racial violence that occurred in nineteenth-century New England. "There are stories about [blacks] being attacked by gangs of white people, in the city of Providence . . . things about black people attacking each other. . . . There's the story about white people burning down a school that a woman in Connecticut put together for black girls. They were so angry with this woman for daring to cultivate these black girls that they stormed the school and burned it down."[73] Peartree, though, opts not to discuss these events with visitors because of their "low tolerance" for these aspects:

> [There are] those kinds of stories. But there's a lot of other stuff, too, so I don't dwell on them. . . . I tell them the story about slavery in a kind of . . . a non-horrific way. I just talk about people who let their slaves go free because they thought it was against the law of God. That's how I interpret it, because . . . the characters that . . . I interpret have that story.[74]

The categorization of historical events into themes in order to produce understanding is not, in itself, the main problem. What is unhelpful is the way the naturalistic ideal tends to limit thinking by imposing a state of suspension of disbelief. Disbelief is an important mechanism that allows a thought process.

In the face of what he saw as the passive acceptance of theatrical narrative in theatre, Bertolt Brecht developed the practices of *Verfremdungseffekt*, in which the performer maintains a space of aesthetic distance between the events portrayed on the stage and the spectator. Rather than becoming immersed in the action (which becomes possible through familiar imagery and psychological realism), Brecht believed that the spectator should intentionally be "defamiliarized" with the events on the stage (this differs from the almost-accidental alienation effect Snow describes as "Brechtian" at Plimoth Plantation). If made strange and unfamiliar, the spectator will leave the play thinking of alternative possibilities to the ending. Seeing the familiar pattern of themes, rising action, climax, and denouement allows the spectator to let the thinking be done for him or her. If disbelief is maintained, though, creating a distance that allows intellectual analysis of the characters and events rather than emotional identification, the spectator will see the events on the stage as just one possibility of many and is encouraged to consider alternatives.[75]

Alternatives to the Naturalistic Mode

Adopting theatrical practices that are governed by strict definitions of theatre grounded in the naturalistic ideal prevents the representation of narratives outside a linear, efficient series of actions intended to get across a specific theme or idea. Jean-François Lyotard, responding to the question "What Is the Postmodern?" articulates that the function of realism is to "protect the consciousness from doubt."[76] Therefore, if living history museums restrict their understanding of representational practices to realism, then the space of doubt—which allows intellectual questioning rather than complacent acceptance—is severely compromised. Perhaps the use of representational practices that maintain discomfort and doubt, rather than soothing the consciousness of the visitors, would allow living history museums more potential for responsibly addressing a multiplicity of narratives than would be available in a more restricted definition of *theatre*.

The protests voiced by critics of the 1994 estate auction at Colonial Williamsburg suggest that scripted, naturalistically staged presentations can often turn the interpretation of history (in this case, black history) into a homogenized drama, which threatens to rule out the range of pasts demanded by all groups of onlookers. Such a criticism ought to be considered before curators at Plimoth Plantation begin to adopt programming in Hobbamock's Homesite that would add first-person performance to the strictly third-person site. It is not simply the use of third-person interpretation at the Homesite that makes for dramatic possibilities for historic discussion with visitors (many, indeed most, historic sites use the third person in their programming and rarely treat their visitors to such heady, thought-provoking discourse). The *difference* in interpretive techniques between the Pilgrim Village and the Homesite is what brings visitors out of the reverie induced by suspension of disbelief in the Pilgrim Village and into very real and present problems today, such as the rights museums have in owning and exhibiting

Native ancestral objects and remains. Wampanoag Native interpreters at Plimoth spatially perturb the linear view of history by disallowing their own bodies to be constructed as past objects and foregrounding themselves as present in the here and now. By doing so, the Native interpreters de-center the practices that have pushed the history of the centuries since 1627 to the margin in the rest of the museum.

But, from my conversations with a public relations staff member at Plimoth Plantation, I found that plans are being made to eventually smooth over the distinctions between the first-person Pilgrim Village and third-person Hobbamock's Homesite.[77] In the institution's eye, to feature first-person interpretation at the Homesite would establish continuity or flow between it and the Pilgrim Village and would do a better job at matching the curatorial style and presentation of the more popular Pilgrim Village.

However, adding first-person is an act of norming that would ultimately disenfranchise the Wampanoag Interpretation Program. The power of difference retained by their strict use of the third person would be de-centered and weakened. The contrasts would be smoothed over and the edges made indistinct. This fuzzy space would no longer retain the same potential for addressing these issues. No longer would the visitor's first question be, "Why don't the Wampanoag interpreters speak in first-person?" (to which the interpreter would reply that the Wampanoag language was forced out of usage by white colonizers, that third-person allows a fuller telling of history, that third-person can allow a discussion of the present as well as a multiplicity of pasts, or some similarly thought-provoking answer). Instead, there would simply be an observation that first-person is used in some places in Hobbamock's Homesite and not others. The lack of a question prevents the thinking about possible answers.

Is abandoning first-person, total living-interpretation a viable option, given that it is upheld as the crown jewel of museum interpretation? Third-person would seem to be much more appropriate for covering the multiplicity of pasts surrounding a portrayed period. Though not as "advanced" or as "sexy" a mode of interpretation, as shown in interviews at Williamsburg, Plimoth, Sturbridge, and other sites, third-person interpretation is perhaps more responsible in the interpretation of historic sites in that it allows a distancing between the spectator and the events depicted.

However, third-person is a double-edged sword as well. As Michel de Certeau writes, third-person discourse—that is, discourse in which the subjectivity of the author is erased with the use of the words *I* and *you*—legitimates itself as objective. Objectivity always uses the third person: "Historians have traditionally attempted to transcend the contingency of discursive scenes by establishing 'fact' through strategies of self-effacement or om-niscience."[78] The third person allows discussion of other possibilities, but, in passing up the subjectivity of the first person, it passes itself off as a voice of institutionally affirmed authority. De Certeau describes discourse about the past as having the status of a discourse of the dead, by virtue of its use of the third person:

> The object circulating in it is only the absent, while its meaning is to be a lan-guage shared by the narrator and his or her readers, in other words, by living beings. Whatever is expressed engages a group's communication with itself through this reference to an absent, third party that constitutes its past. The dead are the objective figure of an exchange among the living. They are the *statement* of the discourse which carries them as an object, but in the guise of an interlocution thrown outside of discourse, in the unsaid.[79]

Thus, while first-person interpretation claims "living" history by bringing historic personae to life via role-play, third-person interpretation commodi-fies history as *dead* objects.[80] By ridding discourse of the reference to an *I* ("The Pilgrims arrived here in 1620" vs. "I arrived here in 1620"), third-person interpreters also rid their discourse of the remnants of explicit subjec-tivity, and, as Roland Barthes writes, "No one is there to assume responsibil-ity for the statement."[81] The saving grace, of course, might be that while the writer of history becomes invisible through operating in the third person, the living history interpreter (though lacking a name tag with the museum's logo) is visibly present in the visitor's touristic encounter with the institu-tion's history.

One way to address some of these issues is to forgo privileging one mode of costumed interpretation over the other and focus instead on highlighting *difference* as a defamiliarization strategy. In the example of the WIP's Hob-bamock's Homesite, it is the difference between the third-person Native in-terpreters and the first-person Pilgrims next-door that causes thinking in the present when moving through a simulation of the past. By defamiliarizing the visitor with the subject of interpretation, the visitor would not be able to sus-pend his or her disbelief and feel at home in the environment, as is currently the goal.

The argument has been made that social (or "everyman's") history helps peo-ple to more easily "associate with the past" than would be the case if museums focused exclusively on the elite (as did Colonial Williamsburg prior to the 1970s).[82] Public relations and curatorial staff, however, capitalize on encourag-ing visitors to identify with the more elite subjects of living history. For instance, a flier I received in the mail from Colonial Williamsburg in January 2001 depicted a gowned noblewoman casting a welcoming look over her shoulder to the viewer. She was in the doorway to a lush, warmly lit, eighteenth-century room filled with gilt paintings and similarly dressed people. "Your Party Awaits" was the caption on the front. The invitation was continued on the reverse: "At last. The office party is over, the family gatherings have passed. Your time is finally your own. We've created a party you've been waiting for." The message was that here, at Colonial Williamsburg, one can not only enter the past, but enter it as one of the elite, at home in the splendor of the aristocracy. Likewise, the Colonial Williamsburg gift catalog encourages people to behave like the aristocracy, by purchasing colonial bedroom sets for thousands of dollars or a set of stationery (150 cards and envelopes) for $120.[83]

Would it be as inviting to enter the squalor of a one-room house in which eight members of a "middling sort" family lived in poverty? I imagine that people would rather associate with the elite than with the common people who sleep on dirt floors. Another example: in a public audience with Patrick Henry that I attended in June 2000, Richard Schumann, the character interpreter portraying Henry, addressed his audience as "gentlemen." Rarely would the audience be referred to as anything but social equals or betters. (Except, that is, in cases where they want to incite contempt for the "bad guy" in the narrative. For instance, in another public spectacle, simulating the morning after the gunpowder was secretly removed from Williamsburg's magazine by Lord Dunmore's forces, the governor's agent arrived to address the crowd as "rabble," ordering them to disperse. Of course, his orders were met with delighted "boos".)

I would like to see how audience reception and discussion would change if, rather than encouraging comfort and familiarity, the gentry of the past were made strange. Consider what would happen if the costumed interpreters portraying the wealthy, landed 1 percent of the population showed disdain toward visitors; if they did not invite them into their homes; if they made visible the tensions existing across economic divides. Another way, perhaps more obvious, would be to break the fourth wall of the eighteenth-century environment and point to disparities in values and politics between it and the present. To do so would allow audiences to distance themselves emotionally and, as Brecht would have it, engage in a more intellectual analysis of the conditions portrayed. Rather than forefathers whose choices were informed by the kernels of the American patriotic spirit that have come to fruition in the twenty-first century, these personae may be regarded as subjects without such easily transferable systems of understanding.

Discomfort—making the familiar strange—has the power to make the past not so easily consumable. It is only when the comfort is perturbed that thinking can take place. While studies show that adult museum visitors learn the best when they are comfortable and perceive their surroundings to be supporting environments free from anxiety, fear, and other negative mental states, these same studies indicate that conflict and controversy can prompt adult learners to learn more.[84] Marilyn Hood finds that visitors learn best when challenged with new experiences.[85] Judy Rand emphasizes that museum visitors are entitled to a "Visitors' Bill of Rights" that includes giving individuals choices in, and control over, what they learn and giving them challenges they are confident they can handle.[86] John H. Falk and Lynn D. Dierking similarly state that human beings learn best when the challenges of the task meet their skills.[87]

Ethical issues especially are a "prime topic" for adult learning sessions, finds another study. "Historically, there has been a tendency to avoid challenging participants on emotional and ethical issues in all types of adult education programs," the study's authors wrote, for fear of "treading on the value systems" of the diverse range of visitors to museum sites. "But in doing so, we neglect an essential component of life and learning."[88] Furthermore, according to Ralph Brockett and Roger Hiemstra, "choosing not to address ethical issues can be very costly in terms of personal and institutional reputation, program effectiveness, and long-term success."[89]

Rex Ellis adamantly maintains that museums not shy away from controversy and the lessons it can teach, no matter how much discomfort such controversy might engender:

> Practitioners of history . . . must be knowledgeable, prepared, and willing to confront the controversies that will inevitably arise. Remember, for every ten who complain, there are hundreds who appreciate the risks taken and the dedication required to go the extra mile to tell a full and inclusive story.[90]

Paul A. Shackel, in *Memory in Black and White: Race, Commemoration and the Post-Bellum Landscape*, offers strategies of discomfort museums can adopt in order to challenge the default to simplistic commemoration of the past by celebratory ideologies. These include "making a lesson out of national disgrace" (rarely, if ever, found at U.S. living museums), like that offered by the commemoration of Japanese internment camps at Manzanar National Historic Site near Lone Pine, California, which creates a moral lesson around the memories of racism and tragedy.[91]

To simply match preconceived, nostalgic notions of the past and to cater to the visitor as someone who would fit easily and comfortably into this environment is to discourage consideration of difference. For example, when I visited the preview of the African-American performance of "Spirit Voices" at Colonial Williamsburg's Carter's Grove on June 6, 2000, the leader of the participatory re-creation of a slave gathering welcomed everyone present (a mostly white audience) to this facet of the eighteenth century. But laced within this welcome environment was an illustration of difference: When drawing people out of the audience to dance with the performers, I was singled out as an alien in this environment. "And you," the leader said, grabbing me by the arm, "since you've been writing the whole time we've been singing and talking, we want you up, too!" She brought me to the front of the group of dancers. "That bespectacled fellow over there," others joined in, "that's one of them 'scholars.'" The moment was couched in humor, but it was clear that my "scholarliness" made me different, and this difference was highlighted. Such discomfort precluded a simple, touristic consumption or identification with black slaves of colonial Virginia.

Practices that adhere to realism impose restraints on thinking, while those that prompt discomfort and anxiety open repressed or previously unexplored trajectories of thought. There are representational practices that have, since the late nineteenth century, put the limitations of realism into question. Given these considerations, specific approaches (such as defamiliarization) should be used at living history sites in order to challenge the current modes of performance and engender new ways to think about and represent the past.

Post-Tourists and Living Museum Performance

> It is the actor's role as a witness which determines the kind of relationship a certain production develops with the historical past.
>
> —Freddie Rokem, *Performing History*

> The tourist is involved in nothing less than the rewriting of the economic and political geography of the world.
>
> —Louis Turner and John Ash, *The Golden Hordes*

In *The Tourist: A New Theory of the Leisure Class*, Dean MacCannell argues that setting off certain spaces as more historically significant than the surrounding area helps satisfy the touristic craving for the authentic. The predicament for MacCannell, writing in 1976, is that he saw a disparity between what the tourist wanted (an authentic experience) and what the tourist got at tourist sites: mere *staged* authenticity.[92] MacCannell differenti-

ates the authentic from the simulation by placing the relationship on a continuum. He uses Erving Goffman's front and back regions and the successive
steps in between them[93] to imply that tourist sites' representations are several
steps removed from the authentic experience. There have been shifts since
1976, however. At this particular historical moment, it may be argued along
with Maxine Feifer and John Urry that the new tourist, or "post-tourist," is
no longer a generalized seeker of the authentic, but rather one who delights
in the *inauthenticity* of the normal tourist experience and finds pleasure in the
multiplicity of tourist games.[94]

In this understanding of the relationship between tourist and tourist site,
each visitor brings a completely different set of expectations and perceptions
to a space and continually realigns herself or himself at each new juncture
between the self and the attraction. Even MacCannell has since written that
a growing number of tourists now seek the "hyperreal" or the virtual: a
heightening of "ho-hum" everyday experiences.[95] In his introduction to the
1999 edition of *The Tourist*, he writes that the tourist is no longer a pilgrim
seeking the authentic but more of a Deleuzian nomad.[96] Perhaps, vis-à-vis
Deleuze's essay "Nomad Art: Space," the touristic mode is becoming a movement no longer organized "optically," but one in which the tourist may
become lost "without landmarks in smooth space." Instead of a line of travel
legitimized by points of origin and destination, the touristic mode gives way
to the abstract or haptic "line of variable direction that describes no contour
and delimits no form."[97] Thus, the post-tourist is less inclined to seek the authentic than to play out one or several of the multiplicity of relationships
outside of the binary of tourist and authentic site.

A post-touristic set of games is easily found in the living history environment. Snow, who suggests that visitors to Plimoth Plantation are never fully
able to immerse themselves into a total living environment because of the
outside distractions of radios, video cameras, and the presence of other
tourists, writes that many younger tourists would rather spend their time in
the Pilgrim Village "Pilgrim-baiting" than paying reverential attention to
the costumed interpreters.[98] Plimoth Plantation, where the staff are known
for their rock-solid ability to stay in character, is a worthy target for those
who solicit touristic pleasure by pointing out airplanes to break the illusion
of the seventeenth century. "This is all part of the play—the game—of the
village," writes Snow.[99]

From my conversations with Carolyn Travers and Cynthia Gedraitis, it
seems Pilgrim-baiters (especially teenagers) are especially prone to notice
and vocalize precise detail in historical environments. In these instances,
however, the details are not seen as markers of authenticity, but quite the

opposite: instead of accepting the museum's selection of details as referents for the actual, such visitors point out interpreters' earring holes and anachronistic oral hygiene as reminders of the artificiality of it all.[100]

So, if indeed the new "role-distanced" tourist is savvy enough to realize that the procedures of museums do not correspond to actual reality, then why is there a disparity between this individual and the perceived tourist to which the museums direct their marketing? For whom are the museum literature, brochures, and signage that boast authenticity, accuracy, and the real? If the post-tourist knows better than to invest in simple representation, why is first-person interpretation atop the evolutionary ladder of museum development?

Third-person interpretation, like that of the Wampanoag interpreters at Plimoth and the African-American guides on Williamsburg's Other Half walking tour, seems better equipped, in this regard, because, in addition to allowing discussion of a multiplicity of narratives and foregrounding the present consequences of political or social action, it would circumvent the temptation for Pilgrim-baiting and its equivalent in colonial Virginia or nineteenth-century New England. Can living history institutions more fully explore these possibilities within first-person programming? Or can they embrace the procedures of what John Urry calls "postmodern museums?" These institutions, in Urry's definition, broaden the category of objects deemed worthy of preservation. Instead of the natural history of a period, they treat "alternative" or "vernacular" histories (social, economic, populist, feminist, industrial, etc.). In short, the emphasis is on *histories* (in the plural). Above all, these are museums that show the wires or explain to visitors how the exhibits have been prepared, including the selection process, in order to demonstrate that their narrative of the subjects of display is only one of many possibilities.[101]

Maybe it is not as simple as all that. Because of the museum effect, and the procedures and structures in place by virtue of the scientific contract, it is impossible to portray a *simulation* of history without it automatically *becoming* history, just as Jean Baudrillard says it is impossible to stage a simulation of a hold-up without the same consequences of a real hold-up:

> The network of artificial signs will become inextricably mixed up with the real elements (a policeman will really fire on sight; a client of the bank will faint and die of a heart attack; one will actually pay you a phony ransom), in short, you will immediately find yourself again, without wishing it, in the real, one of whose functions is precisely to devour any attempt at simulation, to reduce everything to the real—that is, to the established order itself.[102]

In the case of authoritative museums, the signifiers do not reference the past, but stand on their own as a category of the real. Therefore, while neither tourists nor post-tourists believe they are seeing the real *past* or that they are time-traveling to a different temporal space, it is easy, without available conditions for unmasking, to simply assume that this is real, trustworthy history.

There are a couple of ways living museums can consider addressing this phenomenon. First of all, Suzan-Lori Parks, a playwright and theorist, reminds us that, since history often fails to remember certain voices, theatre and performance can serve as incubators for new historical events.

> A play is a blueprint of an event: a way of creating and rewriting history through the medium of literature. Since history is a recorded or remembered event, theatre, for me, is the perfect place to "make" history—that is, because so much of African-American history has been unrecorded, dismembered, washed out, one of my tasks as a playwright is to—through literature and the special strange relationship between theatre and real life—locate the ancestral burial ground, dig for bones, find bones, hear the bones sing, write it down.[103]

Because the just-the-facts approach and reality effect disallow treatment of stories repressed, silenced, and relegated to the margins of historical discourse, performative practices may be used to make *new histories* that more appropriately give voice to the marginal than the one currently available in extant records. On stage in performance, as in Gilles Deleuze and Félix Guattari's "creative fabulation,"[104] the events become just as real as those in legitimate histories, and are "ripe for inclusion in the canon of history."[105] As in the case of artificial insemination, Parks writes, the baby is no less human. She plays upon the notion that what happens on stage *becomes* the event.

History, as postmodern historiography teaches, is not of the past, but happens in the present. It is made each time it is enunciated—not a leftover product of the past giving us a window into its reality. Deleuze and Guattari describe the event as not something that happened at one time, and then disappeared, but a perpetual state of possibles that is actualized in the present. Parks recognizes this and suggests that the performance of the history in the present *is* history in the making. Her image of artificial insemination is resonant with the subject of *making* history at living museums: It is practiced in institutional rare-breeds programming as a way of achieving accuracy and authenticity at Plimoth Plantation, Old Sturbridge Village, Colonial Williamsburg, and elsewhere. The artificially inseminated animals are presented as authentic representations of the livestock that populated the villages and farms of the past. The same could be said for artificially inseminated facts.

Rebecca Schneider uses Parks's *The America Play* (in which the character of Abraham Lincoln is played by a black man), as well as Time and Space Theater Limited's 1988 production of *Cross Way Cross* (in which Lincoln is played by a white woman), to illustrate the ways in which "exercises in error" may be used in performance in order to get history "right." In both cases, actors are cast that cannot easily pass as those individuals they represent, forcing the audience to come to terms with those raced and gendered resistances (or even existences) that have not been recognized in historical accounts.[106] In these examples, the material detail supplied in performance counters that which is traditionally recognized as real or authentic.

Living history museums ought to reexamine their institutional goals and historiographic practices. I have argued that the institutional representation of the past as a realistic, living milieu is increasingly divergent from the many modes of visitor reception and play in a post-touristic field. I have also indicated that the African-American and Native American interpretation programs find that disrupting the mainstream histories at living museums with alternative tactics acquaints more visitors with past inequalities and suffering than if they merely relied on historical record. Furthermore, the "fabulated" histories suggested by Parks and Schneider may be more "true" to the lived past than those that may be corroborated by historical record or archaeological evidence. Given these points, it is apparent that the prevailing model of accurately reconstructing the past through the propagation of detail and heavily researched character performance requires further questioning. The notion of a homogenous continuum of time leads us to believe we can fill in the gaps of knowledge, while at the same time obfuscates the fact that we often determine the shape of the jar first, then pick from the multiplicity of shards based on those that fit. Rather than seeking to fill in the gaps based on contours of the extant, can museums limit themselves to pointing toward that which shapes the gaps? That is, can they seek to probe the gaps like de Certeau's historian, who is no longer an empire builder, but one who comes to circulate *around* acquired rationalizations,[107] to point to the gaps as sites of loss—to the contours of those procedures or obstacles that shape what we cannot see, or are not allowed to see?

Again, in order to answer these questions, it is helpful to look at the missed opportunities at the 1994 estate auction at Williamsburg. In the auction, several stories were told and condensed: Lucy and Daniel were sold to different bidders from counties fifty miles apart, their marriage and family (Lucy was pregnant) broken up. Sukey, a laundress, was purchased by her husband, a "free Negro," who was able to outbid a wealthy white landowner. Another slave, a carpenter, was sold to a white bidder along with his tools.

The staged auction lasted about thirty minutes, but by the end, a clear set of important themes and lessons had emerged to tie the stories together:

1. Whites bought and sold blacks like animal property.
2. Sometimes freed blacks could outbid whites to purchase and free enslaved individuals.
3. Sometimes white masters' desire for profit and/or frugality overpowered the bonds between two human beings.

Several other narratives were possible but were unable to be contained in a dramatic presentation that sought to convey selected historical information and ideas in the most immediate and successful way possible. These other potential stories were left out of the narrative because they would not easily fit into the dramatic structure of singular plot, conflict, rising action, and denouement.

The audience picked up on this limitation (though not in the same terms), and subsequent criticism emerged in the postauction talk.[108] Christy Coleman (who had played Lucy in the performance) fielded questions from the audience. "Where do you show African Americans as fighters?" shouted one voice from a contingent of protesters holding banners demanding "Say No to Racist Shows."[109] After repeating the question over the loudspeaker so that the rest in attendance could hear it, Coleman responded that the AAIP shows resistance in *all* of their programming at Colonial Williamsburg, adding that they show both active and passive resistance (passive resistance, she explained, can be in the form of deciding not to work for the master one day, saying "I'm sick," or breaking a hoe): both forms of resistance were important. This answer did not, apparently, appease the dissatisfied spectators. Another question was hurled from the crowd: "Where was that today?"

When considering the events that transpired at the estate auction, it would seem that visitor/spectator expectations were not fully met and that the ethical, performative, and historiographic responsibilities of the museum left something to be desired. It is vital that the largely undocumented history of black oppression and experience continue to be voiced at such an educational institution and historical tourist mecca as Williamsburg. But fully realized discussion and exploration is hardly possible in a living history sound bite like the estate auction. The most potential for coming to terms with this dilemma does not lie in rewriting the script, nor in revisiting the historical documents upon which it was based, but in looking toward, and harnessing, the points at which the conflict was most visible: in the questions from the disenchanted spectators, the anachronistic bodies of the protestors, or *both*.

Drawing upon existing forms of twentieth- and twenty-first-century perform-ance would both make curatorial decisions and agendas visible to spectators and give these same spectators more agency in determining the trajectory of their encounter with history.

* * *

I devote the remaining pages of chapter 3 to the emergent mode of "second-person interpretation," in which the *visitors* pretend to be part of the past. Second-person must be more radically explored than simply letting vis-itors try out a hoe or a colonial musket. Conner Prairie's "Follow the North Star" Underground Railroad living history program is an important step, in that it puts visitors in the roles of fugitive slaves in rural Indiana, but muse-ums can go even further than merely giving visitors generalized roles based on amalgams of individuals found in historic records. What would happen if the visitor were allowed to be George Washington, Myles Standish, or an-other founding father? What if the visitor-performer, given the circumstances and opportunities historically available, made decisions that did not match historical accounts? Could this generate discussion about the way the past is remembered? Second-person is limited in its current form, but retains in its basic structure a potential for programming that may exceed first- and third-person interpretation in historiographic and performative pedagogy.

In order for these shifts to be possible, the living museum visitor must be treated as a post-tourist, rather than as an uninformed naïf stepping into what he or she regards as a convincing portrayal of the past, suspending dis-belief and playing make-believe (the 1994 estate auction audience, includ-ing the protestors, were such post-tourists: they had had a multiplicity of agendas [tourist games] other than, or in addition to, "stepping back in time"). Post-tourists are creative, politically aware individuals, capable of engaging several performances, social exchanges, narratives, and relation-ships simultaneously—far from the image of the wide-eyed rube fresh out of the SUV. In addition, tourists are performers, too, playing the tourist games to which Urry refers and framing their interaction with the professional in-terpreters in terms of how they want to be perceived as much as they do to gather information or be entertained.

The recent emergence of second-person interpretation can be traced to museums' recognition that visitors desire higher levels of participation in the historic environment than mere spectatorship. Researchers find that visitors do not like lectures (which have lately constituted most museums' adult-learning programs) as much as "active-learning" experiences.[110] This is apparent in living museums' promotional material. While the bulk of programming may be devoted to first-person reenactment, with visitors taking the part of present-day interlocutors, museum brochures and travel literature make heavy use of second-person voice in their advertising copy. The summer 2003 ad campaign at Conner Prairie is a good example:

> Live the life of a Farmer in 1886: Can you handle working in the fields, caring for livestock and living in a farmhouse without modern conveniences?
>
> Live the life of a pioneer in 1836: Are you ready to spin your own wool, tend the garden and learn in a one-room schoolhouse?
>
> Live the life of an American Indian in 1836: Are you prepared to dig out your own canoe and barter with a fur trader for goods?[111]

While the language strongly suggests that the visitors will be the ones doing the "living" at this living history site, a regular visit to the museum will still largely mean being an observer, and "living the life" of any of the above characters will be restricted to the mind's eye. In Conner Prairie's evening and winter activities, such as "Follow the North Star," visitors can come to the museum outside the regular business hours to engage in second-person activities, but they still play amalgams of several documented people.[112]

Museums like Old Sturbridge Village in Massachusetts have special buildings devoted to such hands-on activities as school primers, etiquette books, and puzzles—efforts to counter the stuffy "look-but-don't-touch" history of traditional museums. Sturbridge's "SummerShops" program, billed as "five-day adventures in history" for children ages 8–17, allows day-campers to dress up in 1830s New England costume, learn crafts, go to a one-room schoolhouse, do farm chores, and play period games. The $275 registration fee covers the rental of costumes (the campers get to keep their hats or bonnets at the end of the week).[113] Unlike the amalgams at Conner Prairie second-person programs, participants spend a portion of each day "assuming the role of an actual historical character."[114] A third-person interpreter at the Center Meeting House, one of the restored buildings relocated to Sturbridge to comprise its village, said that it is exciting to see how "representational" the village becomes when it is filled with children in costume.[115]

In addition to the multiple second-person craft and youth day-camp activities, there are also those larger activities (games, dinners, square dances) involving visitor/audience participation—a way of encouraging visitors to get "caught up in the action." A growing staple at museums that focus on the nineteenth century (e.g., Old Sturbridge Village, Greenfield Village, Conner Prairie, Living History Farms), for instance, appears to be period baseball, with the appropriate uniforms and rules: clockwise base-running, underhand pitching, and playing to a score of 21. Old Sturbridge Village visitors can cheer in period parlance. "Encouraging cheers in the early 19th century include Capital!, Well struck!, First rate!, Well played!, Cleverly done!, and Huzzah!"[116] Participants are not to swear, but "Consarn it!" or "Thunderation!" are acceptable and historically accurate substitutes. Visitors to the "base ball" games at Conner Prairie can even play ball with the costumed ballplayers, as I found on my visit in April 2004.

Often, too, reenacted historical *events* (as opposed to the generalized common practices like ballgames and square dances) require the occasional crowds or cast of thousands in order to approximate an accurate picture of that which originally transpired. Colonial Williamsburg makes heavy use of crowd participation, much of which simply means that visitors chant lines on the cues given by the first-person reenactors. One June afternoon in 2000 (which was November 7, 1769, in the historic area), I was one of the hundreds of visitors gathered for the "Convening of the General Assembly." After Williamsburg staff handpicked a selection of middle-aged men from the audience to represent the burgesses marching through the gates of the Capitol building to begin that year's session, the crowd was led in a rousing chorus of "Rule Britannia!" in order to demonstrate that, at least in 1769, ties between Virginia and England were still strong. That was Sunday. By Tuesday morning of that week, we had skipped to April 1775, and the crowd was enlisted in protesting the British governor's middle-of-the-night removal of gunpowder from the Public Magazine, and, later that day, we jeered at the burning effigy of Alfred, Lord North, in protest of growing British sanctions.

With the exception of the 1994 estate auction at Colonial Williamsburg, there is no question of compliance with the rules of these games, post-tourist or no. So effective is the tourist realism and family fun, that to go against the grain and voice alternative histories or to question the agenda of the institution (or to assume a character not assigned by the interpretive staff), would make one a spoilsport. The result is that the visitor is placed into an orchestrated narrative of Democracy and Progress. When there is conflict, it is for the purposes of dramatic tension, spun in terms of building the American Character or tempering the American Democratic Spirit. The economic and social status of visitor role-playing is likewise carefully determined. Rarely at Colonial Williamsburg's events are visitors assigned the economic status below the landowning gentry or the "middling sort" (even though these two categories together comprised only a small percentage of the seventeenth-century Virginia Tidewater population). We are referred to collectively as "gentlemen," but do not retain the rights and privileges of that class: at the estate auction, visitors were not permitted to bid (not that they would have wanted to, unless it was in hopes of, perhaps, freeing a purchased slave). The spectator therefore becomes neutralized and cannot participate in anything resembling what Giorgio Agamben would call a personal history, but rather is absorbed into the sanctioned "state" history of the institution.[117] In Colonial Williamsburg's case, this history is the popular narratives of "Road to Revolution" and "Becoming Americans."

In short, the rules and delineated boundaries of living museums curtail the number of tourist practices and performance possibilities available to visitors. The window is narrowest at Plimoth Plantation, where visitors are explicitly told what is expected of them in the map and guide that comes with admission: "We ask that visitors not wear costumes of any type to avoid confusion with our role players."[118] In other words, visitors are *not* to pretend to be denizens to the past, as it would disrupt the carefully constructed environment into which they are "stepping back" (at other museums, the no-costume rule is bent or is allowed some range of play).[119] Plimoth visitors can try things out (sweep a floor, churn some butter), but always as *themselves*.

The rule might sound cut-and-dried. But, as we know, forgoing costumes of *any* type is impossible in the new age of performance studies, where any clothing choice is a specific act of identity construction and enactment. And visitors may unintentionally blur the distinction between themselves and museum staff. What happens when a busload of Mennonites show up at Plymouth, as happened when I was there in the summer of 2003? The dresses of the sectarian cultural group, especially among the Mennonite women, bear a striking resemblance to those of the Pilgrim women of the seventeenth century. While I did not witness such confusion, I can imagine a visitor approaching a Mennonite and asking about their voyage across the Atlantic on the *Mayflower*.

Second-person programming sticks closely to this formula of assigning visitors the role of largely undocumented "could-have-been" denizens of history. It is therefore limited to generalized craft demonstrations and conjectural daily activities (whether for play, for work, or for military drilling). These practices lack *narrative* or, at best, relegate narrative to the background or the abstract. Activities in which visitors get to participate most fully (i.e., crafts, chores) are not really *events*, per se, but a kind of social history filler—conjectural details that fill in the gaps *between* the events—what Roland Barthes, in "The Reality Effect," called the "interstices" of history.[120]

When second-person *is* a part of an enactment of a lived historical event, it never gives visitors the roles of the protagonists of history. Visitors, even when role-playing, are still multiple steps removed from playing a developed character. In other words, they either "play" present characters engaging past characters in dialogue or, in a demonstration, play an abstract "character" for a professional reenactor who assigns them a role but who does not (as a character) recognize them as one of his or her own, except as a hypothetical in an exchange that is mutually understood between the professional reenactor and layperson visitor as an exercise. The visitor-performers are still from the present, lacking a costume, and participating in a demonstration—not pretending to be from the past.

This is a grave situation: it reinforces the idea that the social history material concerning the lives and activities of women, peasants, children, slaves, and the "middling sort" (shopkeepers and professionals) are of a class of historical material that anyone can do, but that there are still historical events important enough that they should be left only to professionals. In other words, a visitor can step into the role of a faceless, basket-weaving supernumerary from the nineteenth century, but never, within the jurisdiction of the institution, try out being Patrick Henry or George (or Martha) Washington, or a "Pilgrim Father" like Myles Standish or Governor Bradford. So, even though social history's attempts to fill in the "rest of the story" have been in place since the late 1960s, there is no doubt, in the institutions' minds, what the "real" history is when it comes to performance.

To be sure, the boundaries between the past of the museum environment and the present the visitors bring with them are important, and indeed necessary to establish and police the historiographic operation. Freddie Rokem begins his book *Performing History: Theatrical Representations of the Past in Contemporary Theatre* with this same axiom.

> There is room for historians only in a world where it is possible to establish relations between the past and the present. And history can be performed, in the world and on the theatrical stage too, when different structures of time (besides the daily reappearance of the sun), can be distinguished, making it possible to ask not only if the things that appear again [cf. Horatio's line in Act I of *Hamlet*] are natural phenomena but if they are triggered by some kind of agency, creating a pattern, not just a mathematical repetition.[121]

Without an explicit recognition of difference between specific categories of time, a very different mode of historical production would be required—one that would necessitate an as-yet nonexistent kind and structure of museum institution.

An alternative model of second-person can be employed at existing museums while still maintaining the helpful separation of past and present. The trick is to give visitors historic voice within museum-sanctioned tourist practices that allow for both more flexibility than strict one-to-one correspondence between reenactment and historic document and a multiplicity of possible dialogues outside the chosen thematic groupings of current programs.

If second-person programming is to be successful in truly allowing visitors at living museum sites to glean a full scope of the political, racial, and socioeconomic opportunities and limitations of a past milieu, they should be given the roles of documented historic personages (developed characters) in singular, stageable situations where they are presented period information and led to make choices based on their understanding of their role and the sensibilities, relationships, ethics, knowledge, curiosity, and creativity unique to each individual. The outcome of the performance should hinge on these choices, which would generate discussion and, in turn, further restagings.

Rather than starting from scratch, it would be advantageous to start by taking account of what museums already have. At the most fundamental level is the museum industry's commitment to performance in its programming, whether role-playing or noncharacter interpretation. This is promising. Theatre and performance are powerful historiographic tools. If they were not, the stakes would be considerably lower when discussing living history as historiographic operation. As Rokem puts it, theatre more *forcefully* participates in historiographic procedures than other forms of discourse.[122]

For Rokem, the element of live performance that separates it from other historiographic discourses and makes it a more forceful mode of creating and disseminating narratives about the past is the very presence of the human performer: "It is the actor's role as a witness which determines the kind of relationship a certain production develops with the historical past."[123] This is a significant point, as it shifts the primary emphasis away from the document and the archive. It would follow that the *live performer* at living museums, despite the institutions' heavy emphasis on the historic sources in their research and their literature, is what makes the history at living museums compelling to visitors. There are multiple reasons for this, but for Rokem the inciting factor is the actor's ability to tap into and manipulate "theatrical energies":

> They perform the historical figures from the past on the stage, relying on different kinds of theatrical energies. . . . It refers to the restorative potentials of the theatre in trying to counteract the destructive forces of history. The creative energies of the theatre not only are central for the impact of a performance on its spectators, but are crucial for the ways in which such a performance confronts the issues of collective identity and transgression.[124]

The key notions here are that of portraying "historical figures" from the past and the "restorative potential" of this portrayal in redressing some of the negative consequences of the events in our "collective" past. Allowing the visitor to step into the role of a historical figure, and allowing him or her to make decisions in the present when faced with possible choices that would have been available to that figure, would open up heretofore unknown possibilities of rich historical discourse and indeed help to confront "issues of collective identity and transgression." This potential is dissipated when the role of the historical figure is played by a museum employee improvising to a set agenda of the institution: the spectator-visitors are disempowered and unable to participate directly in the historiographic discourse.

The disempowerment stems from the scripted status of the enactment. Only a single, agreed-upon ending is ever possible, and thus, the possibilities for discourse are limited before the enactment is even performed. The creative potential, though, as we know in theatre, is in the rehearsal, as it were, and not in the final performance. In other words, it is in the stages where the end product is not known that the possibilities are infinite. This is especially apparent when the product of the performance does not do justice to the history of the people in the audience. To paraphrase Augusto Boal, the non-elite in most of the world abhors a "closed" theatre, presenting images of a finished world, complete with the values the spectators are expected to passively accept.[125] The theatre of the oppressed, who still do not *know* what their world is like, will exist perpetually in rehearsal. (After formulating his Theatre of the Oppressed in the early 1970s, Boal has worked outside Latin America in more affluent, Westernized, bourgeois communities and has adapted his "social therapy" techniques to answer to more de-centered and ingrained forms of oppression such as loneliness and alienation inculcated by societal values and the media, or "cops in the head.")[126]

Second-person interpretation cannot effectively tap into this potential if it is limited to the "amalgam" or "composite" characters of the past or to the unnamed individuals that fill the interstices of history. The visitor should be allowed to step into the role of those historic personages that are legitimized as real players in historic discourse—not that these people were any more valuable or important than the unrecorded individuals, but they have been, for better or for worse, irrevocably assigned that status by historians. As a revisionist, it pains me to come to this conclusion. But, with the exception of sites that began as museums of "everyman's history" (e.g., Sturbridge, Living History Farms), even post-tourists come to these places in order to encounter the *extra*ordinary individuals of history—the ones they learned about in school, who inhabit and star in their collective mythology.

The similarity between the performed event and the original event is not as important as the *relationship* between the two, to again return to Rokem's statement. The authenticity, in this case, lies not in the accuracy of the depiction, but rather has to do with the theatrical energies and their intensities: the actor, as hyper-historian, "summons a certain kind of energy, which validates the authenticity of the events that are depicted on the stage as historical events."[127] "Errors" or differences between the lived event and its representation can actually be much more productive to discourse than blindly following the "script." Rebecca Schneider's use of "exercises in error" as a means of "getting something right" is a good example, and Rokem treats several instances of Shoah (Holocaust) theatre that exercise subjective and/or abstract representations of the past in order to challenge the ingrained, hegemonic perceptions of it:

> Theatrical performances of and about history reflect complex ideological issues concerning deeply rooted national identities and subjectivities and power structures and can in some cases be seen as a willful resistance to and critique of the established or hegemonic, sometimes even stereotypical, perceptions of the past. They can also provide a direct critique of certain historical figures and their actions. When we move from these forms of ideological critique to blunt revisionism, the moral issues concerning the performances of history become a burning issue. As we know, it is usually the victors, not the victims, who write history. The question is to what extent this is true of those who "perform" it on the stage as well.[128]

Living museums ought to fully embrace the possibilities inherent in playing against the grain of the historic document. The situations must be collected from what we know about the past. But they can be altered, rearranged, and conflated with other histories, especially oral histories and extra-archival resources, to suit the purposes of the exercise and allow for breathing room. The way the enactment proceeds should not be forced to conform to the same trajectory as the archival transcription of it (itself, needless to say, a far-from-infallible, far-from-objective source). Instead, echoing Suzan-Lori Parks, this kind of environmental theatre should be treated as an incubator for new historical events that are just as authentic as those that happened to be written down. "The baby" as per Parks's essay, would be "no less human."[129]

It is not the story or the narrative that is as important as the actor as a *witness* in determining that relationship.[130] At the same time, this does not exempt the facilitators, programmers, and curators from being familiar with the documents upon which the reenactment is based. In fact, it requires the opposite: facilitators must have a rigorous grasp of the archive—certainly one that is no less rigorous than is currently the norm at top institutions—because they must be able to discuss with visitors the historic networks of social and political relationships and obstacles that might need to be taken into account when suggesting change or specific action. They must be aware of documented statements on matters that would be relevant to possible scenarios and be able to compare and contrast *new* outcomes with the historically lived ones.

In addition to museums' fundamental commitment to performance as a building block, the other encouraging element is that one needn't look far in order to find existing models of second-person interpretation that begin to approach what I propose. The available forms of second-person described above, while limited in their current form, can be pushed into new territory. Non–living museums and interpretive centers are doing similar things already: for example, it has been implemented at the newly opened Constitution Center in Philadelphia, where visitors can not only sign their name to the Constitution, but can dissent and write why. They can also be sworn in as president of the United States. Both contain the implicit choice to accept or critique the principles upon which the nation was supposedly founded. The closest model to what I propose is in the U.S. Supreme Court interpretive exhibit, where one can sit on a replica of the Supreme Court bench, listen to historic cases and issue one's own opinion—then see if it matched that of the Court in the actual case.[131] But how would this look at living museums?

Perhaps the most productive applications of second-person living museum programming can draw techniques from the workshops facilitated by Augusto Boal and those who have adapted his work in Europe and North America. "Participatory Theatre as an agent of change is a very familiar concept to practitioners of Augusto Boal's techniques," writes Susan Kattwinkel. "Not only do spectators control the direction of performance but also the theatrical goal is one of efficacy, in which the creation and strengthening of communities is used to change society."[132]

In his "Forum Theatre," Boal invites spectators onto the stage to intervene, participate in, and change the action of a "reconstructed incident," purposefully blurring and erasing the boundaries between spectator and actor maintained in traditional theatre (and living museums) and granting the "spect-actor" the ability to take the representation into her or his own hands. Boal breaks the process into steps: The protagonist (a member of the company) selects from the group of spectators the individuals who will participate in the reconstruction of the incident. He or she provides them with in-struction and the direction needed to act out the scenario. The participants enact it. Then, they repeat the exercise, this time encouraging the new protagonist to fight against the oppression inherent in the relationship. The protagonist fights to impose his or her own will and ideas. This rejection of the "cathartic" nature of accepting the results of the first drama as the only possible outcome allows the protagonist to resist in "real life," having rehearsed it on the stage.[133]

The exercise is most successful, suggests Boal, when the spectators and participants do not know whether the scenario chosen for enactment has been based on a recent event in a newspaper or a historical event from a book. Not knowing the actual outcome of that which they reconstruct, the spectators will not automatically accept a given outcome without understanding other possibilities. Instead, maintains Boal, they will adopt a critical, "comparative" attitude toward the choices and events before them, comparing the historical situation and inequalities to their own lives.[134] This last point is crucial. Any immersive experience in an environment that references the past can be educational, but if it does not offer strategies for conducting one's behavior and working for justice in the present, it falls short.

Michel-Rolph Trouillot exquisitely puts it as follows: while historiographic representation has its own problematic cyclical self-determinacy ("By packaging events within temporal sequences, commemorations adorn the past with certainty: the proof of the happening is in the cyclical inevitability of its celebration"), historical accounts do need to establish some relation to knowledge about the past. But, if engaging the representation gives the viewer some understanding of injustice in the past without an accompanying suggestion of how to approach its current consequences, we should reserve our approval. It is easy, for instance, to denounce slavery in the twenty-first century, but unless its legacy in a racist present is denounced, the representation has lost an opportunity to "increase our ardor for struggles against discrimination."[135]

It is most fitting, in offering a hypothetical example of how such an enactment would look, to consider the 1994 estate auction. I approach the illustration as what Boal called a "reconstructed event" as part of his Forum Theatre, using the term *spectactor* for the museum visitors empowered to make choices and change the action through second-person interpretation. Perhaps it could look something like the following:

1. The facilitators (professional costumed interpreters) present the scenario: portions of the estates of Francis Wilkins, William Kennan (deceased), William Byrd III, Ralph Womely Jr. (deceased), and John

Robinson, Esq., are up for sale in front of Wetherburn's Tavern on Duke of Gloucester Street in order to satisfy court-ordered debt settlements. Characters include the auctioneer, the sheriff, the clerk, the slaves (Sukey, a laundress, from the estate of Mr. Kennan; Billy, a carpenter, from the estate of Mr. Byrd, to be sold with his tools; Daniel, to be sold with his livery, and the pregnant Lucy, house servants from the estate of Mr. Womely), the bidders (Mr. Warren, Mr. Taylowe, Mr. Hubbard, Mr. Page, Mr. Allison, Mr. Nelson, Mr. Prentiss, and John Ashby—a free Negro, the husband of Sukey), and every member of the audience.

2. The "rules" of the performance are established by the auctioning of items on the bill: three parcels of land, linens, tools of husbandry, and so on.

3. The first enslaved individuals are brought to the block. Bidding begins. At any time from this point, any visitor may intervene to stop the action. The facilitators would then invite this individual to the stage to replace (a) the slaves on the block, (b) the bidders, (c) the sheriff, or (d) the auctioneer.

4. The "reconstructed incident" proceeds, this time with spectactors in the roles of the event and making choices based on the situation. Do they (a) continue as before, following the "rules," or (b) protest the situation and look for ways to enact more just actions?

5. Discuss: Who is more empowered to make these choices? The audience? The bidders? The bailiff? Who is the least empowered? What other possibilities or choices were available? How could extreme measures be taken? Could the spectators rush the block and liberate the slaves? Could another audience member have offered to furnish whatever extra funds were needed to help Ashby free his wife, or to help him purchase both Daniel and Lucy? To mobilize political action to try to end slavery as an institution? What historical factors presented obstacles? Racism? The status quo? Deadlocks between economic and ethical factors (Thomas Jefferson, himself a slave owner and the father of illegitimate children by his slave Sally Hemmings, compared the institution to gripping a wolf by the ears: "You cannot let go, yet cannot keep holding on forever")? If the spectators continue as before, why? Did they feel disempowered as perpetuators of the system? Did change seem impossible? What connections can be drawn to the present (i.e., how do present sensibilities, current events, and attitudes inform choices made in the reconstructed incident, and how would these have differed in the eighteenth century)?

6. Reenact the scene from the same place, substituting different spectactors or different characters. What new networks of possibilities emerge? What new discussions are generated?

7. Inform the participants of the outcomes of the auction as transcribed in the newspaper account: Ashby secured his wife, Prentiss won the bid for Billy, Taylowe outbid Allison for Daniel but then lost the bid for Lucy to Nelson (visitors not knowing the end is important—to know the end might limit thinking of other possibilities. Just as the spectators and participants in Boal's theatre are not intimately acquainted with the documents upon which their scenarios are based, living museum visitors might be more prone to adopt a critical, comparative attitude when faced with one possibility out of several that are known to them. That is, they will not simply wait to find out what actually happened).[136] What was different? The same? What emotions does this generate? How might Virginia, America, or the world be different today if events had actually transpired the same ways as the reconstructed incident?

The Williamsburg slave auction is one of many possibilities where past injustices can be brought to light through second-person forum interpretation. Another would be, for instance, a scenario where land is being forcefully taken away from Native peoples. Such events are readily available in the archives of living museums starting with Plimoth and Jamestown/Yorktown in Virginia and extending chronologically to the nineteenth-century sites and geographically to the westernmost American living museums. If and when the second-person interpreters *change* history—making something different from what originally transpired—freeing the slaves, for instance, they will have achieved part of what current programming cannot do: they have been empowered to take charge of the history as protagonists. The visitors will no longer have to cede power and agency in their experience of history to the museum professionals.

The traditional leaning toward more scripted, "finished" theatre can disempower the actors as much as the spectators, as was the case with the 1994 auction, when the interpreters who could normally interact with visitors with ease suddenly found that it was much more difficult and exhausting without their "interpreter hat," because they had to internalize the emotions they sought to represent. By shifting to programming that would break up the action to allow for voicings of opinion and emotion in the present, the emotional strain of keeping quiet in the face of historical injustice could be redressed.

Through examining the other possibilities of how events of the past could have turned out via second-person interpretation, visitors may be reminded that history did not simply unfold in order to conform to some divine or patriotic plan (e.g., Manifest Destiny), nor have events been remembered objectively without historians making explicit choices of what to record and how. Events are remembered depending on whether they can be made to fit templates like Manifest Destiny. But, just as in the case of the estate auction, there have been other possibilities available.

Is this a radical plan? Yes and no. Yes, in that, to those who hold that first-person costumed interpretation is at the top of the evolutionary ladder of living museum programming, this might seem like a move in the wrong direction. No, in that the elements of this post-touristic second-person programming already exist in the field, albeit not yet assembled in this exact manner.

An approach like Forum Theatre, however, may work better in theory than in practice, and there are several concerns that would need to be addressed before anything like it could be successfully implemented at living museums. First of all, Boalian concepts like this have proven difficult to transfer to North American venues, since the politics and systems of oppression here (e.g., segregation) do not parallel those of Boal's initial populations in Brazil, Argentina, and Chile in the 1960s and 1970s:

> The postmodern notion of the exploded and multiple self has replaced the humanist singular and unified self. When Boal's techniques—particularly the more reductive exercises of image theatre and the structure of forum theatre which require relative simplicity to accommodate interventions—are placed within these constructed frameworks of invisible power dynamics and fragmented identity politics, they are somewhat incapacitated and potentially read as dogmatic and shallow.[137]

Mady Schutzman writes that affluent Western participants in Boalian workshops often possess a liminality that allows them to slip between identifying with oppressors and the oppressed. She introduces the concepts of multiple protagonists occupying "oppressive territory," emphasizing spectra of oppressions in order to displace "power dualisms" that often threaten to oversimplify the context of Western political and social systems.[138] "Boal's forum theatre demands distillation into symbolic social roles to facilitate its most critical aspect—spectator intervention," Schutzman writes. "Broader societal solutions cannot be explored in forum."[139] To illustrate the disparity, she offers the example of a situation in which a minority patient does not receive proper medical care. Performing options "at the moment of discrimination" might offer some possibilities for participants in this situation, but there is no possibility to develop and enact "more complex and cooperative schemes to approach the hospital administration, the board of directors, the financiers, or the massive bureaucratic and political apparatus that preserve racism."[140]

Transferring Boal's practices to a historical interpretation of Colonial Virginia, in this case, might actually be easier than it would be to contemporary Western political contexts, because the historic forms of oppression are much more easily identified and embodied (it is easier to perform a site of oppression embodied in a Virginian slave owner than a modern rhizomatic economic bureaucracy). But when it comes to making connections in the present—perhaps attempting to enact parallel situations today—the multifarious nature of oppression would call for the much more complex practices elaborated by Schutzman and other practitioners.[141]

Second, it goes without saying that some may say this is not "real" history, since it is grounded in conjecture, improvisation, and fast-and-loose conflation between past knowledge and present ideas, rather than in the objective archive. This critique would extend from the emphasis the industry currently places on the document, and the fact that authenticity is tied almost inextricably to the just-the-facts approach to living interpretation. This approach, though, is already being challenged by programs within living museums like the Native Wampanoag interpreters at Plimoth and Williamsburg's Other Half tour. In my proposed plan, sharing the documents is part of the process, too, especially when citing how the events have been recorded at the end of the exercise, but only *after* the visitors have grappled with the range of issues and possibilities when confronted with the scenarios and have made a series of choices themselves. If living museums are distinguished from other institutions by their use of performance as historiographic operation, then the sanctity of the document must be deemphasized and more legitimacy ought to be assigned to performance practices in establishing authenticity at these sites.

Third, programmers might be made uncomfortable by the emphasis in this kind of programming on those events and moments in history that center on what we regard today as controversy, injustice, violence, and suffering. This would change the tone considerably from the regular business of history museums, which tends to *celebrate* the past, not point out its atrocities. This, too, is not exactly a new idea, as the 1994 estate auction sought to address the same histories. In that case, these efforts should continue and expand. For decades, living museums have been criticized by Schlereth, Wallace, Huxtable, and many others for omissions of the darker events of the past. Warren Leon and Margaret Piatt add "violence, vigilantism, family discord, labor conflict, minority political movements, and other evidence of conflict" to the list of neglected historical material.[142]

Kevin Walsh reserves the term *postmoral* for those institutions that "neuter" their reproductions of horrible or tragic ordeals of the past.[143] Indeed, all history museums in Walsh's account are guilty of an attack on democracy and people's understanding of their "places" in it: according to Walsh, history museums trivialize the past by separating it out as distant and "other" than the present.[144] "A true democracy," he says, "will offer many and varied forms of museum service. The danger is that we are in fact moving towards an homogenized monopoly of form which in itself is an attack on democracy."[145] Walsh's prescription is to look to those museums that are local in their democracy and public service and which teach their own people about *their* place. He cites emergent "eco-museums" and interactive video programs: "Essentially, interactive video offers the potential for greater democracy in access to information about the past and can allow people to develop their own cognitive maps and thus, a sense of place."[146] Though Walsh is getting at the same kinds of ideas of visitor agency, I would hope that the second-person living history model I propose could go much further than interactive video.

Fourth, the success of the operation relies on engaged, imaginative, "posttouristic" visitors and their willingness to participate. True, these visitors may not always be around and therefore are not to be taken for granted. Culture, background, comfort level, and shyness, as well as many other elements, are factors just as they are in the classroom. For instance, living history programmers have found that native Minnesotans (like myself), shy and often passive-aggressive, do not like interacting with character interpreters. At least that's what accounts and statistics would indicate: a study conducted by the Minnesota Historical Society about its premier living history site, Fort Snelling (a museum depicting the nineteenth-century outpost of the same name), showed that respondents who had not yet been to the fort "don't like the idea of costumed guides interacting with the public. . . . They ask, 'Who are those strange people dressed in strange clothes, and do I have to talk to them?'" John Crippen, director of Metro-Area historic sites says that once people visit, they "warm to the idea," but "the site also needs noncostumed guides for people who don't think they want to play act in the 1800s."[147] Site Manager Stephen Osman and Assistant Site Manager Thomas Shaw told me as much when I interviewed them separately two years earlier.[148]

Finally, what if museums say, "This is not what visitors want?" Frankly, this is the most irresponsible argument—if not the weakest. Museums have been instrumental in producing and shaping visitor desire from the start, not the other way around. According to Tony Bennett, the political purposes behind developing public museums in the nineteenth century were to bring citizens to a higher cultural consciousness. It was based on the scientific assumption that well-planned civic additions of libraries, parks, and museums could divert those who would otherwise tend toward drunken idleness. The museum, in polar opposition to the amusement park and the fairgrounds, Bennett writes, was a Foucaultian site of power—a site of confinement and discipline that would rein in these nineteenth-century incontinent impulses.[149]

There is precedent, then, for museums to *create* audience expectations—not conform to them. When they deny this responsibility, they pander to the lowest common denominator, rather than pushing the envelope. Allowing public opinion to shape what is exhibited in museums can have grave consequences. (Witness the *Enola Gay* fiasco at the Smithsonian's Air and Space Museum in the 1990s: the exhibit planned for the historic B-29 bomber had included a large panoramic room showing only the devastation that occurred when the bomb was dropped on Hiroshima and, elsewhere, signage asking visitors to consider, in light of the exhibited evidence, if the bombing was justified, i.e., would a Japanese invasion of the United States have been certain? Public critiques ranging from the "poor taste" of the exhibit to what some veterans, conservatives, and the U.S. Air Force considered the "inappropriate" treatment of Japanese as "victims" rather than aggressors resulted in postponement of the project until the interpretation and approach changed.)[150] It will be difficult work to create new visitor expectations, but not, by any means, new ground.

* * *

In the preceding pages, I have presented a critique of the current historiographic practices living museums conduct through the use of costumed performance. First-person enactments of historical events, while held in esteem and often offering profound and emotional representations of the past, frequently disempower both visitors and performers as a result of defaulting to the cathartic, scripted performances associated with traditional theatre and drama. The recent development of second-person interpretation programs allows more room for visitor choice and personal engagement with museum historiography, but exists only in limited form, because visitors are allowed to play parts of only unnamed or amalgam individuals of the past who have not been assigned prominent status by historians as figures with agency and capacity for change. These limitations can be addressed by looking to the work of Boal, Parks, Rokem, Schneider, and others and adopting a model that would allow the visitors to step into second-person interpretation that lets them assume the role of characters faced with social and political choice, as well as include space for multiple counterenactments and discussions. I also addressed possible critical reactions to this model.

A final question might be on readers' minds: Would this kind of historiography still be *fun*? After all, that is the main reason people visit living museums. Or is it, in fact, distasteful to have any fun at all when faced with the historical accounts of injustice and suffering I describe above? My question in response is, does *fun* always have to be equated with depoliticization? Does it have to be free of confrontation, differing opinions, struggle, or thinking? Can one only have fun if safe from information or images that will be disturbing or unnerving? In the end, it depends on the definition of *fun*. Certainly, Urry's term for the interactions visitors engage at tourist attractions—*games*—would suggest some amount of room for this possibility. Theatre, as Horace reminds us, has within its constitution the dual function to instruct and to delight (though some interpreters object that the latter ought to be restricted to theme parks). And, more importantly, in his discourse on time, history, and the remembering of events, Agamben finds "joy" at the end of the historiographic process only when the individual can liberate himself or herself from the dominant ideologies of state, institution, or historian that prevent personal connections with his or her history.[151] With such stakes, it is worth asking at these museums not only how "fun" can be the means to an end (learning), but also the other way around.

Notes

1. Gilles Deleuze, "Nomad Art: Space," in *The Deleuze Reader*, ed. Constantin V. Boundas (New York: Columbia University Press, 1993), 167.

2. Blau, in a question-and-answer session following the presentation of his paper "The Soul Complex of Strindberg: Suffering, Suffocation, Scopophilia, and the Seer," delivered at the University of Minnesota Department of Theatre Arts and Dance Symposium "Staging Strindberg in the 21st Century," 17 February 2001.

3. Snow, *Performing the Pilgrims: A Study of Ethnohistorical Role-Playing at Plimoth Plantation* (Jackson: University Press of Mississippi, 1993), 143ff.

4. Snow, *Performing the Pilgrims*, 45, 44, 124ff.

5. Snow, *Performing the Pilgrims*, 125ff.

6. Snow, *Performing the Pilgrims*, 127.

7. Snow, *Performing the Pilgrims*, xxi.

8. Anne Bogart, *Anne Bogart: Viewpoints*, ed. Michael Dixon and Joel A. Smith (Lyme, NH: Smith & Kraus, 1995), 208.

9. "Visitor's Companion" (December 1990), 10–16, quoted in Richard Handler and Eric Gable, *The New History in an Old Museum: Creating the Past at Colonial Williamsburg* (Durham, NC: Duke University Press, 1999), 8.

10. Manager, Theatrical Productions Department, Colonial Williamsburg, personal interview, 7 June 2000.

11. "The Reminiscences of Mrs. Albert M. Sneed" (H. J. Campbell, Oral History Collection, Colonial Williamsburg Foundation Archives, 1946), cited in Handler and Gable, *New History in an Old Museum*, 184.

12. Carolyn Travers, personal interview, 15 June 2000.

13. Emily James, personal interview, 8 June 2000.

14. Third-person costumed interpreter, Hobbamock's Homesite, personal interview, 17 June 2000.

15. Laura Peers, "Playing Ourselves: Native Histories, Native Interpreters, and Living History Sites" (Ph.D. dissertation, McMaster University, 1996), 3. See also my essay "Recreation and Re-Creation: On-Site Historical Reenactment as Historiographic Operation at Plimoth Plantation," *Journal of Dramatic Theory and Criticism* (Fall 2002).

16. Peers, "Playing Ourselves," 10.

17. James Deetz and Patricia Scott Deetz, *The Times of Their Lives: Life, Love, and Death in Plymouth Colony* (New York: Freeman, 2000), 289.

18. Marge Bruchac, personal interview, 20 June 2000.

19. Employee in living history management (name withheld by request), personal interview, June 2000.

20. Staff member, Interpretive Program Development, Colonial Williamsburg, personal interview, 8 June 2000.

21. Cynthia Gedraitis, personal interview, 15 June 2000.

22. Kate Hill, personal interview, 19 June 2000.

23. Kate Hill, personal interview, 19 June 2000.

24. Kate Hill, personal interview, 19 June 2000.

25. Staff member, Interpretive Program Development, Colonial Williamsburg, personal interview, 8 June 2000.

26. Toni Brennan, personal interview, 7 June 2000.

27. Bill Barker, personal interview, 7 June 2000.

28. Bill Barker, personal interview, 7 June 2000.

29. First-person costumed interpreter (Lydia Maria Child), Old Sturbridge Village, personal interview, 19 June 2000.

30. Third-person costumed interpreter, Pioneer Village, Salem, MA, personal interview, 16 June 2000.

31. First-person costumed interpreter (George Washington), Colonial Williamsburg, personal interview, 5 June 2000.

32. First-person costumed interpreter (George Washington), Colonial Williamsburg, personal interview, 5 June 2000.

33. Third-person costumed interpreter, Pioneer Village, Salem, MA, personal interview, 16 June 2000.

34. Third-person costumed interpreter, Pioneer Village, Salem, MA, personal interview, 16 June 2000.

35. Skansen refers to its costumed docents as "hosts" and "hostesses," though they fulfill the same function as do interpreters in U.S. open-air museums. Annika Johansson, assistant director of the host and hostess program at Skansen, explained their roles, noting that individual hosts are free to temporarily assume a historic character: "Our hosts working in the buildings, they're not *actors*. . . . They are *interpreters—historical interpreters*. And of course they can sometimes enter a role in a way, because, as you've seen, they are dressed up, like matching the period of the building that they are working in. If they want to, sometimes, they can enter that role . . . , depending on what the visitor wants to do, or wants to know. But it's not that they pretend or are in the role at the time. They talk, they tell about the buildings and the life that went on, but not as a person from the time" (personal interview, 8 July 2002).

36. Costumed hostess at Oktorps-Gården, Skansen, personal interview, 8 July 2002.

37. Costumed hostess at Ekshärads-Gården, Skansen, personal interview, 8 July 2002.

38. *Plimoth Plantation*, VHS (Glastonbury, CT: VideoTours, 1989).

39. Mark Howell, personal interview, 7 June 2000.

40. Third-person costumed interpreter, Jamestown Settlement, personal interview, 4 June 2000.

41. Third-person costumed interpreter, Jamestown Settlement, personal interview, 4 June 2000.

42. William Sommerfield, interview by Lynn Neary, "Adventures in Re-creating History," *Talk of the Nation*, National Public Radio, 5 July 2004; my emphasis.

43. Staff member, Theatrical Productions Department, Colonial Williamsburg, personal interview, 7 June 2000.

44. Snow, *Performing the Pilgrims*, 137.

45. Cary Carson, "Colonial Williamsburg and the Practice of Interpretive Planning in American History Museums," *Public Historian* 20.3 (Summer 1998), 11ff.

46. Christy Coleman Matthews, "Twenty Years Interpreting African American History: A Colonial Williamsburg Revolution," *History News* 54 (Spring 1999), 9–10.

47. Anders Greenspan, *Creating Colonial Williamsburg* (Washington, DC: Smithsonian Institution Press, 2002), 164.

48. Barbara Kirshenblatt-Gimblett, *Destination Culture*, 173.

49. Donald Garfield, "Too Real for Comfort," *Museum News* 74.1 (January–February 1995): 9.

50. Garfield, "Too Real for Comfort," 9.

51. Matthews, 10.

52. Garfield, "Too Real for Comfort," 10. For a discussion of whether the "realism" of a performed estate auction is the best way to educate museum visitors about

African American and slave history, see Bruce McConachie, "Slavery and Authenticity: Performing a Slave Auction at Colonial Williamsburg," *Theatre Annual* 51 (1998), 71–81.

53. Christy Coleman Matthews, personal interview, 9 May 2000.

54. Christy Coleman Matthews, personal interview, 9 May 2000.

55. Christy Coleman Matthews, personal interview, 9 May 2000.

56. Bruce McConachie, "Slavery and Authenticity: Performing a Slave Auction at Colonial Williamsburg," *Theatre Annual* 51 (1998), 71–72.

57. McConachie, "Slavery and Authenticity," 74.

58. Rex Ellis, "Interpreting the Whole House," in *Interpreting Historic House Museums*, ed. Jessica Foy Donnelly (Walnut Creek, CA: AltaMira, 2002), 78.

59. Richard Schechner, "Restoration of Behavior," *Studies in Visual Communication* 7.3 (Summer 1981).

60. Snow, *Performing the Pilgrims*, 147.

61. Snow, *Performing the Pilgrims*, 147.

62. Snow, *Performing the Pilgrims*, 148.

63. Carson, "Colonial Williamsburg," 49.

64. See James Henry Breasted, *Ancient Records of Egypt* (Chicago: University of Chicago Press, 1906).

65. Looking for evidence of dramatic impulses or "stage directions," writes Kobialka, scholars like E. K. Chambers or Karl Young take a text describing the proper manner in which monks should conduct the night office before the Easter Mass and make it into a record of early English drama. See Michal Kobialka, *This Is My Body: Representational Practices in the Early Middle Ages* (Ann Arbor: University of Michigan Press, 1999).

66. See Pierre-Louis Duchartre, *The Italian Comedy: The Improvisation, Scenarios, Lives, Attributes, Portraits and Masks of the Illustrious Characters of the Commedia dell'Arte*, trans. Randolph T. Weaver (New York: John Day, 1929), and Giacomo Oreglia, *The Commedia dell'Arte*, trans. Lovett F. Edwards (London: Methuen, 1968).

67. See Luis Valdez, *Luis Valdez—Early Works: Actos, Bernabé, and Pensamiento Serpentino* (Houston: Arte Publico, 1990), and Augusto Boal, *Theater of the Oppressed*, trans. Charles A. McBride and Maria-Odilia Leal McBride (New York: Urizen Books; London: Pluto, 1979).

68. See Deleuze, "Nomad Art," 166.

69. I borrow the phrase "just-the-facts" from Handler and Gable (*New History in an Old Museum*, 978ff), who use it to identify a mode of interpretation limited to that which may be proven beyond reasonable doubt by documented evidence.

70. Handler and Gable, *New History in an Old Museum*, 86.

71. Michael Lang, "Marketing Historical Resources" (master's thesis, University of Calgary, 1991), quote on 58.

72. Michael Hall, program interpreter at Plimoth Plantation, personal interview, 15 June 2000.

73. Guy Peartree, personal interview, 20 June 2000.

74. Guy Peartree, personal interview, 20 June 2000.

75. See Bertolt Brecht's "Notes to *The Rise and Fall of the City of Mahoganny*" (1930), "The *Verfremdungseffekt* in the Chinese Theatre" (1936), "Über Experimentelles Theater" (1939), etc.

76. Jean-François Lyotard, "Answer to the Question, 'What Is the Postmodern?'" trans. Don Barry, in *The Postmodern Explained*, ed. Julian Pefanis and Morgan Thomas (Minneapolis: University of Minnesota Press, 1992), 5.

77. Public relations staff member, Plimoth Plantation, personal interview, 15 June 2000. See chapter 1 for full quote.

78. Tom Conley, introduction to Michel de Certeau, *The Writing of History*, trans. Tom Conley (New York: Columbia University Press, 1988), xx.

79. De Certeau, *Writing of History*, 46.

80. Third-person discourse in the past tense tends to be reserved for those events and individuals that are no longer with us. Richard Liebmann-Smith, musing on his high school alumni newsletter's mistaken report of his recent death, described how language denotes the life/death status of the subject: "The best way to tell if you're dead, I figured, is to carefully observe the behavior of the people around you. Do they seem to be looking through you rather than at you? Do they talk about you in the third person or the past tense? ('Dad always liked mashed potatoes' as opposed to 'please pass the mashed potatoes, Dad.') Do they turn pale at the sight of you? Do they keep trying to put coins on your eyes?" ("Not Dead Yet," *New York Times Magazine*, 13 May 2001, 68).

81. Roland Barthes, "Le discours de l'histoire," 71, quoted in de Certeau, *Writing of History*, 46.

82. Susan K. Irwin, "Popular History: Living-History Sites, Historical Interpretation, and the Public" (master's thesis, Bowling Green State University, 1993), 42.

83. *Williamsburg Spring 2001 Catalogue* (Williamsburg, VA: Colonial Williamsburg Foundation), 18.

84. See John H. Falk and Lynn D. Dierking, *Lessons without Limit: How Free-Choice Learning Is Transforming Education* (Walnut Creek, CA: AltaMira, 2002), 15, and Marilyn G. Hood, "Staying Away: Why People Choose Not to Visit Museums," in *Reinventing the Museum: Historical and Contemporary Perspectives on the Paradigm Shift*, ed. Gail Anderson (Walnut Creek, CA: AltaMira, 2004), 151.

85. Hood, "Staying Away," 151.

86. Judy Rand, "The Visitors' Bill of Rights," in Anderson, *Reinventing the Museum*, 158–59.

87. Falk and Dierking, *Lessons without Limit*, 15.

88. Bonnie Sachatello-Sawyer, Robert A. Fellenz, Hanly Burton, Laura Gittings-Carlson, Janet Lewis-Mahony, and Walter Woodbaugh, *Adult Museum Programs: Designing Meaningful Experiences* (Walnut Creek, CA: AltaMira, 2002), 130.

89. Ralph Brockett and Roger Hiemstra, "Philosophical and Ethical Considerations," in *Program Planning for the Training and Continuing Education of Adults*, ed. Peter S. Cookson (Malabar, FL: Krieger, 1998), 131.

90. Ellis, "Interpreting the Whole House," 75–76.

91. Paul A. Shackel, *Memory in Black and White: Race, Commemoration, and the Post-Bellum Landscape* (Walnut Creek, CA: AltaMira, 2003), 198.

92. Dean MacCannell, *The Tourist: A New Theory of the Leisure Class* (Berkeley: University of California Press, 1999), 99.

93. Erving Goffman, *The Presentation of Self in Everyday Life* (Garden City, NY: Doubleday, 1959).

94. See Maxine Feifer, *Tourism in History: From Imperial Rome to the Present* (New York: Stein & Day, 1985), and John Urry, *The Tourist Gaze: Leisure and Travel in Contemporary Societies* (London: Sage, 1990).

95. Dean MacCannell, "Virtual Reality's Place," *Performance Research* 2.2 (Summer 1997).

96. MacCannell, *Tourist*, xxiii.

97. Deleuze, "Nomad Art," 177.

98. Snow, *Performing the Pilgrims*, 207–8, 160.

99. Snow, *Performing the Pilgrims*, 219n7.

100. Carolyn Travers, personal interview, 15 June 2000; Cynthia Gedraitis, personal interview, 15 June 2000.

101. Urry, *Tourist Gaze*, 128–31. Living history museums and other historic reconstructions, writes Laura Peers, are still a far cry from the postmodern institutions Urry describes. This is especially true of the sites that treat Native histories. They continue to be "silent about the curatorial decisions that affect their production, and they silence many of the questions and perspectives involved in such creations. . . . By allowing the visitor to believe that the reconstruction is an exact replica of what the site really looked like at a given moment in history, sites give visitors free rein to interpret what they actually see—which they do in light of popular discourses about the past and especially about the frontier, rather than discourses about the creation of historic sites or the politics and constraints of representing the past" (Peers, "Playing Ourselves," 116–17).

102. Jean Baudrillard, "The Precession of Simulacra," in *Simulation and Simulacra*, trans. Sheila Faria Glaser (Ann Arbor: University of Michigan Press, 1994), 20.

103. Suzan-Lori Parks, "Possession," in *The America Play, and Other Works* (New York: Theatre Communications Group, 1995), 5.

104. See Gilles Deleuze and Félix Guattari, *What Is Philosophy?* trans. Hugh Tomlinson and Graham Burchell (New York: Columbia University Press, 1994). Creative fabulation, according to the authors, is that which has nothing to do with a memory, but is that in which novelists engage when writing a story or artists when they paint an image (171–72).

105. Parks, "Possession," 5.

106. Rebecca Schneider, "Flesh Memory and the Logic of the Archive; or, Driving the Lincoln," paper delivered at the Australasian Drama Studies Association Meetings, Newcastle, Australia, July 2000.

107. De Certeau, *Writing of History*, 79.

108. Many visitors and audience members were generous and supportive of the auction. The questions ranged from whether the events they portrayed were from actual documented records to the absence of last names of the slave characters.

109. *Publick Times: An Estate Auction*, VHS (Williamsburg, VA: Colonial Williamsburg Productions, 1994).

110. Sachatello-Sawyer et al., *Adult Museum Programs*, xxiiff.

111. "Live Some History," brochure, Conner Prairie, Summer 2003.

112. Visitor services representative, Conner Prairie, telephone interview, 4 August 2003.

113. Old Sturbridge Village, "Send the Kids on a History Adventure this Summer," e-mail newsletter, 20 June 2003.

114. "SummerShops at Old Sturbridge Village 2003," brochure, Old Sturbridge, Inc., 2003.

115. Third-person costumed interpreter, Old Sturbridge Village, personal interview, 24 June 2003.

116. Old Sturbridge Village Educators' Newsletter, 12 June 2003.

117. Giorgio Agamben, "Time and History: Critique of the Instant and the Continuum," in *Infancy and History: Essays on the Destruction of Experience*, trans. Liz Heron (London: Verso, 1993), 91.

118. Plimoth Plantation map/guide, Summer 2003.

119. The SummerShops program at Sturbridge is a prime example (and Colonial Williamsburg annually invites girls to attend in costume with their historic American Girl dolls). Sturbridge, at the time of writing, had just added a new program called "kids in costume" on weekends throughout the summer. Regular visitors can pay $25 to dress their children in period costume throughout the day of their visit (www.osv.org).

120. Roland Barthes, "The Reality Effect," in *The Rustle of Language*, trans. Richard Howard (New York: Hill & Wang, 1986), 142.

121. Freddie Rokem, *Performing History: Theatrical Representations of the Past in Contemporary Theatre* (Iowa City: University of Iowa Press, 2000), xi.

122. Rokem, *Performing History*, 3.

123. Rokem, *Performing History*, 9.

124. Rokem, *Performing History*, 3. Rokem discusses theatrical energies in full in chapter 4 of *Performing History*.

125. Augusto Boal, "Theatre as Discourse," in *The Twentieth Century Performance Reader*, ed. Michael Huxley and Noel Witts (London: Routledge, 1996), 85.

126. See Augusto Boal, *The Rainbow of Desire: The Boal Method of Theatre and Therapy*, trans. Adrian Jackson (London: Routledge, 1995), 40ff, and "The Cop in the Head: Three Hypotheses," *Drama Review* 34.3 (1990). See also Mady Schutzman and Jan Cohen-Cruz, eds., *Playing Boal: Theatre, Therapy, Activism* (London: Routledge, 1994), 4.

127. Rokem, *Performing History*, 101–2.

128. Rokem, *Performing History*, 8.

129. Parks, "Possession," 5.

130. In this sense, a stricter definition would favor the term *discourse* over *narrative*. Gérard Genette notes that *discourse* has an "I" and a "thou," has adverbial and pronomial indicators, and has present, present perfect, and future verb tenses, while *narrative* is limited to the third person and the preterit or pluperfect verb tense; see "Boundaries of Narrative," *New Literary History* 8.1 (Autumn 1976).

131. See "High-tech Meets History in a More Perfect Union: A New Museum Brings the Constitution to Life," *Chicago Tribune*, 13 July 2003, and "1787 and All That: Walking Through Amendments and Rubbing Elbows with Founding Fathers at the New Constitution Center," *New York Times*, 17 August 2003.

132. Susan Kattwinkel, introduction to *Audience Participation: Essays on Inclusion in Performance*, ed. Susan Kattwinkel (Westport, CT: Praeger, 2003), xiii.

133. Boal, "Theatre as Discourse," 92. Boal has reexamined the notion of catharsis since *Theatre of the Oppressed*, now allowing that a form of catharsis can be found at the moment the spect-actor is dynamized toward action; see Boal, *Rainbow of Desire*. For examples of Theatre of the Oppressed and Forum Theatre techniques, see Augusto Boal, *Games for Actors and Non-Actors*, trans. Adrian Jackson (London: Routledge, 1992); Boal, *Theatre of the Oppressed*; Boal, *Rainbow of Desire*; Schutzman and Cohen-Cruz, *Playing Boal*; and *Como Querem Beber Agua: Augusto Boal and Theatre of the Oppressed in Rio De Janeiro*, dir. Robert Morelos (Queensland: Center for Innovation in the Arts, Queensland University of Technology, 1995).

134. Boal, "Theatre as Discourse," 91.

135. Michel-Rolph Trouillot, *Silencing the Past: Power and the Production of History* (Boston: Beacon Press, 1997), 116, 150.

136. If some know the end already, that is all right, too, as this may also be an engaging teaching tool. As Marvin Carlson writes, the audience delights in, and is engaged by, instances of irony resulting from situations in which they know more about the protagonist's fate than the protagonist (e.g., Oedipus); see Carlson, *The Haunted Stage: Theatre as Memory Machine* (Ann Arbor: University of Michigan Press, 2001), 30–31. Living museums already make use of these situations for the delight of the audience. When Colonial Williamsburg hosts a "public audience" with Patrick Henry, Thomas Jefferson, or George Washington in the early 1770s, we listen to their philosophies, pronouncements, and what they would do if they were in charge, knowing—unlike their characters—that they *will* go on to become important revolutionaries or even presidents, or even that the colonies will win.

137. Mady Schutzman, "Brechtian Shamanism: The Political Therapy of Augusto Boal," in Schutzman and Cohen-Cruz, 140.

138. Schutzman, "Brechtian Shamanism," 149.

139. Schutzman, "Brechtian Shamanism," 145.

140. Schutzman, "Brechtian Shamanism," 145.

141. See, for instance, Lib Spry, who finds "power-over" is a more helpful term than "oppression" in her TO workshops in Canada ("Structures of Power: Toward a Theatre of Liberation," Schutzman and Cohen-Cruz, 174). See also the work of Jan

Cohen-Cruz in Minnesota and New York: "Mainstream or Margin: U.S. Activist Performance and Theatre of the Oppressed," Schutzman and Cohen-Cruz, 110ff, and "Boal at NYU: A Workshop and its Aftermath," *The Drama Review* 34.3, 35–42.

142. Warren Leon and Margaret Piatt, "Living-History Museums," in *History Museums in the United States: A Critical Assessment*, ed. Warren Leon and Roy Rosenzweig (Urbana: University of Illinois Press, 1989), 69.

143. Kevin Walsh, *The Representation of the Past: Museums and Heritage in the Postmodern World* (London: Routledge, 1992), 2.

144. Walsh, *Representation of the Past*, 4.

145. Walsh, *Representation of the Past*, 183.

146. Walsh, *Representation of the Past*, 168–69.

147. "Fort Snelling Hopes History Has a Future," *Star Tribune* (Minneapolis), 18 February 2002.

148. Personal interviews, 13 May 2000.

149. See Tony Bennett, *The Birth of the Museum: History, Theory, Politics* (London: Routledge, 1995), chaps. 1 and 2.

150. See Martin Harwit, *An Exhibit Denied* (New York: Copernicus, 1996); Frank Rich, "The Nation's Basement," *New York Times*, 22 June 1996; and Shackel, *Memory in Black and White*, 203–4.

151. As discussed in chapter 2, Agamben writes that authentic history is achieved only in moments of *cairós*, during which, by her or his own initiative, the individual "grasps favourable opportunity and chooses his own freedom in the moment." A "cairological" time is a time of genuine joy, a time of authentic revolution ("Time and History," 104).

Conclusion

Like other living history museums such as Williamsburg and Old Sturbridge Village, to name but two, Plimoth Plantation is a construction of a past world done as carefully and thoroughly as research permits. However, it does not, and cannot, constitute a *re-creation* of the village as it was in the early seventeenth century. One hopes, however, that should the original inhabitants reappear, while they would not recognize the little community in all of the details that it possessed in their time, they would at least feel somewhat at home in their surroundings.

—James Deetz and Patricia Scott Deetz, *The Times of Their Lives*

Whatever this new understanding of the past holds to be irrelevant— shards created by the selection of materials, remainders left aside by an explication—comes back, despite everything, on the edges of discourse or in its rifts and crannies: "resistances," "survivals," or delays discreetly perturb the pretty order of a line of "progress" or a system of interpretation.

—Michel de Certeau, *The Writing of History*

As I indicated in chapter 1, the discourse informing accounts of the emergence of living history museums in the twentieth century is linked to a narrative of development from simple to complex over time. Because of the limits imposed by this evolutionary model, those who write about museums, and those who work at them, speak of their own positions as occupying the tip of the arrow of progress: all that has occurred before has formed the stepping-stones leading up to the current moment and—à la the survival of the fittest—those practices that have *not* worked have been (or will be) filtered out of current programming, leaving today's museums the best of all possible models. These assumptions do not leave room to consider alternative models of perform-ance. The sheer momentum of the progress already under way, it would ap-pear, makes it difficult for museums to change trajectories. "We may not be the most accurate now," the argument goes, "but someday, when somebody else is sitting in this chair. . . ." Such statements, though, are spoken from the curatorial sites of authority. A close-range movement through the field re-veals the perceptions that first-person costumed interpretation holding to a naturalistic mode of performance is not necessarily the best of all possible models. In many cases, it does not allow "connection" with the visitor and, in most cases, leaves nothing but a singular moment of the past to be exam-ined. Moreover, in an increasingly post-touristic world, visitors' expectations are shifting from hopes for an encounter with an authentic environment to one that offers a wider range of tourist play.

Likewise, the governing perceptions of time and history at living museums do not allow the historical event to be talked about as anything other than a developmental point along a continuum of such points leading to the pres-ent and beyond. With this notion, it makes sense that history can be "un-done," or traced backward to a past point. The moment itself may be ir-recoverable, but if crack teams of historical scientists and museum curators work long and hard enough, they will rediscover its lost or forgotten rem-nants. Eventually, following this logic to its conclusion, it will be possible to re-create the moment with absolute precision. Museums, as I found in my re-search and interviews, tend to condition their programming with this prin-ciple of "undoing history."

Just as curators and staff understand their own positions as the farthest point along a timeline of progressing museum development, so too do they imply that ideals of American character, freedom, and democracy, since they are still with us, must be powerful enough to have survived all this time. Therefore, these must have been the very same ontological principles that guided the everyday lives of the people of the past. Again, the problem is that this notion leaves little room to consider alternate histories which do not fit this narrative, especially the histories of countermovements: black, Native, or women's histories that did not leave the type of authoritative evidence that historical scientists look for. If the continuum of precise and homoge-neous instants were to be removed, it would be possible to regard the past moment as a site of emergence in a plane of imminent becomings, of which we, too, are a part. Articulation of the past, then, would not be seen as an arrangement of artifacts from another time as much as a collection of statements in the present.

In the face of these concerns, I offered in chapter 2 a new historiography of living history museum performance by avoiding explanations of emergence and development due to transcendental motivators such as progress, the human instinct to perform, survival of the fittest, backbone-forming cycles of conflict and resolution, and so forth. Instead, I offered a nomadological approach, moving through the field of living history museums and articulating the way I perceive that certain statements about living history have been organized. It seems, for example, as though living history practices have changed at various moments not because of progress, but rather because there were concomitant events that informed what was possible to stage. Notions of an American identity crisis in the 1950s did not allow museums like Colonial Williamsburg to perform anything other than a conservative, patriotic Virginia colony where the forefathers hammered out the precepts that would guide our nation in times of anxiety. Notions of loss and disconnection from the land in the 1970s, on the other hand, informed the marketing of history as a place where one could relieve the stresses and dangers of the city and technology.

Social history practices, while allowing the voicing of several narratives not possible before, are now considered a huge step in the direction of a more scientifically accurate portrayal of the past: since women, blacks, and poor people are highlighted in museum histories, a much fuller scope of the past is available to visitors. Because social history programming was laid over the existing notions of time and history, however, what resulted was that the selected histories of these groups merely reinforce narratives not dissimilar to those of the 1950s. America remains a nation built upon the ideals of freedom and hard work, and these individuals, though less empowered, were equally influenced by the American ideal and contributed to the building of what we have today. Furthermore, economic, social, and political factors limit the incorporation of social history programming at museums. This is most apparent at Colonial Williamsburg, where the handful of African-American interpreters are supposed to represent the 50-plus percent of Williamsburg's population in the late eighteenth century who were either slaves or "free Negroes."

Finally, though the work of Stephen Eddy Snow and others has established that living history programming can confidently be called "theatre" and "performance," chapter 3 showed that the way performance is understood and practiced at these institutions is limited by a severely reductive definition of *theatre* as a text-based, representational mode of performance.

Thus, discussion of whether or not living history interpretation is theatre becomes one of binary opposition: either living history is *not* theatre because it does not use a script or it *is* theatre *in spite of* not using a script. In addition, the modes of performance considered to be the best are those which incorporate "realistic" first-person interpretation in naturalistic environments with rigorous attention to detail. Coupled with the museums' explicit mandate to be true to the past by showing only that which has been gleaned from historical evidence (and the dutiful disposal of inaccuracies as they are discovered), the visitor is left with a staged narrative that makes only the "real stuff" visible. This real stuff is then condensed to what can be expressed in a developmental story with the intent to transmit an idea or theme to a family audience (i.e., "Becoming Americans").

That this understanding of performance limits how theatre and performance may be discussed is one problem. Far more troubling is the manner in which living history museums' ideal mode of representation limits historical discourse. The closer a museum gets to the model of perfect, first-person interpretation based on documented sources, the more possibilities are silenced. (Groups within the museums, however, find ways to challenge this mainstreaming of the historical narrative. Native histories at Plimoth Plantation, for instance, would be compromised were it not for the Wampanoag Interpretation Program's resistance against the more normative first-person interpretation used by the costumed Pilgrims. At Colonial Williamsburg, African-American staff tactically insert narratives from oral history that counter those of the more conservative "just-the-facts" approach.)

In all of these cases—the written history of living museums, the institutional understandings of time and space, the approach to the past, and the models of performance used in representing the past—there exist tendencies to reduce, confine, stabilize, interpret, simplify, sharpen, and focus. These tendencies are the most threatening to thought. As I suggested at the end of chapter 3, it would be more responsible to seek those practices that would open up discourse, trouble the narratives, ask questions, tease out limits of understanding, make visible the gaps, insert anxiety, and foment doubt. By exploring these strategies, it may be possible to, in the words of Michel de Certeau, "discreetly perturb the pretty order of a line of 'progress' or a system of interpretation."

My hope is that the critiques and suggestions presented here may prompt a response from scholars and the living museum industry that would "muddy the waters" of the discourse. Opening the discussion to consider ideas that lie outside current museum performance programming perturbs the misleading and disempowering assumption that the problems of living history have easy solutions "further down the line." It is important to vigilantly question the stakes and goals of institutional representation of history. Whose goals will be met if museums eventually "undo history" to arrive at total accuracy in interpretation? As Laura Peers points out, authenticity and accuracy are often irrelevant to "those who are waging larger battles against ignorance, prejudice, and racism."[1] For these individuals, whose histories have *not* always been seen fit to remember, it is more important to bear witness to a lived experience in the present than to agonize over accurately re-creating a documented—yet largely incomplete—historical moment. Alternative modes of performance hold potential for filling those gaps where naturalism and just-the-facts fall short in answering a historically perpetuated injustice. In these cases, it would seem appropriate to take up Suzan-Lori Parks's suggestion that theatre or performative sites can be incubators for the *creation* of historical events, rather than simply showcases for the recorded ones.[2]

Notes

1. Laura Peers, "'Playing Ourselves': Native Histories, Native Interpreters, and Living History Sites" (Ph.D. dissertation, McMaster University, 1996), 165.

2. Suzan-Lori Parks, "Possession," in *The America Play, and Other Works* (New York: Theatre Communications Group, 1995), 4–5.

APPENDIX

~

Selected Living History Programming Sites

United States

Agricultural Heritage Center and Museum
P.O. Box 1076
Boerne, Texas 78006
www.agmuseum.org

Apple River Fort State Historic Site
P.O. Box 206
Elizabeth, Illinois 61028
www.appleriverfort.com

Buffalo Gap Historic Village
P.O. Box 818
Buffalo Gap, Texas 79508
www.buffalogap.com

Burritt on the Mountain
3101 Burritt Drive
Huntsville, Alabama 35801
www.burrittmuseum.com

Claude Moore Colonial Farm at Turkey Run
6310 Georgetown Pike
McLean, Virginia 22101
www.1771.org

Colonial Michilimackinac
P.O. Box 370
Mackinac Island, Michigan 49757
www.mackinacparks.com

Colonial Pennsylvania Plantation
Ridley Creek State Park
Media, Pennsylvania 19063
www.colonialplantation.org

Colonial Williamsburg Foundation
P.O. Box 1776
Williamsburg, Virginia 23187-1776
www.history.org

Columbia Gold Mining Town
P.O. Box 1824
Columbia, California 95310
www.columbiacalifornia.com

Conner Prairie
13400 Allisonville Road
Fishers, Indiana 46038-4499
www.connerprairie.org

Cracker Country
Florida State Fair Authority
Cracker Country
P.O. Box 11766
Tampa, Florida 33680
www.crackercountry.org

Dallas Heritage Village at Old City Park
1515 S. Harwood
Dallas, Texas 75215
www.oldcitypark.org

Delaware Agricultural Museum and Village
866 North DuPont Highway
Dover, Delaware 19901
www.agriculturalmuseum.org

El Rancho de las Golondrinas
334 Los Pinos Road
Santa Fe, New Mexico 87507
www.golondrinas.org

Farmers' Museum
P.O. Box 30
Cooperstown, New York 13326
www.farmersmuseum.org

The Fort at No. 4
267 Springfield Road, Rt. 11
P.O. Box 1336
Charlestown, New Hampshire 03603
www.fortat4.com

Fort Ticonderoga
P.O. Box 390
Ticonderoga, New York 12883
www.fort-ticonderoga.org

Fort Walla Walla
755 Myra Road
Walla Walla, Washington 99362
www.fortwallawallamuseum.org

Freetown Village
P.O. Box 1041
Indianapolis, Indiana 46206-1041
www.freetown.org

Frontier Culture Museum
1290 Richmond Road
Staunton, Virginia 24401
www.frontiermuseum.org

Genesee Country Village and Museum
1410 Flint Hill Road
Mumford, New York 14511
www.gcv.org

George Ranch Historical Park
Richmond, Texas 77469
www.georgeranch.org

Graeme Park
859 County Line Road
Horsham, Pennsylvania 19044
www.ushistory.org/graeme

Greenfield Village
The Henry Ford
20900 Oakwood Boulevard
Dearborn, Michigan 48124-4088
www.hfmgv.org

Hagley Museum and Library
298 Buck Road East
Wilmington, Delaware 19807
www.hagley.lib.de.us

Hale Farm and Village
Western Reserve Historical Society
10825 East Boulevard
Cleveland, Ohio 44106
www.whrh.org/halefarm

Hancock Shaker Village
P.O. Box 927
Pittsfield, Massachusetts 01202
www.hancockshakervillage.org

Harper's Ferry National Historic Park
P.O. Box 65
Harpers Ferry, West Virginia 25425
www.nps.gov/hafe/home.htm

Historic Cold Spring Village
720 Route 9
Cape May, New Jersey 08204
www.hcsv.org

Historic Collinsville
4711 Weakley Road
Southside, Tennessee 37171
www.historiccollinsville.com

Historic Fort Snelling
Minnesota Historical Society
345 W. Kellogg Boulevard
St. Paul, Minnesota 55102-1906
www.mnhs.org/places/sites/hfs

Historic Hudson Valley
150 White Plains Road
Tarrytown, New York 10591
www.hudsonvalley.org

Historic Latta Plantation
5225 Sample Road
Huntersville, North Carolina 28078
www.lattaplantation.org

Historic Mount Vernon
3200 Mount Vernon Memorial
   Highway
Mount Vernon, Virginia 22121
www.mountvernon.org

Historic Richmondtown
441 Clarke Avenue
Staten Island, New York 10306
www.historicrichmondtown.org

Historic St. Mary's City
P.O. Box 39
St. Mary's City, Maryland 20686
www.stmaryscity.org

Homestead Prairie Farm
Macon County Conservation
    District
3939 Nearing Lane
Decatur, Illinois 62521
www.maconcountyconservation.org/
    historic.htm

Hope Lodge
553 S. Bethlehem Pike
Fort Washington, Pennsylvania
    19034
www.ushistory.org/hope

Howell Living History Farm
101 Hunter Road
Titusville, New Jersey 08560
www.howellfarm.com

Knott's Berry Farm
8039 Beach Boulevard
Buena Park, California 90620
www.knotts.com

Landis Valley Museum
2451 Kissel Hill Road
Lancaster, Pennsylvania 17601
www.landisvalleymuseum.org

Living History Farms
2600 111th Street
Urbandale, Iowa 50322
www.lhf.org

Los Encinos State Historic Park
16756 Moorpark St.
Encino, California 91436-1068
http://los-encinos.org

**Meadowcroft Museum of Rural
    Life**
401 Meadowcroft Road
Avella, Pennsylvania 15312
www.meadowcroftmuseum.org

Missouri Town 1855
8010 East Park Road
Lee's Summit, Missouri 64015
www.co.jackson.mo.us/rec_hs_mt
    .shtml

Monticello
Thomas Jefferson Foundation
P.O. Box 316
Charlottesville, Virginia 22902
www.monticello.org

Museum Village
1010 Route 17M
Monroe, New York 10950
www.museumvillage.org

Mystic Seaport
75 Greenmanville Avenue
Mystic, Connecticut 06355-0990
www.mysticseaport.org

Naper Settlement
523 South Webster Street
Naperville, Illinois 60540
www.napersettlement.org

Newbold-White House
Hertford, North Carolina
www.newboldwhitehouse.com

North West Company Fur Post
P.O. Box 51
Pine City, Minnesota 55063
www.mnhs.org/places/sites/nwcfp

Ohio Village
1982 Velma Ave.
Columbus, Ohio 43211
www.ohiohistory.org/places/ohvillag

Old Barracks Museum
Barrack Street
Trenton, New Jersey 08608
www.barracks.org

Old Bethpage Village Restoration
Reception Center
Round Swamp Road
Old Bethpage, New York 11804
www.oldbethpage.org

Old Cowtown Museum
1871 Sim Park Drive
Wichita, Kansas 67203
www.old-cowtown.org

Old Fort Niagara
P.O. Box 169
Youngstown, New York 14174-0169
www.oldfortniagara.org

Old Salem
P.O. Box F
Salem Station
Winston-Salem, North Carolina
27108-0346
www.oldsalem.org

Old Sturbridge Village
1 Old Sturbridge Village Road
Sturbridge, Massachusetts 01566
www.osv.org

Old World Wisconsin
S103 W37890 Highway 67
Eagle, Wisconsin 53119
www.wisconsinhistory.org/oww

Oliver H. Kelley Farm
15788 Kelley Farm Rd.
Elk River, Minnesota 55330
www.mnhs.org/places/sites/ohkf/

Oxon Cove Park and Oxon Hill Farm
6411 Oxon Hill Road
Oxon Hill, Maryland 20745
www.nps.gov/oxhi

Philadelphia Zoo
3400 West Girard Avenue
Philadelphia, Pennsylvania
19104-1196
www.philadelphiazoo.org

Philip Foster Farm
29912 SE Highway 211
Eagle Creek, Oregon 97022
www.philipfosterfarm.com

Pioneer Village
Essex National Heritage Association
221 Essex Street, Suite 41
Salem, Massachusetts 01970
www.essexheritage.org/sites/
pioneer_village.shtml

Plimoth Plantation
137 Warren Avenue
Plymouth, Massachusetts 02360
www.plimoth.org

Polynesian Cultural Center
55-370 Kamehameha Highway
Laie, Hawaii 96762
www.polynesia.com

Pomeroy Living History Farm
20902 NE Lucia Falls Road
Yacolt, Washington 98675
www.pomeroyfarm.org

Quiet Valley Living Historical
   Farm
1000 Turkey Hill Road
Stroudsburg, Pennsylvania 18360
www.quietvalley.org

Rock Ledge Ranch Historic Site
1401 Recreation Way
Colorado Springs, Colorado 80905
www.rockledgeranch.com

Roth Living Farm Museum of
   Delaware Valley College
Route 202 & Hancock Road
North Wales, Pennsylvania 19454
www.devalcol.edu/roth

Sam Houston Memorial Museum
P.O. Box 2057
Huntsville, Texas 77341
www.shsu.edu/~smm_www

Sauder Village
22611 State Route 2
Archbold, Ohio 43502
www.saudervillage.org

Sauer-Beckmann Living History
   Farm
Lyndon B. Johnson State Park and
   Historic Site
P.O. Box 238
Stonewall, Texas 78671
www.tpwd.state.tx.us/spdest/
   findadest/parks/lyndon_b_
   johnson/#sauer

Southern Oregon Historical
   Society
106 N. Central
Medford, Oregon 97501
www.sohs.org

Strawbery Banke Museum
P.O. Box 300
Portsmouth, New Hampshire 03802
www.strawberybanke.org

USS *Constellation*
Pier 1
301 East Pratt Street
Baltimore, Maryland 21202-3134
www.constellation.org

Westville Village
P.O. Box 1850
Lumpkin, Georgia 31815
www.westville.org

Wheaton History Center
606 N. Main Street
Wheaton, Illinois 60187
www.wheaton.lib.il.us/whc

Wylie House Museum
307 E. Second Street
Bloomington, Indiana 47401
www.indiana.edu/~libwylie

Canada

Doon Heritage Crossroads
10 Huron Road at Homer Watson
  Boulevard
Kitchener, Ontario N2P 2R7
www.region.waterloo.on.ca/doon

Elderfield Old-Time Farm
Valley 1-8
Hornby Island, British Columbia
  V0R 1Z0
www.hornbyisland.com/elderfield

Fort Calgary Historic Park
750 9th Avenue SE
P.O. Box 2100
Station M (#106)
Calgary, Alberta T2P 2M5
www.fortcalgary.com

Fort Edmonton Park
7000-143 St.
Edmonton, Alberta
www.edmonton.ca/fort

Fort George National Historic Site
P.O. Box 787
26 Queen Street
Niagara-on-the-Lake, Ontario L0S
  1J0
www.pc.gc.ca/lhn-nhs/on/fortgeorge

Fort William Historical Park
1350 King Road
Thunder Bay, Ontario P7E 1L7
www.fwhp.ca

**Fortress of Louisbourg National
  Historic Site**
259 Park Service Road
Louisbourg, Nova Scotia
  B1C 2L2
www.louisbourg.ca/park

Green Gables Heritage Place
2 Palmer's Lane
Charlottetown, Prince Edward
  Island C1A 5V6
www.pc.gc.ca/lhn-nhs/pe/
  greengables

Heritage Park Historical Village
1900 Heritage Drive SW
Calgary, Alberta T2V 2X3
www.heritagepark.ab.ca

King's Landing
20 Kings Landing Road
Kings Landing, New Brunswick E6K
  3W3
www.gnb.ca/kingslanding

Lang Pioneer Village
104 Lang Road
Keene, Ontario
www.langpioneervillage.ca

Lower Fort Garry National
Historic Site
5925 Highway 9
St. Andrews, Manitoba R1A 4A8
www.parkscanada.gc.ca/garry

Sainte-Marie among the Hurons
Highway 12 East

Midland, Ontario L4R 4K8
www.saintemarieamongthehurons
.on.ca

Sherbrooke Village
42 Main Street
Sherbrooke, Nova Scotia
museum.gov.ns.ca/sv

Upper Canada Village Heritage
Park
13740 County Road 2
Morrisburg, Ontario K0C 1X0
www.uppercanadavillage.com

Europe

ASTRA Open Air Museum in
Dumbrava Sibiului
2400 Sibiu, Calea Rasinari
Romania
www.itcnet.ro/sibiu/engl/
dumbra_e.htm

Austrian Outdoor Museum in
Stubing
Österreichisches Freilichtmuseum
Stübing
A-8114 Stübing
Austria
www.freilichtmuseum.at

Beamish
County Durham
England
www.beamish.org.uk

Benjamin Franklin House
36 Craven Street

London WC2N 5NF ·
England
www.benjaminfranklinhouse.org

Jamtli Open Air Museum
Box 709
831 28 Östersund
Sweden
www.jamtli.com

Natural History Museum
Cromwell Road
London SW7 5BD
England
www.nhm.ac.uk

Norsk Folkemuseum
Museumsveien 10, Bygdøy
N-0287 Oslo
Norway
www.norskfolke.museum.no

Roman Open Air Museum
Römisches Freilichtmuseum
D-72379 Hechingen-Stein
Germany
www.villa-rustica.de

Sagalund
Museivägen 7
25700 Kimito
Finland
www.sagalund.fi

Skansen
Box 27807
115 93 Stockholm
Sweden
www.skansen.se

Statek Hyperion
Černotín 13+37
334 01 pošta Přeštice
Czech Republic
www.cernotin.com

Africa

Shakaland
Protea Hotel Shakaland
14km past Eshowe on R66

Eshowe 3815
South Africa

New Zealand

Howick Historical Village
Bells Road, Lloyd Elsmore Park
Pakuranga, Auckland

New Zealand
www.fencible.org.nz

Bibliography

Books, Articles, and Dissertations

Abing, Laura E. "Old Sturbridge Village: An Institutional History of a Cultural Artifact." Ph.D. dissertation, Marquette University, 1997.

Abramov Levy, Barbara, Sandra MacKenzie Lloyd, and Susan Porter Schreiber. *Great Tours! Thematic Tours and Guide Training for Historic Sites*. Walnut Creek, CA: AltaMira, 2001.

Adorno, Theodor. "Commitment." In *The Essential Frankfurt School Reader*, eds. Andrew Arato and Eike Gebhardt. Oxford: Basil Blackwell, 1978.

Agamben, Giorgio. *Remnants of Auschwitz: The Witness and the Archive*. Trans. Daniel Heller-Roazen. New York: Zone Books, 1999.

———. "Time and History: Critique of the Instant and the Continuum." In *Infancy and History: Essays on the Destruction of Experience*, trans. Liz Heron. London: Verso, 1993.

Alderson, William T., and Shirley Payne Low. *Interpretation of Historic Sites*. 2nd ed., rev. Nashville, TN: American Association for State and Local History, 1985.

Alexander, Edward P. *Museums in Motion*. Walnut Creek, CA: American Association for State and Local History, 1996.

———. *Museums in Motion: An Introduction to the History and Functions of Museums*. Nashville: American Association for State and Local History, 1979.

America's Historylands: Touring Our Landmarks of Liberty. Washington, DC: National Geographic Society, 1967.

Anderson, Benedict. *Imagined Communities*. London: Verso, 1983.

Anderson, Gail, Ed. *Reinventing the Museum: Historical and Contemporary Perspectives on the Paradigm Shift*. Walnut Creek, CA: AltaMira, 2004.

Anderson, Jay. "Living History: Simulating Everyday Life in Living Museums." *American Quarterly* 34:3 (1982).

———. *A Living History Reader: Volume One: Museums*. Nashville: American Association for State and Local History, 1991.

———. *The Living History Sourcebook*. Nashville: American Association for State and Local History, 1985.

———. *Time Machines: The World of Living History*. Nashville: American Association for State and Local History, 1984.

Ashworth, G. J., and J. E. Tunbridge. *The Tourist-Historic City*. London: Belhaven Press, 1990.

Baguley, David, ed. *Critical Essays on Emile Zola*. Boston: G.K. Hall, 1986.

Baker, Andrew, and Warren Leon. "Old Sturbridge Village Introduces Social Conflict into Its Interpretive Story." *History News* (March 1986).

Baker, James. "Haunted by the Pilgrims." In *The Art and Mystery of Historical Archaeology: Essays in Honor of James Deetz*, eds. Anne Elizabeth Yentsch and Mary C. Beaudry. Boca Raton, FL: CRC Press, 1992.

———. *Plimoth Plantation: Fifty Years of Living History*. Plymouth: Plimoth Plantation Publications, 1997.

Baker, Keith Michael. *Inventing the French Revolution: Essays on the French Political Culture in the Eighteenth Century*. New York: Cambridge University Press, 1990.

Balme, Christopher B. "Staging the Pacific: Framing Authenticity in Performances for Tourists at the Polynesian Cultural Center." *Theatre Journal* 50.1 (March 1998).

Bank, Rosmarie K. "Meditations upon Opening and Crossing Over: Trangressing the Boundaries of Historiography and Tracking the History of Nineteenth-Century American Theatre." In *Of Borders and Thresholds: Theatre History, Practice and Theory*, ed. Michal Kobialka. Minneapolis: University of Minnesota Press, 1999.

———. *Theatre Culture in America, 1825–1860*. Cambridge, UK: Cambridge University Press, 1997.

Barthes, Roland. "The Reality Effect." In *The Rustle of Language*, trans. Richard Howard. New York: Hill & Wang, 1986.

Baudrillard, Jean. "The Precession of Simulacra." In *Simulacra and Simulation*, trans. Sheila Faria Glaser. Ann Arbor: University of Michigan Press, 1994.

———. *Simulacra and Simulation*. Trans. Sheila Glaser. Ann Arbor: University of Michigan Press, 1994.

———. *The System of Objects*. Trans. James Benedict. London: Verso, 1996.

Benjamin, Walter. "Theses on the Philosophy of History." In *Illuminations: Essays and Reflections*, trans. Hannah Arendt. New York: Schocken, 1969.

Bennett, Tony. *The Birth of the Museum: History, Theory, Politics*. London: Routledge, 1995.

Berg, William J., and Laurey K. Martin. *Emile Zola Revisited*. New York: Twayne, 1992.

Blatti, Jo, ed. *Past Meets Present: Essays about Historic Interpretation and Public Audiences*. Washington, DC: Smithsonian Press, 1987.

Blau, Herbert. "Notes from the Underground." In *Sails of the Herring Fleet: Essays on Beckett.* Ann Arbor: University of Michigan Press, 2000.

Boal, Augusto. "The Cop in the Head: Three Hypotheses." *Drama Review* 34.3 (1990).

———. *Games for Actors and Non-Actors.* Trans. Adrian Jackson. London: Routledge, 1992.

———. *The Rainbow of Desire: The Boal Method of Theatre and Therapy.* Trans. Adrian Jackson. London: Routledge, 1995.

———. "Theatre as Discourse." In *The Twentieth Century Performance Reader*, eds. Michael Huxley and Noel Witts. London: Routledge, 1996.

———. *Theater of the Oppressed.* Trans. Charles A. and Maria-Odilia Leal McBride. New York: Urizen Books; London: Pluto, 1979.

Bogart, Anne. *Anne Bogart: Viewpoints.* Eds. Michael Dixon and Joel A. Smith. Lyme, NH: Smith & Kraus, 1995.

Boorstin, Daniel. *The Image: A Guide to Pseudo Events in America.* New York: Atheneum, 1962.

———. "Past and Present in America: A Historian Visits Colonial Williamsburg." *Commentary* 25 (1958).

Boundas, Constantine, ed. *The Deleuze Reader.* New York: Columbia University Press, 1993.

Bourdieu, Pierre. *Distinction: A Social Critique of the Judgement of Taste.* Trans. Richard Nice. Cambridge: Harvard University Press, 1984.

Bourdieu, Pierre, and Loïc J. D. Wacquant. *An Invitation to Reflexive Sociology.* Chicago: University of Chicago Press, 1992.

Bourne, Russell. *The Red King's Rebellion: Racial Politics in New England, 1675–1678.* New York: Atheneum, 1990.

Bowden, Henry W., and James P. Ronda, eds. *John Eliot's Indian Dialogues: A Study in Cultural Interaction.* Westport, CT: Greenwood, 1980.

Boyarin, Jonathan. *Remapping Memory: The Politics of TimeSpace.* Minneapolis: University of Minnesota Press, 1994.

Brandt, Anthony. "A Short Natural History of Nostalgia." *Atlantic Monthly* (December 1978).

Breasted, James Henry. *Ancient Records of Egypt.* Chicago: University of Chicago Press, 1906.

Brecht, Bertolt. *The Rise and Fall of the City of Mahoganny.* Trans. W. H. Auden and Chester Kallman. Boston: D. R. Godine, 1976.

———. *Über Experimentelles Theater.* Frankfurt: A. M. Suhrkamp, 1970.

———. "The *Verfremdungseffekt* in the Chinese Theatre." In *Brecht on Theatre*, trans. John Willett. New York: Hill & Wang, 1964.

Breen, T. H. *Imagining the Past: East Hampton Histories.* Reading, MA: Addison-Wesley, 1989.

Brockett, Ralph, and Roger Hiemstra. "Philosophical and Ethical Considerations." In *Program Planning for the Training and Continuing Education of Adults*, ed. Peter S. Cookson. Malabar, FL: Krieger, 1998.

Brown, Patricia Leigh. "Away from the Big House: Interpreting the Uncomfortable Parts of History." *History News* (March/April 1989).

Bryan, Charles F., Jr. "Marketing History: How Far Have We Come? How Far Do We Go?" *History News* (July/August 1989).

Buck, Elizabeth. *Paradise Remade: The Politics of Culture and History in Hawaii.* Philadelphia: Temple University Press, 1993.

Bumiller, Elisabeth. "Weekend Excursion: Colonial Myth and Reality." *New York Times,* 4 June 1999.

Burcaw, G. Ellis. *Introduction to Museum Work.* Nashville: American Association for State and Local History, 1983.

Carlson, Marvin. *The Haunted Stage: Theatre as Memory Machine.* Ann Arbor: University of Michigan Press, 2001.

Carr, David. *The Promise of Cultural Institutions.* Walnut Creek, CA: AltaMira, 2003.

Carson, Cary. "Becoming Americans: Our Struggle to Be Both Free and Equal; A Plan of Thematic Interpretation." January 1996 Training Edition. Williamsburg, VA: Colonial Williamsburg Foundation, 1996.

———. "Colonial Williamsburg and the Practice of Interpretive Planning in American History Museums." *Public Historian* 20.3 (Summer 1998).

———. "Historical Associations Take Stand against Political Interference in History Museums." *Perspectives: Newsletter of the American Historical Association* 34.5 (1 May 1996).

———. "Living Museums of Everyman's History." *Harvard* (Summer 1981).

———. "Lost in the Fun House: A Commentary on Anthropologists' First Contact with History Museums." *Journal of American History* 81.1 (June 1994): 137–45.

———. "Mirror Mirror on the Wall, Whose History Is the Fairest of Them All?" *The Public Historian* 17.4 (Fall 1995).

Chothia, Jean. *Andre Antoine.* New York: Cambridge University Press, 1991.

Cohen-Cruz, Jan. "Mainstream or Margin: U.S. Activist Performance and Theatre of the Oppressed." In *Playing Boal: Theatre, Therapy, Activism,* eds. Mady Schutzman and Jan Cohen-Cruz. London: Routledge, 1994.

Cole, David. *The Theatrical Event: A Mythos, A Vocabulary, A Perspective.* Middletown, CT: Wesleyan University Press, 1975.

Cole, Toby. and Helen Krich Chinoy, eds. *Directors on Directing.* New York: Bobbs-Merril, 1963.

Coleman Matthews, Christy. "Twenty Years Interpreting African American History: A Colonial Williamsburg Revolution." *History News* 54 (Spring 1999).

Coleridge, Samuel Taylor. "Progress of the Drama." In *Dramatic Theory and Criticism: Greeks to Grotowski,* ed. Bernard E. Dukore. Fort Worth, TX: Harcourt, 1976.

Colonial Williamsburg: Official Guidebook. Colonial Williamsburg Foundation, 1985.

Colonial Williamsburg: The First Twenty-five Years: A Report by the President as of December 31, 1951. Williamsburg, VA: Colonial Williamsburg, Inc., 1951.

"Colonial Williamsburg Expands 'Days in History' in 2000 to Delve Deeper into Virginia's Road to Revolution." Colonial Williamsburg press release, 2000.

Colonial Williamsburg Foundation, *Redefining Family: Resource Book 1997*. Williamsburg, VA: Colonial Williamsburg Foundation, 1997.

"Colonial Williamsburg Podcasts Debut." In *Colonial Williamsburg: The Journal of the Colonial Williamsburg Foundation* (Autumn 2005).

Comte, August. *"Cours de Philosophie Positive," Auguste Comte and Positivism: The Essential Writings*. Trans. Gertrud Lenzer. New Brunswick, NJ: Transaction, 1998.

Cook, Peter W. "The Craft of Demonstrations." *Museum News* 53:3 (November 1974).

Copel, Melinda. "The 1954 Limon Company Tour to South America: Goodwill Tour or Cold War Cultural Propaganda?" In *José Limón*, ed. June Dunbar. New York: Routledge, 2000.

Crippen, John. "Fort Snelling Hopes History Has a Future," *Minneapolis Star Tribune*, 18 February 2002, A1, A8.

Davies, Charlotte Aull. *Reflexive Ethnography: A Guide to Researching Selves and Others*. London: Routledge, 1999.

De Certeau, Michel. *Heterologies: Discourse on the Other*. Trans. Brian Massumi. Minneapolis: University of Minnesota Press, 1986.

———. "History, Ethics, Science and Fiction." In *Social Science as Moral Inquiry*, eds. Norma Haan et al. New York: Columbia University Press, 1983.

———. *The Practice of Everyday Life*. Trans. Steve Rendall. Berkeley: University of California Press, 1984.

———. *The Writing of History*. Trans. Tom Conley. New York: Columbia University Press, 1988.

Deetz, James. *In Small Things Forgotten: An Archaeology of Early American Life*. New York: Doubleday, 1996.

———. *Invitation to Archaeology*. Garden City, NY: Natural History Press, 1967.

———. "The Link from Object to Person to Concept." In *Museums, Adults, and the Humanities*, ed. Zipporah W. Collins. Washington, DC: American Association of Museums, 1981.

———. "A Sense of Another World: History Museums and Cultural Change." *Museum News* 58.5 (May–June 1980).

Deetz, James, and Patricia Scott Deetz. *The Times of Their Lives: Life, Love, and Death in Plymouth Colony*. New York: Freeman, 2000.

Deleuze, Gilles. *Cinema*. Vol. 1, *The Movement Image*. Trans. Hugh Tomlinson and Barbara Habberjam. Minneapolis: University of Minnesota Press, 1986. Vol. 2, *The Time Image*. Trans. Hugh Tomlinson and Robert Galeta. Minneapolis: University of Minnesota Press, 1989.

———. *Foucault*. Trans. Sean Hand. Minneapolis: University of Minnesota Press, 1986.

———. "Music and Ritornello." In *The Deleuze Reader*, ed. Constantin V. Boundas. New York: Columbia University Press, 1993.

———. "Nomad Art: Space." In *The Deleuze Reader*, ed. Constantin V. Boundas. New York: Columbia University Press, 1993.

———. "On Philosophy." In Negotiations: 1972–1990, trans. Martin Joughin. New York: Columbia University Press, 1995.

Deleuze, Gilles, and Félix Guattari. What Is Philosophy? Trans. Hugh Tomlinson and Graham Burchell. New York: Columbia University Press, 1994.

Descartes, René. "A Discourse on Method." In A Discourse on Method and Selected Writings, trans. John Veitch. New York: Dutton, 1951.

Dormon, James H. "American Popular Culture and the New Immigration Ethnics: The Vaudeville Stage and the Process of Ethnic Ascription." Amerikastudien (American Studies) 36.2 (1991).

Duchartre, Pierre-Louis. The Italian Comedy: The Improvisation, Scenarios, Lives, Attributes, Portraits and Masks of the Illustrious Characters of the Commedia dell'Arte. Trans. Randolph T. Weaver. New York: John Day, 1929.

Eco, Umberto. Travels in Hyper Reality: Essays. Trans. William Weaver. San Diego: Harcourt Brace Jovanovich, 1986.

Eisenstein, Sergei. "Montage of Attractions." Trans. Daniel and Eleanor Gerould. In Dramatic Theory and Criticism: Greeks to Grotowski, ed. Bernard E. Dukore. Fort Worth, TX: Harcourt, 1974.

Eley, Geoff, and Keith Nield. "Why Does Social History Ignore Politics?" Social History 5 (May 1980).

Ellis, Rex M. "Interpreting the Whole House." In Interpreting Historic House Museums, ed. Jessica Foy Donnelly. Walnut Creek, CA: AltaMira, 2002.

———. "Presenting the Past: Education, Interpretation, and the Teaching of Black History at Colonial Williamsburg." Ph.D. dissertation, College of William and Mary, 1989.

———. "Re: Living History: Bringing History into Play." American Visions 7:6 (December/January 1992).

Elmer, Jonathan. "The Archive, the Native American, Jefferson's Convulsions." Diacritics 28.4 (Winter 1998).

Erisman, Wendy Elizabeth. "Forward into the Past: The Poetics and Politics of Community in Two Historical Re-Creation Groups." Ph.D. dissertation, University of Texas at Austin, 1998.

"Evaluation of the Becoming Americans Theme and Redefining Family Story Line: Summary of Findings." Williamsburg, VA: Randi Korn and Associates, October 1997.

Fahrenthold, David A. "Living-History Museums Struggle to Draw Visitors: Creativity Drives Changes in Hunt for Attendance." Washington Post, 25 December 2005.

Fairburn, Miles. Social History: Problems, Strategies and Methods. New York: St. Martin's, 1999.

Falk, John H., and Lynn D. Dierking. Learning from Museums: Visitor Experiences and the Making of Meaning. Walnut Creek, CA: AltaMira, 2000.

———. Lessons without Limit: How Free-Choice Learning Is Transforming Education. Walnut Creek, CA: AltaMira, 2002.

———. The Museum Experience. Washington, DC: Whalesback Books, 1992.

Feifer, Maxine. Tourism in History: From Imperial Rome to the Present. New York: Stein & Day, 1985.

Flynn, Thomas R. "Reconstituting Praxis: Historialization as Re-enactment." *American Catholic Philosophical Quarterly* 70:4 (Autumn 1996).

Fortier, John. "Thoughts on the Re-creation and Interpretation of Historical Environments." In *Schedule and Papers of the Third International Congress of Maritime Museums.* Mystic Seaport, CT, 1978.

Foucault, Michel. *The Archaeology of Knowledge.* Trans. A. M. Sheridan Smith. New York: Pantheon, 1972.

———. "Of Other Spaces." Trans. Jay Miskowiek. *Diacritics* 16.1 (Spring 1986).

———. "Politics and the Study of Discourse." In *The Foucault Effect: Studies in Governmentality,* eds. Graham Burchell, Colin Gordon, and Peter Miller. London: Harvester, 1981.

Gable, Eric, and Richard Handler. "In Colonial Williamsburg, the New History Meets the Old." *Chronicle of Higher Education,* 30 October 1998.

Gable, Eric, Richard Handler, and Anna Lawson. "On the Uses of Relativism: Fact, Conjecture, and Black and White Histories at Colonial Williamsburg." *American Ethnologist* 19.4 (November 1992).

Gardner, James B., and George Rollie Adams, eds. *Ordinary People and Everyday Life: Perspectives on the New Social History.* Nashville: American Association for State and Local History, 1983.

Garfield, Donald. "Too Real for Comfort." *Museum News* 74.1 (January–February 1995).

Geertz, Clifford. *The Interpretation of Cultures: Selected Essays.* New York: Basic Books, 1973.

———. "Thick Description: Toward an Interpretive Theory of Culture." In *The Interpretation of Cultures: Selected Essays.* New York: Basic Books, 1973.

Genette, Gérard. "Boundaries of Narrative." *New Literary History* 8.1 (Autumn 1976).

Gibb, James G., and Karen Lee Davis. "History Exhibits and the Theories of Material Culture." *Journal of American Culture* 12.2 (Summer 1989).

Goffman, Erving. *The Presentation of Self in Everyday Life.* Garden City, NY: Doubleday, 1959.

Goldberg, Roselee. *Performance Art: From Futurism to the Present.* New York: Abrams, 1979.

Golub, Spencer. *Evreinov, the Theatre of Paradox and Transformation.* Ann Arbor, MI: UMI Research Press, 1984.

———. *The Recurrence of Fate: Theatre and Memory in Twentieth-Century Russia.* Iowa City: University of Iowa Press, 1994.

Gordon, Mel, ed. *Dada Performance.* New York: PAJ, 1987.

———. *Expressionist Texts.* New York: PAJ, 1986.

Greene, Jack P. "The New History: From Top to Bottom," *New York Times,* 8 January 1975.

Greenspan, Anders. *Creating Colonial Williamsburg.* Washington, DC: Smithsonian Institution Press, 2002.

Grein, A. A. J. T. Grein: The Story of a Pioneer. London: John Murray, 1936.

Griffin, Penny. *Arthur Wing Pinero and Henry Arthur Jones*. New York: St. Martin's Press, 1991.

Gurian, Elaine Heumann. "What Is the Object of This Exercise?" In *Reinventing the Museum: Historical and Contemporary Perspectives on the Paradigm Shift*, ed. Gail Anderson. Walnut Creek, CA: AltaMira, 2004.

Gutek, Gerald, and Patricia Gutek. *Experiencing America's Past: A Travel Guide to Museum Villages*. Columbia: University of South Carolina Press, 1994.

Handler, Richard. "Overpowered by Realism: Living History and the Simulation of the Past." *Journal of American Folklore* 100.397 (1987): 338.

Handler, Richard, and Eric Gable. *The New History in an Old Museum: Creating the Past at Colonial Williamsburg*. Durham, NC: Duke University Press, 1999.

Harwit, Martin. *An Exhibit Denied*. New York: Copernicus, 1996.

Heidegger, Martin. *Being and Time*. Trans. John Macquarrie and Edward Robinson. Oxford: Basil Blackwell, 1967.

Henderson, John A. *The First Avant-Garde, 1887–1894: Sources of the Modern French Theatre*. London: George G. Harrap, 1971.

Hewison, Robert. *The Heritage Industry: Britain in a Climate of Decline*. London: Methuen, 1987.

"High-Tech Meets History in a More Perfect Union: A New Museum Brings the Constitution to Life." *Chicago Tribune* (13 July 2003, sec. 8): 1, 6–7.

Hobsbawm, Eric, and Terence Ranger, eds. *The Invention of Tradition*. Cambridge, UK: Cambridge University Press, 1983.

Holzer, H. "Turning Back the Calendar to 1627 at Plimoth Plantation." *American History Illustrated* 20.7 (1985).

Hood, Marilyn G. "Staying Away: Why People Choose Not to Visit Museums." *Museum News* (April 1993). Reprinted in *Reinventing the Museum: Historical and Contemporary Perspectives on the Paradigm Shift*, ed. Gail Anderson. Walnut Creek, CA: AltaMira, 2004.

Hudson, Kenneth. *A Social History of Museums: What the Visitors Thought*. Humanities Press, 1975.

Hueumann Gurian, Elaine. "What Is the Object of This Exercise?" In *Reinventing The Museum: Historical and Contemporary Perspectives on the Paradigm Shift*, ed. Gail Anderson. Walnut Creek, CA: AltaMira, 2004.

Innes, Christopher. *Modern British Drama: 1890–1990*. Toronto University Press, 1992.

Irwin, Susan K. "Popular History: Living History Sites, Historical Interpretation and the Public." Master's thesis, Bowling Green State University, 1993.

Jakle, John A. *The Tourist: Travel in Twentieth-Century North America*. Lincoln: University of Nebraska Press, 1985.

Jamestown Settlement: Recreating America's First Permanent English Settlement. Williamsburg, VA: Bitcast, 1995.

Jennys, Susan. "The Great Buckskinner Debate." *Harpers* 286:1714.

Jones, Sally. "The First But Not the Last of the Vanishing Indians: Edwin Forrest and the Mythic Re-Creations of Native Population." In *Dressing in Feathers: The Con-*

struction of the Indian in American Popular Culture, ed. S. Elizabeth Bird. London: Routledge; Boulder, CO: Westview, 1996.

Karp, Ivan, and Steven D. Lavine, eds. *Exhibiting Cultures: The Poetics and Politics of Museum Display*. Washington, DC: Smithsonian, 1991.

Karp, Walter. "My Gawd, They've Sold the Town." *American Heritage* 32.5 (August/September 1981).

Kattwinkel, Susan, ed. *Audience Participation: Essays on Inclusion in Performance*. Westport, CT: Praeger, 2003.

Kirby, Michael, and Victoria Nes Kirby, eds. *Futurist Performance*. New York: PAJ, 1986.

Kirshenblatt-Gimblett, Barbara. "Afterlives." *Performance Research* 2.2 (Summer 1997).

———. *Destination Culture: Tourism, Museums, and Heritage*. Berkeley: University of California Press, 1998.

Kleberg, Lars. *Theatre as Action: Soviet Russian Avant-Garde Aesthetics*. Houndmills, Hampshire, UK: Macmillan, 1993.

Kobialka, Michal. "Historical Events and the Historiography of Tourism." *Journal of Theatre and Drama* 2 (1996).

———. *This Is My Body: Representational Practices in the Early Middle Ages*. Ann Arbor: University of Michigan Press, 1999.

Kobialka, Michal, ed. *Of Borders and Thresholds*. Minneapolis: University of Minnesota Press, 2000.

Kocher, A. Lawrence, and Howard Dearstyne. *Colonial Williamsburg: Its Buildings and Gardens*. Williamsburg, VA: Colonial Williamsburg, 1949.

Kopper, Philip. *Colonial Williamsburg*. New York: Henry N. Abrams, 1986.

Krugler, John D. "Behind the Public Presentations: Research and Scholarship at Living History Museums of Early America." *William and Mary Quarterly* 48.3 (July 1991).

———. "Stepping Outside of the Classroom: History and the Outdoor Museum." *Journal of American Culture* 12.2 (Summer 1989).

Kushner, Tony. "Playwright's Notes." In *Angels in America: Millennium Approaches*. New York: Theatre Communications Group, 1992.

Landesman, Peter. "A Crisis of Fakes." *New York Times Magazine* (18 March 2001).

Lang, Michael. "Marketing Historical Resources." Master's thesis, University of Calgary, 1991.

Lawless, Elaine J. *Holy Women, Wholly Women: Sharing Ministries of Wholeness through Life Stories and Reciprocal Ethnography*. Philadelphia: University of Pennsylvania Press, 1993.

Lawson, Anna Logan. "'The Other Half': Making African-American History at Colonial Williamsburg." Ph.D. dissertation, University of Virginia, 1995.

Leon, Warren, and Margaret Piatt. "Living History Museums." In *History Museums in the United States: A Critical Assessment*. Ed. Warren Leon and Roy Rosenzweig. Urbana: University of Illinois Press, 1989.

Levy, Barbara Abramoff, Sandra McKenzie Lloyd, and Susan Porter Schreiber. *Great Tours! Thematic Tours and Guide Training for Historic Sites.* Walnut Creek, CA: AltaMira, 2001.

Liebmann-Smith, Richard. "Not Dead Yet." *New York Times Magazine* (13 May 2001).

"Living History: Getting Closer to Getting It Right." *Early American Life* 21.3 (June 1990).

Loeb, Robert, Jr. *Meet the Real Pilgrims: Everyday Life on Plimouth Plantation in 1627.* Garden City, NY: Doubleday, 1979.

——. *New England Village: Everyday Life in 1810.* Garden City: Doubleday, 1979.

Lowenthal, David. *The Past Is a Foreign Country.* Cambridge, UK: Cambridge University Press, 1985.

——. "Past Time, Present Place: Landscape and Memory." *Geographical Review* 65:1 (January 1975).

——. *Possessed by the Past: The Heritage Crusade and the Spoils of History.* New York: Free Press, 1996.

Lynch, Kevin. *What Time Is This Place?* Cambridge, MA: MIT Press, 1972.

Lyotard, Jean-François. "Answer to the Question, 'What Is the Postmodern?'" Trans. Don Barry. In *The Postmodern Explained*, eds. Julian Pefanis and Morgan Thomas. Minneapolis: University of Minnesota Press, 1992.

——. "A Monument of Possibles." In *Postmodern Fables*, trans. Georges van den Abeele. Minneapolis: University of Minnesota Press, 1997.

——. *The Postmodern Explained.* Trans. Don Barry et al; eds. Julian Pefanis and Morgan Thomas. Minneapolis: University of Minnesota Press, 1992.

MacCannell, Dean. *The Tourist: A New Theory of the Leisure Class.* Berkeley: University of California Press, 1999.

——. "Virtual Reality's Place." *Performance Research* 2.2 (Summer 1997).

Magelssen, Scott. "Performance Practices of (Living) Open-Air Museums (And a New Look at 'Skansen' in American Living Museum Discourse)." *Theatre History Studies* 24 (June 2004).

——. "Recreation and Re-Creation: On-Site Historical Reenactment as Historiographic Operation at Plimoth Plantation." *Journal of Dramatic Theory and Criticism* (Fall 2002).

——. "Resuscitating the Extinct: The Back-Breeding of Historic Animals at U.S. Living History Museums." *Drama Review* 47.4 (Winter 2004).

——. "Stepping Back in Time: The Construction of Different Temporal Spaces at Living History Museums in the United States." *Theatre Annual* 57 (2004).

——. "'This Is a Drama—You Are Characters': The Tourist as Fugitive Slave in Conner Prairie's 'Follow the North Star.'" *Theatre Topics* (Spring 2006).

——. "The Vulgar Representation of Time: Time Space and Living History Museums." *California State University, Stanislaus, Journal of Research* (Fall 2001).

Mandell, Patricia. "Details, Details, Details." *Americana* 17.5 (November–December 1989).

Matthews, Christy Coleman. "Twenty Years Interpreting African American History: A Colonial Williamsburg Revolution." *History News* 54 (Spring 1999).

McCallum, Kent, ed. *Old Sturbridge Village: A Visitor's Guide.* Sturbridge, MA: Old Sturbridge, 1999.

McConachie, Bruce. "Slavery and Authenticity: Performing a Slave Auction at Colonial Williamsburg." *Theatre Annual* 51 (1988).

Melzer, Annabelle. *Latest Rage the Big Drum: Dada and Surrealist Performance.* Ann Arbor, MI: UMI Research Press, 1980.

Messenger, Phyllis Mauch. *The Ethics of Collecting Cultural Property.* Albuquerque: University of New Mexico Press, 1999.

Miller, Anna Irene. *The Independent Theater in Europe.* New York: Ray Long & Richard R. Smith, 1931.

Nabokov, Vladimir. *The Annotated Lolita.* Ed. Alfred Appel Jr. New York: McGraw-Hill, 1970.

———. "On a Book Entitled *Lolita.*" In *The Annotated Lolita,* ed. Alfred Appel Jr. New York: McGraw-Hill, 1970.

Neustadt, Kathy. *Clambake: A History and Celebration of an American Tradition.* Amherst: University of Massachusetts Press, 1992.

Nietzsche, Friedrich. "On the Uses and Disadvantages of History for Life." In *Untimely Meditations,* ed. Daniel Breazeale; trans. R. J. Hollingdale. Cambridge, UK: Cambridge University Press, 1997.

Novick, Peter. *That Noble Dream: "The Objectivity Question" and the American Historical Profession.* Cambridge, UK: Cambridge University Press, 1988.

Nugent, Walter T. K. *Structures of American Social History.* Bloomingon: Indiana University Press, 1981.

O'Brian, Michael. *McCarthy and McCarthyism in Wisconsin.* Columbia: University of Missouri Press, 1980.

Old Sturbridge Visitor 36.2 (Summer 1996).

Old Sturbridge Visitor 37.3 (Fall 1997).

Old Sturbridge Visitor 38.1 (Spring 1998).

O'Leary, Cecilia Elizabeth. *To Die For: The Paradox of American Patriotism.* Princeton, NJ: Princeton University Press, 1999.

Omert, Michael. *Official Guide to Colonial Williamsburg.* Williamsburg, VA: Colonial Williamsburg Foundation, 1998.

Oreglia, Giacomo. *The Commedia dell'Arte.* Trans. Lovett F. Edwards. London: Methuen, 1968.

Orvell, Miles. *The Real Thing: Imitation and Authenticity in American Culture, 1880–1940.* Chapel Hill: University of North Carolina Press, 1989.

Osterud, Nancy Grey. "Living Living History: First-Person Interpretation at Plimoth Plantation, Plymouth, Massachusetts." *Journal of Museum Education* 17.1 (Winter 1992).

Parks, Suzan-Lori. *The America Play and Other Works.* New York: Theatre Communications Group, 1995.

———. "Possession." In *The America Play, and Other Works*. New York: Theatre Communications Group, 1995.

Peers, Laura. "'Playing Ourselves': Native Histories, Native Interpreters, and Living History Sites." Ph.D. dissertation, McMaster University, 1996.

Peterson, David. "There Is No Living History, There Are No Time Machines." *History News* 43.5 (1988).

Phillip, Mary Christine. "To Reenact or Not to Reenact: Disputes over Staging of Slave Auction Shows." *Black Issues in Higher Education* 11:18.

Prater, Brian. "History Camps for Curious Kids." *Americana* 20:2 (April 1992).

Pratt, Mary Louise. *Travel Writing and Transculturation*. London: Routledge, 1992.

Preserving America's Past. Washington, DC: National Geographic Society, 1983.

Rancière, Jacques. *The Names of History: On the Poetics of Knowledge*, trans. Hassan Melehy. Minneapolis: University of Minnesota Press, 1994.

Rand, Judy. "The Visitors' Bill of Rights." In *Reinventing the Museum: Historical and Contemporary Perspectives on the Paradigm Shift*, ed. Gail Anderson. Walnut Creek, CA: AltaMira, 2004.

Rich, Frank. "The Nation's Basement." *New York Times* (22 June 1996).

Roach, Joseph. *Cities of the Dead: Circum-Atlantic Performance*. New York: Columbia University Press, 1996.

Roddewig, Richard J. "Selling America's Heritage." *Preservation Forum* 2 (Fall 1988).

Rokem, Freddie. *Performing History: Theatrical Representations of the Past in Contemporary Theatre*. Iowa City: University of Iowa Press, 2000.

Ronsheim, Robert D. "Is the Past Dead?" *Museum News* 53:3 (November 1974).

Roth, Stacy F. *Past into Present: Effective Techniques for First-Person Historical Interpretation*. Chapel Hill: University of North Carolina Press, 1998.

Rountree, Helen C. "Powhattan Indian Women: The People Captain John Smith Barely Saw." *Ethnohistory* 45.1 (Winter 1998).

Rousseau, Jean-Jacques. "The Letter to M. D'Alambert on the Theatre." In *Politics and the Arts*, trans. Allan Bloom. Ithaca: New York, 1960.

Rydell, Robert W. *All the World's a Fair*. Chicago: University of Chicago Press, 1984.

Sachatello-Sawyer, Bonnie, Robert A. Fellenz, Hanly Burton, Laura Gittings-Carlson, Janet Lewis-Mahony, and Walter Woolbaugh. *Adult Museum Programs: Designing Meaningful Experiences*. Walnut Creek, CA: AltaMira, 2002.

Samuel, Raphael, and Gareth Stedman Jones, eds. *Culture, Ideology and Politics*. London: Routledge, 1982.

Schechner, Richard. "Believed-in Theatre." *Performance Research* 2.2 (Summer 1997).

———. "Restoration of Behavior." *Studies in Visual Communication* 7.3 (Summer 1981).

Schlereth, Thomas. "It Wasn't That Simple." *Museum News* 56:1 (January/February 1978).

Schneider, Rebecca. "Flesh Memory and the Logic of the Archive; or, Driving the Lincoln." Paper delivered at the Australasian Drama Studies Association Meetings, Newcastle, Australia, July 2000.

Schutzman, Mady. "Brechtian Shamanism: The Political Therapy of Augusto Boal." In *Playing Boal: Theatre, Therapy, Activism*, eds. Mady Schutzman and Jan Cohen-Cruz. London: Routledge, 1994.

Schutzman, Mady, and Jan Cohen-Cruz, eds. *Playing Boal: Theatre, Therapy, Activism*. London: Routledge, 1994.

"1787 and All That: Walking through Amendments and Rubbing Elbows with Founding Fathers at the New Constitution Center." *New York Times* (17 August 2003).

Shackel, Paul A. *Memory in Black and White: Race, Commemoration, and the Post-Bellum Landscape*. Walnut Creek, CA: AltaMira, 2003.

Shakespeare, William. "A Midsummer Night's Dream." In *The Riverside Shakespeare*. Dallas: Houghton-Mifflin, 1974.

Sheperd-Barr, Kirsten. *Ibsen and Early Modernist Theatre: 1890–1900*. Westport, CT: Greenwood, 1997.

Sidford, Holly. "Stepping into History." *Museum News* 53:5 (November 1974).

Slotkin, Richard. *Gunfighter Nation: The Myth of the Frontier in Twentieth-Century America*. New York: Atheneum, 1992.

Slotkin, Richard, and James K. Folsom, eds. *So Dreadfull a Judgement: Puritan Responses to King Philip's War, 1676–1677*. Middletown, CT: Wesleyan University Press, 1978.

Smith, Valerie L. *Hosts and Guests: The Anthropology of Tourism*. University of Philadelphia Press, 1989.

Snow, Stephen Eddy. *Performing the Pilgrims: A Study of Ethnohistorical Role-Playing at Plimoth Plantation*. Jackson: University Press of Mississippi, 1993.

———. "Plimoth Plantation: Living History as Blurred Genre." *Kentucky Folklore Record* 32.1, 2 (January/June 1986).

Spivak, Gayatri Chakravorty. "Can the Subaltern Speak?" In *Marxism and the Interpretation of Culture*, ed. Cary Nelson and Larry Grossberg. Chicago: University of Illinois Press, 1988.

The Spivak Reader. Eds. Donna Landry and Gerald MacLean. New York: Routledge, 1996.

Spradley, James P. *The Ethnographic Interview*. New York: Holt, Rinehart and Winston, 1979.

Spry, Lib. "Structures of Power: Toward a Theatre of Liberation." In *Playing Boal: Theatre, Therapy, Activism*, eds. Mady Schutzman and Jan Cohen-Cruz. London: Routledge, 1994.

Stanislavsky, Konstantin. *An Actor Prepares*, trans. Elizabeth Reynolds Hapgood. New York: Theatre Arts, 1936.

———. *Building a Character*. Trans. Elizabeth Reynolds Hapgood. New York: Theater Arts, 1949.

———. *Creating a Role*. Trans. Elizabeth Reynolds Hapgood. New York: Theater Arts, 1961.

Starobinski, Jean. "The Idea of Nostalgia." *Diogenes* 54 (Summer 1966).

States, Bert O. "The Actor's Presence," in *Acting (Re)Considered: Theories and Practices*, ed. Phillip B. Zarrilli. London: Routledge, 1995.

Stewart, Kathleen. "Nostalgia—A Polemic." In *Rereading Cultural Anthropology*, ed. George E. Marcus. Durham, NC: Duke University Press, 1992.

Stover, Kate F. "Is It *Real* History Yet? An Update on Living History Musuems." *Journal of American Culture* 12.2 (Summer 1989).

Strindberg, August. "Preface to *Miss Julie*." Trans. E. M. Sprinchorn. In *Dramatic Theory and Criticism: Greeks to Grotowski*, ed. Bernard E. Dukore. Fort Worth, TX: Harcourt, 1976.

———. *Strindberg: Five Plays*. Trans. Harry G. Carlson. Berkeley: University of California Press, 1983.

Sussman, Vic. "From Williamsburg to Conner Prairie." *U.S. News and World Report* 107:4 (24 July 1989).

Taine, Hippolyte A. *History of English Literature*. Trans. H. Van Laun. New York: F. Ungar, 1965.

Tilden, Freeman. *Interpreting Our Heritage*. 3rd ed. Chapel Hill: University of North Carolina Press, 1977.

Toffler, Alvin. *Future Shock*. New York: Random House, 1970.

Tomkins, T. "Small Beer, Large Pigs, and the Anglo-Dutch War of 1627." *Museum* 44:3 (1992).

Trouillot, Michel-Rolph. *Silencing the Past: Power and the Production of History*. Boston: Beacon Press, 1997.

Turner, Louis, and John Ash. *The Golden Hordes: International Tourism and the Pleasure Periphery*. London: Constable, 1975.

Urdang, Laurence. *The Timetables of American History*. New York: Simon & Schuster, 1981.

Urry, John. *The Tourist Gaze: Leisure and Travel in Contemporary Societies*. London: Sage, 1990.

Valdez, Luis. *Luis Valdez—Early Works: Actos, Bernabé, and Pensamiento Serpentino*. Houston: Arte Publico, 1990.

Van West, Caroll, and Mary S. Hoffschwelle. "'Slumbering on Its Old Foundations': Interpretation at Colonial Williamsburg." *South Atlantic Quarterly* 83 (Spring 1984).

Vattimo, Gianni. *The Transparent Society*. Trans. David Webb. Baltimore, MD: Johns Hopkins University Press, 1992.

Villa Bryk, Nancy E. "Infusing the House with Characters." In *Interpreting Historic House Museums*, ed. Jessica Foy Donnelly. Walnut Creek, CA: AltaMira, 2002.

Wallace, Michael. *Mickey Mouse History and Other Essays on American Memory*. Philadelphia: Temple University Press, 1996.

———. "Visiting the Past: History Museums in the United States." *Radical History Review* 25 (1981): 63–96.

Walsh, Kevin. *The Representation of the Past: Museums and Heritage in the Postmodern World*. London: Routledge, 1992.

Waxman, Samuel. *Antoine and the Theatre Libre*. New York: Benjamin, 1926.

Webb, T. D. "Highly Structured Tourist Art: Form and Meaning of the Polynesian Cultural Center." *Contemporary Pacific* 6.1 (Spring 1994).

Wells, Robert B. *Daylight in the Swamp*. Ashland, WI: Northwood, 1987.

Weschler, Lawrence. "Inhaling the Spore: Field Trip to a Museum of Natural (Un)history." *Harper's* (September 1994).

———. *Mr. Wilson's Cabinet of Wonder*. New York: Pantheon, 1995.

Wheeler, Tim. "Living History to Go: The Short Order Interpreter." In *Annual Proceedings of the Meetings Held at Ottowa, Santa Fe, and Old Sturbridge: 1978–1980*, ed. Virginia Briscoe. Washington, DC: Association for Living History Farms and Agricultural Musuems, 1981.

White, Hayden. "The Value of Narrativity in the Representation of Reality." *Critical Inquiry* 7.1 (Autumn 1980).

Wiencek, Henry. *An Imperfect God: George Washington, His Slaves, and the Creation of America*. New York: Farrar, Straus and Giroux, 2003.

Williamsburg Spring 2001 Catalogue. Williamsburg, VA: Colonial Williamsburg Foundation, 2001.

Yasuhide, Kawashima. "The Pilgrims and the Wampanoag Indians, 1620–1691: Lethal Encounter." *Oklahoma City University Law Review* 23.1–2 (Spring/Summer 1998).

Young, Karl. *Drama of the Medieval Church*. Oxford, UK: Clarendon, 1933.

Zola, Émile. "Naturalism and the Stage." In *The Experimental Novel, and Other Essays*, trans. Belle M. Sherman. New York: Cassell, 1893.

Zunz, Olivier, ed. *Reliving the Past: The Worlds of Social History*. Chapel Hill: University of North Carolina Press, 1985.

———. "The Synthesis of Social Change: Reflections on American Social History." In *Reliving the Past: The Worlds of Social History*, ed. Olivier Zunz. Chapel Hill: University of North Carolina Press, 1985.

Personal Interviews

Bill Barker, first-person interpreter (Thomas Jefferson), Colonial Williamsburg, 7 June 2000.

Chris Benedetto, third-person interpreter, sawpit, Pioneer Village, Salem, MA, 16 June 2000.

Bentley Boyd, reporter, *Daily Press* (Newport News, VA), Colonial Williamsburg, 7 June 2000.

Jim Bradley, public relations, Colonial Williamsburg, 8 June 2000.

Toni Brennan, first-person interpreter, Colonial Williamsburg, 7 June 2000.

Marge Bruchac, first-person interpreter (Molly Geet), Old Sturbridge Village, 20 June 2000.

Joel Garcia, noncostumed third-person interpreter, Colonial Williamsburg, 3 June 2000.

Cynthia Gedraitis, supervisor, Colonial Interpretation Department, Plimoth Plantation, 15 June 2000.

Michael Hall, program interpreter, Plimoth Plantation, 15 June 2000.

Kate Hill, third-person interpreter, Center Meeting House, Old Sturbridge Village, 19 June 2000.

Mark Howell, program manager, Colonial Williamsburg, 7 June 2000.

Emily James, first-person interpreter, Colonial Williamsburg, 8 June 2000.

Annika Johansson, assistant director, Hosts Program, Skansen, Stockholm, Sweden, 8 July 2002.

Susan Kline, associate director, Education Department, Old Sturbridge Village, 21 June 2000.

Jack Larkin, chief historian, Old Sturbridge Village, 21 June 2000.

Christy Coleman Matthews, president, Charles H. Wright Museum of African American History, telephone interview, 9 May 2000.

Rosemarie McAphee, training, Education Division Training, Colonial Williamsburg, 7 June 2000.

Stephen Osman, site manager, Historic Fort Snelling, 13 May 2000.

Guy Peartree, first-person interpreter (Guy Scott), Old Sturbridge Village, 20 June 2000.

Richard Schumann, first-person interpreter (Patrick Henry), Colonial Williamsburg, 6 June 2000.

Thomas Shaw, assistant site manager, Historic Fort Snelling, 13 May 2000.

Martha Sulya, first-person interpreter, Plimoth Plantation, 15 June 2000.

Carolyn Travers, research librarian, Plimoth Plantation, 15 June 2000.

John Truelson, Rare Breeds Program, Plimoth Plantation, 17 June 2000.

Walt Woodward, director of education, Plimoth Plantation, 15 June 2000.

Anonymous Interviews

Third-person costumed interpreter, "Livestock in the 18th Century" Program, Colonial Williamsburg, 3 June 2000.

Third-person costumed interpreter #1, Powhattan Native Encampment, Jamestown Settlement, Jamestown-Yorktown Foundation, 4 June 2000.

Third-person costumed interpreter #2, Powhattan Native Encampment, Jamestown Settlement, Jamestown-Yorktown Foundation, 4 June 2000.

Third-person costumed interpreter #3, Powhattan Native Encampment, Jamestown Settlement, Jamestown-Yorktown Foundation, 4 June 2000.

Third-person costumed interpreter, blacksmith shop, James Fort, Jamestown Settlement, 4 June 2000.

Third-person costumed interpreter, Le Corps de Garde (Arms and Armor Building), James Fort, Jamestown Settlement, 4 June 2000.

Third-person costumed interpreter, Discovery, James Fort, Jamestown Settlement, 4 June 2000.

Third-person costumed interpreter, farmlife area, Yorktown Victory Center, 4 June 2000.

Third-person costumed interpreter, musket drilling, Yorktown Victory Center, 4 June 2000.

Third-person costumed interpreter, apothecary, Yorktown Victory Center, 4 June 2000.

Third-person costumed interpreter, tobacco farm, Yorktown Victory Center, 4 June 2000.

Third-person costumed interpreter, kitchen worker, Yorktown Victory Center, 4 June 2000.

First-person costumed interpreter #1 (George Washington), Colonial Williamsburg, 4 June 2000.

Program manager, Colonial Williamsburg, 6 June 2000.

First-person costumed interpreter #2 (eighteenth-century actor), "Theatre on the Road to Revolution," Colonial Williamsburg, 6 June 2000.

First-person costumed interpreter #3 (eighteenth-century actor), "Theatre on the Road to Revolution," Colonial Williamsburg, 6 June 2000.

Manager, Theatrical Productions, Colonial Williamsburg, 7 June 2000.

Third-person costumed interpreter, windmill, Colonial Williamsburg, 7 June 2000.

Third-person costumed interpreter, Randolph House outbuilding, Colonial Williamsburg, 7 June 2000.

Staff member, interpretive program development, Colonial Williamsburg, 8 June 2000.

Public relations staff member, Plimoth Plantation, 15 June 2000.

Third-person costumed interpreter, Pioneer Village, Salem, Massachusetts, 16 June 2000.

Third-person costumed Native interpreter (Tim), roundhouse, Hobbamock's Homesite, Plimoth Plantation, 17 June 2000.

Third-person costumed Native interpreter, Hobbamock's Homesite, Plimoth Plantation, 17 June 2000.

Artisan (ribbons), Carriage House Craft Center, Plimoth Plantation, 17 June 2000.

Artisan (ceramics), Carriage House Craft Center, Plimoth Plantation, 17 June 2000.

First-person costumed interpreter #1, Parsonage, Old Sturbridge Village, 19 June 2000.

First-person costumed interpreter #2, Parsonage, Old Sturbridge Village, 19 June 2000.

Third-person costumed interpreter, Tin Shop, Old Sturbridge Village, 19 June 2000.

First-person costumed interpreter (Lydia Maria Child), Parsonage Barn, Old Sturbridge Village, 19 June 2000.

Third-person costumed interpreter, Towne Family Farm, Old Sturbridge Village, 19 June 2000.

Third-person costumed interpreter, Main Farm, Old Sturbridge Village, 19 June 2000.

First-person costumed interpreter (women's charitable organization worker), Parsonage, Old Sturbridge Village, 20 June 2000.

Third-person costumed interpreter, Bank, Old Sturbridge Village, 20 June 2000.

Third-person costumed hostess, Oktorps-Gården, Skansen, Stockhom, Sweden, 8 July 2002.

Third-person costumed hostess, Ekshärads-Gården, Skansen, Stockhom, Sweden, 8 July 2002.

Third-person costumed interpreter, Village Common, Old Sturbridge Village, 24 June 2003.

Third-person costumed interpreter, Greenfield Village, 2 July 2003.

Conner Prairie Visitor Services representative, telephone interview, 4 August 2003.

Audiovisual Sources

"Adventures in Re-creating History," hosted by Lynn Neary. *Talk of the Nation*, National Public Radio, 5 July 2004.

Battleship Potempkin. Dir. Sergei Eisenstein. Image Entertainment, 1998.

Colonial Williamsburg. VideoTours, Inc., 1993.

Como Querem Beber Agua: Augusto Boal and Theatre of the Oppressed in Rio De Janeiro. Dir. Robert Morelos. Queensland: Center for Innovation in the Arts, Queensland University of Technology, 1995.

Old Sturbridge Village: Growing Up in New England. Video. VideoTours, Inc., 1991.

Old Sturbridge Village: Official Video. Video. VideoTours, Inc., 1989.

Plimoth Plantation. VHS. Glastonbury, CT: VideoTours, 1989.

Publick Times: An Estate Auction. VHS. Williamsburg, VA: Colonial Williamsburg Foundation, 1994.

Williamsburg: The Story of a Patriot. Williamsburg, VA: Colonial Williamsburg Foundation, 1957.

Websites

Colonial Williamsburg. www.history.org.

Manning, Steve. "A Short History of Station Wagons in the USA." www.stationwagon.com/history.html.

Marshall, Malissa. Review of *Reliving the Past: The Worlds of Social History* (1985). www.ist-socrates.berkeley.edu/~mescha/bookrev/zunzh.html.

Nanepashemet [Anthony Pollard]. "Wampanoag Cultural Survival: The Dynamics of a Living Culture." http://groups.msn.com/traditions/nativeamerican.msnw?action=get_message&mview=1&id_message=15874.

New York Times Online. Wednesday, 13 June 2001. www.nytimes.com.

Old Sturbridge Village. www.osv.org.

Plimoth Plantation. www.plimoth.org.

Strawbery Banke Museum. www.strawberybanke.org.

Sultzman, Lee. "Wampanoag History." www.tolatsga.org/wampa.html.

Brochures and Travel Literature

Briggs, Rose T. *Plymouth Rock: History and Significance.* Sign. Plymouth, MA: 1968.

"Vacation Planner." Brochure. Colonial Williamsburg Foundation, 2000.

"Colonial Williamsburg." Brochure. Colonial Williamsburg Foundation, 2000.

A Handbook for the Exhibition Buildings of Colonial Williamsburg, Incorporated. Guide. Williamsburg: Colonial Williamsburg Foundation, August 1936.

"Living History in the National Park Service." Brochure. Washington, DC: National Park Service, 1976.

Conner Prairie Brochure: "Live Some History." Brochure. Indianapolis: Conner Prairie, Summer 2003.

"Old Sturbridge Village Lodges and Oliver Wight House." Brochure. Old Sturbridge Village, 2000.

Old Sturbridge Village Educators' Newsletter, 12 June 2003.

Pecoraro, Michelle. "The Nye Barn: A Rare Breeds Exhibit." Plimoth Plantation press release, 2000.

———. "Hobbamock's [Wampanoag Indian] Homesite." *Backgrounder.* Plimoth Plantation Press Release, 2000.

Pioneer Village Map/Guide. Salem, MA, 2000.

Plimoth Plantation: A Pictoral Guide. Little Compton, RI: Fort Church, 1997.

"Plimoth Plantation Rare Breeds Program." Pamphlet. Plimoth Plantation, 1995.

"Send the Kids on a History Adventure this Summer," E-mail newsletter, Old Sturbridge Village, 20 June 2003.

"Step Back in Time at Plimoth Plantation." Brochure. Plimoth Plantation Publications, 199[?].

"SummerShops at Old Sturbridge Village 2003," Brochure, Old Sturbridge, Inc., 2003.

"Welcome to Plimoth Plantation!" Guide and map. Plimoth Plantation Publications, 199[?].

"Welcome to Sturbridge Village" Guide and map. Old Sturbridge Village, 19 June 2000.

Yorktown Victory Center. Brochure and guide. Jamestown Yorktown-Foundation, 2000.

"Your Party Awaits." Promotional flier. Colonial Williamsburg Foundation, 2001.

Index

About the Author

Scott Magelssen teaches theatre history, dramaturgy, and performance studies at Augustana College in Rock Island, Illinois, where he lives with his wife, Theresa, and son, Trygg. He is also a theatre practitioner and has worked as a director and dramaturg. Scott holds a Ph.D. in theatre history, theory, and dramatic literature from the University of Minnesota and has presented and published several essays on living history museums, historiography, and performance.